EYEWITNESS TRAVEL GUIDES

UMBRIA

DK

P9-DDF-761

LONDON, NEW YORK,
MELBOURNE, MUNICH AND DELHI
www.dk.com

PRODUCED BY Fabio Ratti Editoria Srl, Milan, Italy

PROJECT EDITORS Mattia Goffetti, Silvia Riboldi
EDITOR Marina Beretta
DESIGNERS Modi Artistici, Tiziano Perotto

CONTRIBUTORS
Giovanni Francesio, Marina Dragoni,
Patrizia Masnini

PHOTOGRAPHER
Ghigo Roli

ILLUSTRATOR
Elisabetta Mancini

CARTOGRAPHY
Laura Belletti

Dorling Kindersley Limited
PUBLISHING MANAGERS Fay Franklin, Kate Poole
SENIOR ART EDITOR Marisa Renzullo
TRANSLATOR Fiona Wild
EDITOR Emily Hatchwell
CONSULTANT Jeffrey Kennedy
FACTCHECKER Leonie Loudon
PRODUCTION Sarah Dodd

Reproduced in Singapore by Colourscan
Printed and bound by L. Rex Printing Company Limited, Chin.a

First American Edition, 2004

02 03 04 05 10 9 8 7 6 5 4 3 2 1

Published in the United States by
DK Publishing, Inc., 375 Hudson Street,
New York, New York 10014.

ISSN 1479-344X

ISBN 0-7566-0298-X

FLOORS ARE REFERRED TO THROUGHOUT IN ACCORDANCE WITH EUROPEAN USEAGE;
IE THE "FIRST FLOOR" IS THE FLOOR ABOVE GROUND LEVEL

**The information in this
Eyewitness Travel Guide is checked annually**.
Every effort has been made to ensure that this book is as up-to-date
as possible at the time of going to press. Some details, however,
such as telephone numbers, opening hours, prices, gallery hanging
arrangements and travel information are liable to change. The
publishers cannot accept responsibility for any consequences arising
from the use of this book, nor for any material on third party
websites, and cannot guarantee that any website address in this
book will be a suitable source of travel information. We value the
views and suggestions of our readers very highly. Please write to:
Publisher, DK Eyewitness Travel Guides,
Dorling Kindersley, 80 Strand, London WC2R 0RL, Great Britain.

CONTENTS

Dispute in the Temple, detail,
Cappella Baglioni, Spello

INTRODUCING
UMBRIA

Opening of the traditional Corsa
all'Anello in Narni

◁ Looking over the city of Spoleto, with the cathedral in the foreground

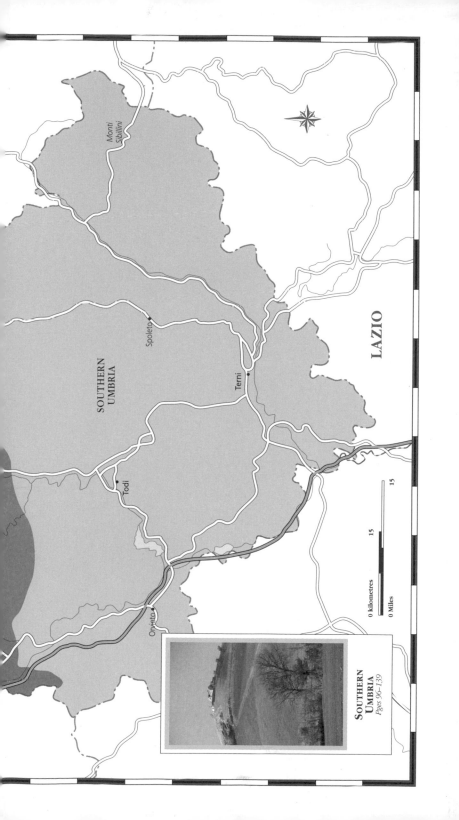

Monti
Sibillini

SOUTHERN
UMBRIA

Spoleto

Terni

Todi

Orvieto

LAZIO

0 kilometres   15

0 Miles   15

**SOUTHERN
UMBRIA**
Pages 96–139

EYEWITNESS TRAVEL GUIDES

UMBRIA

The medieval Piazza della Repubblica in Foligno

Typical ceramic plate from Deruta

The spectacular Cascata delle Marmore, near Terni

Basilica di San Francesco, Assisi

HOW TO USE THIS GUIDE

THIS GUIDE helps you to get the most out of your visit to Umbria by giving detailed descriptions of sights, practical information and expert advice. *Introducing Umbria* sets the region in its geographical, cultural as well as historical context.

Umbria Area by Area describes the main sightseeing areas, with maps, detailed illustrations and photographs. Hotels, restaurants and shops are covered in *Travellers' Needs*, while the *Survival Guide* contains invaluable practical advice.

UMBRIA AREA BY AREA

Umbria has been divided into two sightseeing areas, each with its own colour-coded thumb tab: a key to the colours used is on the inside front cover. Each area has its own chapter, which opens with a *Pictorial Map* with a numbered list of the sights described. There is a *Road Map* and a key to symbols inside the back cover.

Each area has a colour-coded thumb tab.

1 Introduction

The landscape, history and character of each region is described here, showing how the area has developed over the centuries and what it offers to the visitor today.

A locator map shows the area in relation to the region as a whole. It is identified by its colour-coding.

2 Pictorial Map

This gives an illustrated overview of the whole area. All the sights covered in the chapter are numbered and there are also useful tips on getting around by car and public transport.

Features and story boxes highlight special aspects of an area or sight.

3 Detailed Information

All the important towns and other places of interest are described individually. They are listed in order, following the numbering on the *Pictorial Map*. Within each entry there are details on the important buildings and other major sights.

4 Major Towns
All the important towns are described individually. Within each entry there is further detailed information on all the main sights. The Town Map *shows their location.*

A Visitors' Checklist provides the practical details needed to plan a visit, including local transport and details for the local tourist office.

The Town Map shows all the key sights, along with train and bus stations, car parks, churches and tourist offices.

5 The Top Sights
All the most important sights have two or more pages devoted to them. Historic buildings and churches are dissected to reveal their interiors, and museums and galleries have colour-coded floorplans.

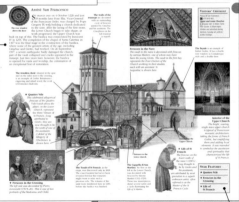

Stars indicate the features you should not miss.

6 Areas of Natural Beauty and National Parks
Parks and nature reserves are described in detail and illustrated with a pictorial map. Roads are shown, together with scenic routes, picnicking areas and campsites.

The scale bar makes it possible to judge distances. The compass shows due north.

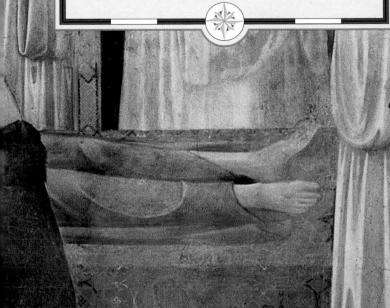

INTRODUCING
UMBRIA

Putting Umbria on the Map

O<small>F ALL THE REGIONS</small> that make up the Italian peninsula, Umbria is the only one to be totally landlocked. The region covers 8,450 sq km (3,260 sq miles), of which three-quarters belongs to the province of Perugia and one-quarter to the province of Terni. Plains make up less than one-tenth of the total area, the rest being taken up with hills and mountains. The main river is the Tiber (il Tevere) and the highest peak is Monte Redentore, at 2,450 m (8,050 ft). Lake Trasimeno, west of Perugia, is the largest inland lake in central Italy.

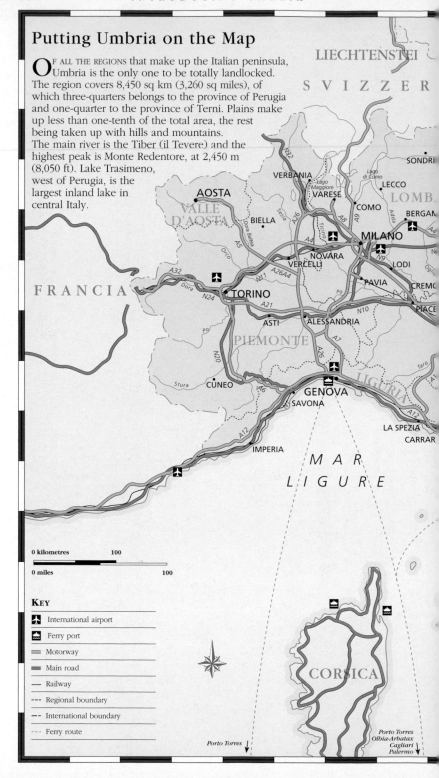

KEY

✈	International airport
⛴	Ferry port
▬	Motorway
▬	Main road
—	Railway
---	Regional boundary
--	International boundary
---	Ferry route

A PORTRAIT OF UMBRIA

UMBRIA IS A LAND APART, *with its own singular character and identity. At the geographical centre of Italy, it is known, thanks to its lushness, as the peninsula's "Green Heart"; its rolling hills and fertile plains are studded with picturesque towns, castles and monasteries, recalling millennia of human habitation.*

Small in comparison to its neighbouring regions, at just 8,450 sq km (3,260 miles), with barely a million inhabitants, Umbria nevertheless radiates a powerful image, both in Italy and abroad. Elemental features of its reputation are its unspoilt landscape, its inimitable art and architecture, and, perhaps most significantly, its deeply mystical heritage. Add to that the region's famously fine cuisine and exuberant festivals and it is no wonder that Umbria has developed a cachet all its own.

Recent decades have witnessed the arrival of a breed of "New Umbrians", neo-settlers who have migrated here, maybe from Milan, Manchester or Manhattan. It is not unusual, while exploring the region's splendidly scenic roads and byways, to come across American couples enjoying the view, monks with typically Nordic features, or Italian ex-urbanites who have chosen a new, more relaxed way of life in this idyllic, largely rural setting.

St Francis, fresco in the Basilica of Assisi

TIMELESS LANDSCAPES

Umbria's pristine natural loveliness is certainly a major enticement. The landscape ranges from the great green slopes and peaks of the Monti Sibillini and the mountain chains that border Le Marche to the gentle hills and plains around Assisi and Perugia; from the roaring waters of the Cascata delle Marmore to the subtle sibilance of the wind among the

The hamlet of Castelluccio, in a spectacular spot close to the Monti Sibillini

◁ Flag-wavers in medieval costume at the Corsa all'Anello at Narni

Piece of traditional Umbrian fabric

reeds on the shores of Lake Trasimeno. Green – the colour which has, in effect, become the region's popular "trademark" – is very much a reality here and dominates the scenery. However, the beauty of the environment alone does not fully account for Umbria's undeniable mystique. The fields, the olive groves, the forests of beech, holm oak and chestnut are inevitably set off by evocative vestiges of a long-standing human presence.

Umbrian potter at work

SUBLIME ARCHITECTURE AND ART

Whether in the form of a town, a village or a medieval monastery, an ancient farmhouse, a dry-stone wall or a ruined church, architecture is essential to the region's spirit. Whether grand or rustic, Roman, Romanesque or Renaissance, such architectural heritage conveys a timeless feel that is distinctively Umbrian. It evokes a symbiosis of man and nature that has flourished since the days of the primordial Umbri and Etruscans, and later the Romans, down to modern Italians.

Umbria's cities and towns are among Italy's most gorgeous. Perugia, Assisi, Gubbio, Orvieto, Spoleto, Todi – the very names are synonymous with the perfection of the medieval hill town. They are approachable, human in scale, but also filled with world-class masterpieces of architecture and art in recognizably Umbrian style. Some of Italy's finest palaces and civic structures are here, as well as some of its most resplendent churches, while Umbrian painters such as Perugino helped set the standard for sheer beauty in the High Renaissance.

Lying at the crossroads between Rome and Florence, the region has been embellished by the works of many renowned artists, including Cimabue, Giotto, Piero della Francesca, Simone Martini, Fra Angelico, Filippo Lippi, Luca Signorelli, Ghirlandaio, Raphael and Gian Lorenzo Bernini. At the same time, venerable Umbrian crafts, especially ceramics and textiles, have been famous for centuries.

Nor should the ancient remains be overlooked. Throughout Umbria, the Romans left behind superb gates,

The renowned Basilica di San Francesco in Assisi

A snapshot of daily life in Assisi, visited by millions of tourists every year

towers, bridges and even a still-functioning theatre or two, while the archaeological finds dating back to Etruscan times and beyond are immensely rich and displayed in beautifully appointed museums.

One insightful observer of Italian life wrote, "With its millennia of infiltration, art has saturated the soul – everyone here lives art, whether they know it or not." This is nowhere more true than in Umbria.

A PLACE OF SPIRITUALITY

Most appealing to many modern newcomers is Umbria's glowing spiritual legacy. The birthplace of St Francis, St Clare and Jacopone da Todi has become the home of many spiritual centres and teachers of every persuasion. Retreats here are not only Christian, but are affiliated with all beliefs, everyone apparently drawn by the ineffable meditative power of the place. Overwhelmingly, it is a venue of peace, as embodied in the Marcia per la Pace (Walk of

Peace) from Perugia to Assisi, which takes place every other autumn. Many global spiritual leaders have promoted greater understanding here, including the Dalai Lama.

INVITING HOSPITALITY

Visitors attracted more by earthly pleasures are well satisfied, too. Umbria's robust and tasty cuisine consists of dishes that combine the best of local culinary traditions, while taking full advantage of the produce and game of the region – highlighting wild mushrooms, black truffles and wild boar *(cinghiale)*.

Hospitality is an art form here, too. Every city, town or village proudly rivals its neighbours with its age-old festivals, as well as its gastronomic specialities. In the countryside, *agriturismo* (farm lodgings) has become a reliable alternative to standard hotel accommodation, offering a delightful first-hand taste of authentic Umbrian life.

Decades of modernization have tested the traditional values of the region, and the disastrous earthquake of 1997 has left its mark in others, but the quintessential allure of Umbria remains intact.

Apparition at Arles, **Upper Church, Assisi**

The Landscape of Umbria

The rare red lily

THE MOUNTAINS OF UMBRIA are of comparatively recent origin. The fact that the region's topography developed relatively late, together with the presence of still-active powerful tectonic forces, mean that there is a heightened risk of earthquakes in Umbria. Once cultivated up to fairly high altitudes, the mountains have now been largely abandoned by farmers. Rolling hills made up of fertile but often fragile terrain border the highest peaks; centuries of cultivation have given them their current shape. In Umbria's southwestern corner, and around Orvieto, the land is of volcanic origin. Lake Trasimeno, in the northwest, is the most important lake in Central Italy.

A bright field of sunflowers, widely cultivated in Umbria

THE MOUNTAINS

The average height of the mountains in Umbria is around 1,000 m (3,280 ft). Most of the range consists of karst limestone and is riddled with caves and subterranean galleries and rivers. The vegetation most characteristic of this environment is beech forest and upland pasture. Among the wildlife found in the mountains are birds of prey, wildcats and several kinds of wolf.

Wolves *became extinct in Umbria in the 18th century but have reappeared in the protected Monti Sibillini. There is a greater chance of seeing them in winter, when they come down to the valley.*

This Apennine edelweiss *lives on calcareous crags. Similar to alpine edelweiss, it is distinguished by its spathulate leaves (that is, wide at the tip and narrow at the base).*

THE HILLS

The climate in the hills is milder than that at higher altitudes, and is also less polluted than on the plain. For this reason, the hills of Umbria have been settled and cultivated since ancient times. In areas not given over to farmland and olive groves there are oaks, holm oaks and, lower down, mixed woodland and scrub.

The wild boar *is one of the most common mammals in the hills. Its meat is prized.*

Acorns

The olive *is one of the most important agricultural products in Umbria. Olives produced in the area around Trevi (see p107) are especially highly regarded.*

CULTIVATION OF THE PLAINS

The few areas of plain found in Umbria lie along river courses and include the Valle Umbra (between Assisi and Spoleto), the Valle del Paglia (in the southwest), and the plains of Terni and Gubbio. Reclamation in these areas in the years after World War II has created very fertile land, where farming is now carried out on an industrial scale (where possible, producing forced and cash crops), although man has been present here since ancient times. The plants found are those commonly seen in cultivated fields.

Lapwings *form flocks in cultivated fields and in pastureland during the winter season.*

The corn cockle (Agrostemma githago) *was once widespread on cultivated land. It is now rare, owing to the use of herbicides by farmers.*

THE PLAINS

In general, every area of flat ground in Umbria occupies the site of an ancient lake or marsh, and is therefore especially fertile. These plains are now primarily given over to cultivation (grapevines and olives, for example). As a consequence, the land is not known for its varied wildlife, although rodents and small predators, such as foxes, are common.

Grain *was once grown as animal fodder, while today, increasingly, it is grown in industrial quantities.*

The fox *is a highly adaptable mammal which manages to live in all kinds of habitat. In cultivated fields, foxes find shelter among the hedgerows.*

LAKES, RIVERS AND MARSHLAND

Lake Trasimeno is a place that has a fascinating history, with a tradition of fishing going back to ancient times. Rivers in Umbria include the Tiber (il Tevere), the Velino and the Nera; the last boasts the spectacular manmade waterfall, the Cascata delle Marmore, and some particularly fine scenery. Freshwater fish and other species abound in the wild.

A trout *is camouflaged among the stones on the river bed thanks to its marbled colouring.*

Freshwater crabs *live in reed beds and are active mainly at night. Their presence indicates good water quality.*

Nature Reserves in Umbria

Logo of the Sistema Parchi Umbri

Although nature plays a fundamental role in the overall image of the region, Umbria has been rather slow to set up protected parks and reserves. The creation of parks has frequently been opposed at a local level (the inhabitants are exceedingly passionate about hunting), and their establishment has been achieved largely by balancing the demands of nature with those of the development of the economy and the tourist trade.

Together with the Umbrian portion of the Parco Nazionale dei Monti Sibillini (part of a great series of protected areas in the Apennines, safeguarding the principal mountain masses in the chain), Umbrian parks today protect around seven per cent of the terrain in the region. These parks can be divided into two categories: "mountain parks", which are those along the border with Le Marche, and "water parks", which are focused around the lakes and water courses of the region.

The Parco Regionale del Lago Trasimeno (see pp92–3) covers 13,200 ha (32,600 acres) and includes the lake shores – thereby safeguarding the water and banks – but not the tourist resorts around the lake. The perimeter of Lake Trasimeno measures around 60 km (37 miles).

The Parco Fluviale del Tevere (see p133) extends from the gates of Todi as far as Alviano, along the banks of the longest river in central Italy, the Tiber. The park protects some 7,925 ha (19,585 acres), over a length of 50 km (31 miles).

The Oasis of Alviano (see p127) is an ecosystem that serves as a breeding ground for numerous species of water birds, as well as an important source of food for rare birds such as cranes, wild geese and ospreys.

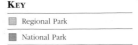

| 0 kilometres | 15 |
| 0 Miles | 15 |

KEY

- Regional Park
- National Park

Città di Castello
Umbertide
LAKE TRASIMENO
Perugia
Orvieto
Todi
LAGO DI CORBARA
Alviano
Nar
N221 N257 N3bis N219 N75bis N599 N220 N317 Tevere N71 N397 N3bis N79bis N448 N205

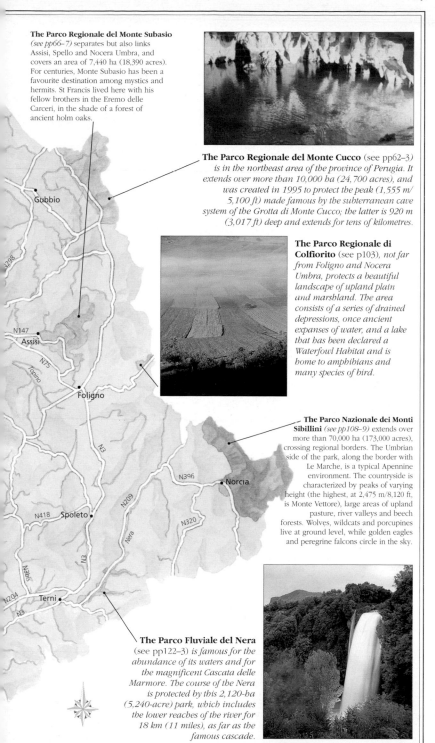

The Parco Regionale del Monte Subasio
(see pp66–7) separates but also links
Assisi, Spello and Nocera Umbra, and
covers an area of 7,440 ha (18,390 acres).
For centuries, Monte Subasio has been a
favourite destination among mystics and
hermits. St Francis lived here with his
fellow brothers in the Eremo delle
Carceri, in the shade of a forest of
ancient holm oaks.

The Parco Regionale del Monte Cucco (see pp62–3)
*is in the northeast area of the province of Perugia. It
extends over more than 10,000 ha (24,700 acres), and
was created in 1995 to protect the peak (1,555 m/
5,100 ft) made famous by the subterranean cave
system of the Grotta di Monte Cucco; the latter is 920 m
(3,017 ft) deep and extends for tens of kilometres.*

**The Parco Regionale di
Colfiorito** (see p103), *not far
from Foligno and Nocera
Umbra, protects a beautiful
landscape of upland plain
and marshland. The area
consists of a series of drained
depressions, once ancient
expanses of water, and a lake
that has been declared a
Waterfowl Habitat and is
home to amphibians and
many species of bird.*

**The Parco Nazionale dei Monti
Sibillini** *(see pp108–9)* extends over
more than 70,000 ha (173,000 acres),
crossing regional borders. The Umbrian
side of the park, along the border with
Le Marche, is a typical Apennine
environment. The countryside is
characterized by peaks of varying
height (the highest, at 2,475 m/8,120 ft,
is Monte Vettore), large areas of upland
pasture, river valleys and beech
forests. Wolves, wildcats and porcupines
live at ground level, while golden eagles
and peregrine falcons circle in the sky.

The Parco Fluviale del Nera
(see pp122–3) *is famous for the
abundance of its waters and for
the magnificent Cascata delle
Marmore. The course of the Nera
is protected by this 2,120-ha
(5,240-acre) park, which includes
the lower reaches of the river for
18 km (11 miles), as far as the
famous cascade.*

Outdoor Activities

G IVEN THE BEAUTY OF THE LANDSCAPE in Umbria, nature and the great outdoors should feature in every visitor's trip to the region. Furthermore, open-air sports are increasingly well catered for, and in every part of the region. Just as pilgrims flock to Assisi from all four corners of the globe, it is equally easy to encounter a whole range of languages among a crowd of canoeists sweeping its way down the Nera or the Tiber, or among the hang-gliding community taking off from Monte Cucco or from the windswept uplands of the Monti Sibillini.

More everyday activities should not be forgotten either, particularly as they constitute one of the best ways of seeing and appreciating this beautiful region: consider going on a long bicycle ride through the hills, past farms and ancient abbeys, or on a gentle horse-ride through one of the greenest, most fascinating and relaxing landscapes in Italy.

Hiking in one of the magnificent valleys of the Monti Sibillini

Horse-riding just outside the historic town of Spello

HORSE-RIDING

I N UMBRIA THERE are many stables and farm holiday (*agriturismo*) businesses that can organize horse-riding trips. As well as being an enjoyable sport, riding offers a closer and more natural view of the countryside than is possible with conventional means of transport.

Many Umbrian horse-riding stables belong to national associations, such as ANTE (Associazione Nazionale Turismo Equestre), and can offer trekking in all the most beautiful areas of the region, including the hills around Assisi, Città della Pieve and Bettona, the shores of Lake Trasimeno, the slopes of Monte Subasio and the steep bridle paths of the Valnerina. Treks that last for several days or more are available from various equestrian clubs, or you can apply directly to ANTE.

WALKING AND CYCLING

N O EQUIPMENT IS required to enjoy walking: all you need is a good view, decent weather, paths to follow and a destination, whether it be historical or natural.

The Monti Sibillini national park, to present the most enticing example, has always been one of the best-loved destinations among walkers in Umbria (along with the neighbouring park areas in the nearby region of Le Marche). In the colder seasons, however, it is also possible to find routes at lower altitudes, such as the bridle paths that link the towns and villages.

The routes that connect Umbria's most famous towns and villages are very popular with cyclists: the gradients are not excessive and the varied landscape provides plenty of interest along the way. Bridle paths and footpaths at higher altitudes are also used by mountain bikers. There are now more than 600 km (373 miles) of mountain biking trails in the region. Brochures and information about walking and cycling are available from tourist offices.

ROCK CLIMBING, CAVES AND GORGES

N OT ALL THAT LONG AGO, all that one had to choose from was mountaineering. Today, various rock climbing sports are popular in Italy, and there are all kinds of cliff faces to use. In Umbria, any visitor in search of a vertical cliff face will feel at home on certain cliffs in the Monti Sibillini and in the village of Ferentillo, where there are numerous suitable sites: rock climbing is such a big thing here that there is even a climbing guide dedicated to the area. Umbria is also a place that finds much favour among speleologists. The biggest attraction is the cave system beneath Monte Cucco, on the border with Le Marche (not far from that region's famous caves, the Grotte di Frasassi). There are also caves worth visiting in the mountains near Terni.

A sport that has taken hold in Umbria, which developed out of speleology – the equipment used is much the same – is "torrentismo", or canyoning, the sport of navigating steep-sided gorges. The most famous and popular sites are found in the Valnerina (Fosso di Rocca Gelli and Forra del Casco), on Monte Cucco (Forra di Riofreddo), and in the hills surrounding Lake Corbara (Gole di Prodo).

It is important to make clear that all of the above are extreme sports, and that they can all be exceedingly dangerous. Anyone trying them out for the first time should ensure that they are accompanied by an expert.

An Umbrian cave, and one of many visiting speleologists

HANG-GLIDING AND CROSS-COUNTRY SKIING

WIND, UNLIMITED vistas and serious gradients are the three ingredients necessary for hang-gliding and paragliding. Umbria has plenty of all three. Famous locations for this exciting but daredevil sport are Monte Cucco and the Monti Sibillini, where the isolated, high-altitude village of Castelluccio di Norcia is now one of the most popular destinations for hang-gliding

Hang-gliding on the slopes of Monte Vettore

aficionados, who come here from all over the world.

The topography of the Umbrian mountains does not much favour downhill skiing, however; few of the slopes are steep enough, and the lower altitudes are not suitable for the building of ski lifts or ski resorts of any great size. To compensate, the great Apennine uplands provide perfect cross-country territory. Skiers can follow the beaten tracks or, better still, ski along snow-covered bridle paths and footpaths.

SHOOTING RAPIDS

IN SPRING, the many rivers and water courses that cross Umbria, almost all of them torrential, are an irresistible attraction for canoeists from all over Europe. As the water rises and the rapids swell, canoes, kayaks and rubber rafts appear as if from nowhere along the banks of the rivers Nera and Tiber.

The Nera offers a range of experiences and caters to various levels of difficulty, up to the highest level, requiring considerable skill and expertise. This river also offers the extraordinary sight

Shooting the rapids on the Nera

of the Cascata delle Marmore (*see pp122–3*), which is the principal starting point for rafting trips. The stretch of the Tiber below Todi is one of the most popular routes for river rafting and other excursions, but you can also join the Tiber further north, at Città di Castello, allowing you to cross virtually the entire region.

A non-competitive descent from Todi to Rome takes place every year from the end of April to early May. It is open to everyone and is very popular. There are also good river-rafting sites from the Monti Sibillini down to the Valnerina.

SAILING ON THE LAKES

LAKE TRASIMENO is clearly the most obvious place for holidaymakers in land-locked Umbria to go sailing and windsurfing. Visitors can bring their own boats or make use of the craft available for hire. There are numerous regattas. Other stretches of water that are at least partially equipped for sailing, windsurfing and other water sports include Lago di Piediluco and Lago di Corbara, both in southern Umbria.

You can also go water skiing on Lake Trasimeno, but you must first apply for a permit from the office of the Provincia di Perugia.

Sailing boats manoeuvring on Lake Trasimeno

In the Footsteps of St Francis

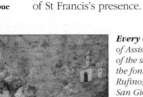

FRANCIS WAS BORN IN ASSISI in 1181–82, and grew up to be a bright, cultured and even ambitious youth. A military career was chosen as the means by which he could rise up through the social hierarchy, and he enrolled in the army that Walter of Brienne was preparing for the Crusades. However, illness brought Francis back to Assisi, where he experienced his conversion and where he began his charity work. The story of his life, marvellously illustrated in the frescoes in the upper church at Assisi, provides us with a picture of a man drawn to nature, poverty and prayer. They also inspire us to go and explore the many places in Umbria that retain the memory of St Francis's presence.

St Francis, attributed to Cimabue

Isola Maggiore, on Lake Trasimeno, was the home of one of the first communities of the Friars Minor at the beginning of the 13th century. St Francis spent a long Lenten period with them here.

Every church, every corner *of Assisi bears traces of the life of the saint. He was baptized in the font in the cathedral of San Rufino; next to the church of San Giorgio was his school; and the Chiesa Nuova was constructed on the very spot where Francis is thought to have been born. Left,* St Francis gives his cloak to a poor man, *with a view of Assisi in the background.*

One of the most famous episodes *in the life of the saint is undoubtedly his preaching to the birds. The stone on which the scene is said to have taken place is in the church of San Francesco in Bevagna (see p104). Right,* Francis preaches to the birds.

Near the Fonti del Clitunno *(see p107), in the church of San Pietro di Bovara, is a Crucifix which spoke to St Francis. (The more famous talking Crucifix is in the Basilica di Santa Chiara, see p70.) Left,* The Saint in Ecstasy.

CITTÀ DI CASTELLO

Tiber

AREZZO

LAKE TRASIMENO

Nestore

Chiani

Paglia

LAKE CORBARA

LAKE ALVIANO

KEY

▬	Trail of St Francis
═	Other roads
≈	River

0 kilometres   20

0 miles   20

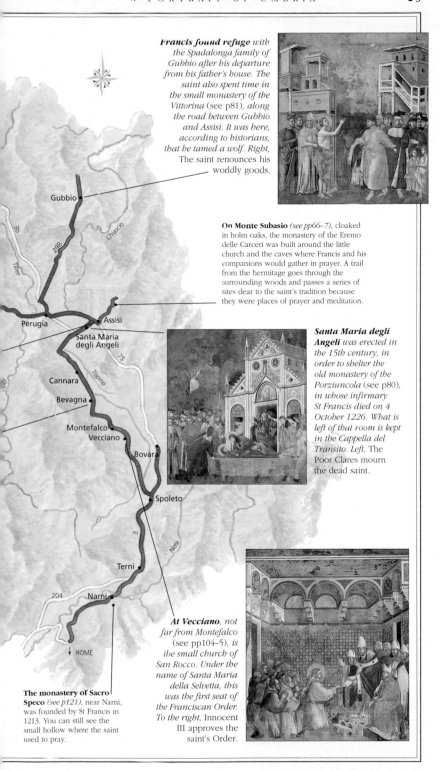

Francis found refuge with the Spadalonga family of Gubbio after his departure from his father's house. The saint also spent time in the small monastery of the Vittorina (see p81), along the road between Gubbio and Assisi. It was here, according to historians, that he tamed a wolf. Right, The saint renounces his worldly goods.

On Monte Subasio *(see pp66–7)*, cloaked in holm oaks, the monastery of the Eremo delle Carceri was built around the little church and the caves where Francis and his companions would gather in prayer. A trail from the hermitage goes through the surrounding woods and passes a series of sites dear to the saint's tradition because they were places of prayer and meditation.

Santa Maria degli Angeli *was erected in the 15th century, in order to shelter the old monastery of the Porziuncola (see p80), in whose infirmary St Francis died on 4 October 1226. What is left of that room is kept in the Cappella del Transito. Left, The Poor Clares mourn the dead saint.*

At Vecciano, *not far from Montefalco (see pp104–5), is the small church of San Rocco. Under the name of Santa Maria della Selvetta, this was the first seat of the Franciscan Order. To the right, Innocent III approves the saint's Order.*

The monastery of Sacro Speco *(see p121)*, near Narni, was founded by St Francis in 1213. You can still see the small hollow where the saint used to pray.

Art in Umbria

THE REGION OF UMBRIA as it is defined today was established only after the unification of Italy in 1861. In the preceding centuries, Umbria's towns and cities formed part of a political and artistic mosaic which extended from Tuscany to the Adriatic coast, without precise boundaries. In art, as in politics, there was plenty of opportunity for contacts and exchanges with other regions. Two crucial highlights stand out in the long history of art in Umbria: the founding and construction of the basilica of St Francis in Assisi – with the contribution of great artists, from Umbria and from other parts of Italy – and the golden age of the city of Perugia.

Etruscan bronze

Tempietto del Clitunno, detail of the front

Cast of stone with Umbrian inscription, 2nd century BC

ORIGINS

UMBRIA WAS POPULATED from the sixth millennium BC. Interesting ceramic finds from that time have been discovered near Norcia and Parrano (outside Orvieto). With the passing of the millennia, a community of shepherds – part of what scholars describe as the Apenine civilization – developed in the mountains. Around the 16th century BC, they started to produce elegant pottery, decorated with geometrical motifs. The burial site at Monteleone di Spoleto dates back to these very early civilizations. Archaeologists discovered a bronze cart here, and this is now in the Metropolitan Museum in New York. During the first millennium BC, Umbrian land was divided between two very different peoples: the Etruscans, who settled on the west bank of the Tiber, with the key towns of Perugia and Orvieto, and the Umbri, about whom little is still known, who were on the Tiber's east bank and in the Apennine mountains.

THE ROMANS

THE ROMAN CONQUEST of Umbria was slow but inexorable. If one had to choose a symbolic historical date for the arrival of the Romans in Umbria, it would be 219 BC, the year in which the Via Flaminia was opened. This Roman road became the main communication route through the region for centuries.

The presence of the Romans led to a great push in building and civil engineering: theatres, public works as well as roads were built. In terms of sculpture dating from the Roman age, many marble and some bronze statues survive. The latter include the extraordinary

Male statue, 1st century AD

statue of Germanicus, found in Amelia and returned there only recently after a long and controversial residence in Perugia *(see p126)*. One can also see well-preserved Roman buildings, such as the amphitheatre in Gubbio *(see p58) and the* Temple of Minerva in Assisi *(see p71)*.

Christianity reached Umbria in around the 3rd and 4th centuries AD: of particular interest from this period are the church of San Salvatore in Spoleto *(see p115)* and the little temple at the Fonti di Clitunno *(see p107)*, both of which show clearly how early Christian architecture was inspired by the Roman and classical traditions. Another important church from the early Christian era in Umbria is San Michele Archangelo, or Sant'Angelo, in Perugia *(see p91)*, which was influenced by Byzantine architecture.

THE MIDDLE AGES

POLITICALLY SPLIT between Byzantium (on the west bank of the Tiber) and the Lombard dominion (on the east bank), Umbria was subject to a range of influences in the field of art. Even though few works of art have survived from the second half of the first millennium, and even though the buildings that remain have often been extensively remodelled, it is known that the 9th century was a period of significant development in Umbria. Cathedrals were founded all over the region and were often adorned with great pictorial cycles (now mostly lost). The main centre for this boom was the Lombard stronghold of Spoleto *(see pp110–15)*, where even today you can admire the reliefs on the façade of San Pietro and the frescoes in the churches of San Gregorio and San Paolo inter Vineas.

The cloister of the abbey of Sassovivo, near Foligno, was built using Roman columns and arches.

Detail of the façade of San Pietro in Spoleto

ASSISI

IN 1228, LESS THAN TWO years after the death of St Francis, and at the wishes of Frate Elia (who took it upon himself to hide the body of the saint), construction of the basilica of San Francesco in Assisi *(see pp72–3)* began. This was a truly crucial moment, since the work on the basilica was to influence the art and architecture of both Umbria and nearby regions for centuries to come. The basilica in Assisi is still one of the most important monuments of Western art today.

The first frescoes were commissioned in 1254 from an anonymous Umbrian artist, known as the Maestro di San Francesco, who is regarded as having operated

GIOTTO

Presumed self-portrait

Born in 1267, Giotto di Bondone probably trained at the Florentine workshop of Cimabue. While it is thought that Giotto contributed to the frescoes in the basilica of St Francis in Assisi, it is now accepted that the cycle of the *Life of St Francis* was not his work but that of Roman painters. Giotto's great works include a *Last Judgment* and *Stories from the Life of the Virgin* in the Cappella degli Scrovegni in Padua and the bell tower for the duomo in Florence, a project that he directed up to his death in 1337.

a workshop of the highest quality. Then, from the end of the 13th century, great masters were summoned from outside the region – among them Cimabue and Giotto – to decorate the walls of the upper and lower churches. Their work would become a model for Umbrian painters later on. Work on the two basilicas continued for more than two centuries, with contributions by other great names from the history of Italian art, including Simone Martini and Pietro Lorenzetti. In parallel with the spreading of the Franciscan faith, so too

Painted Cross, Maestro di San Francesco, 1272

the pictorial style created in Assisi gained ground, and was imitated and reproduced in many new Franciscan churches all over Italy.

On 26 September 1997 this immense inheritance risked being lost forever. The entire complex was badly damaged by a violent earthquake, and parts of the vault in the upper church collapsed. Through the extraordinarily hard work of restorers, fragments of frescoes were saved and reinstalled where possible, but many vaults remain blank. The basilica remains magnificent but tarnished.

Vault of the Evangelists, Cimabue (1240–1302), Basilica of Assisi

PERUGINO

Pietro Vannucci, or Perugino, was born in Città della Pieve in 1452 and died in Fontignano in 1523. He was influenced by the work of Piero della Francesca and Verrocchio, in whose workshop the painter trained early on. Works in Rome include *Handing the Keys to St Peter* in the Sistine Chapel (1481), in the Vatican. In Florence are a *Lamentation* (Palazzo Pitti, 1494) and a *Crucifixion* (Santa Maddalena de' Pazzi, 1493). He also painted frescoes in the Sala dell'Udienza in the Collegio del Cambio, Perugia. His work can be found in several of the smaller towns of Umbria, particularly near Lake Trasimeno *(see p95).*

Epiphany, 1475–78, detail

age came here, including: Piero della Francesca, Fra Angelico (who contributed to the decoration of the cathedral in Orvieto), Filippo Lippi (who would later be called to Spoleto to fresco the cathedral apse), and also Agostino di Duccio. A cycle of frescoes (1498–1500) painted by Perugino in the Collegio del Cambio was to exert a great influence over painters such as Pinturicchio and the young Raphael, who produced some of his early work in Perugia.

In this same period – in Perugia as well as in other cities in Umbria – a new style of architecture began to change the look of the old medieval city spaces, with new palaces being erected for noble merchant families. Influences in this field came from Rome, Urbino or from the great cities of nearby Tuscany.

An example of Umbrian art by the Maestro di Città di Castello

was one of the first of its kind to be built in Italy. To celebrate this magnificent achievement a fountain was built in Piazza IV Novembre, featuring sculptures by Nicola and Giovanni Pisano *(see p87).*

THE 16TH CENTURY IN PERUGIA

TOWARDS THE MIDDLE of the 15th century, the city of Perugia was rich and cosmopolitan. The great Italian painters of the

THE UMBRIAN SCHOOL

IT WAS BECAUSE OF the influence of the great artists who were attracted to Umbria in the second half of the 15th century that a regional school

PERUGIA'S GOLDEN AGE

THE POSITION OF Perugia, on the Via Flaminia and Via Amerina, at the junction of routes of communication between Rome and the Adriatic coast, made the city vulnerable to conquest. After invasions by the Goths and Lombards, the foundation of the cathedral (by the 10th century) marked the first stage in Perugia's rebirth in the Middle Ages.

For around three centuries, the commune of Perugia grew in power, riches and possessions. Signs of the prosperity of this age are the walls and city gates, though an even greater indication is the aqueduct, which brought water to the city centre and

Polyptych, Niccolò di Liberatore known as l'Alunno, 1471

developed in its own right, liberated from the Gothic models that had influenced art in the previous centuries. The principal artists to learn lessons from the Florentine Renaissance were, besides Perugino, Niccolò Alunno, Antonio Mezzastris, Matteo da Gualdo, from around Foligno, and Benedetto Bonfigli, of Perugia. In the first half of the 16th century, the most representative name is that of Giovanni di Pietro, or Spagna. The Umbrian school lost its originality and died out rapidly with the advent of Mannerism.

Coronation of the Virgin, 1511, Spagna

THE DOMINATION OF ROME

WHEN THE POWER of the communes *(see pp42–3)* gave way to papal rule, great military structures were built: Antonio da Sangallo the Younger designed Perugia's Rocca Paolina *(see p84)* and the Pozzo di San Patrizio in Orvieto *(see p138)*. Vignola worked on the Castellina in Norcia *(see p116)*.

By the end of the 16th century all the major artists of the time were working in Rome – not only Italians, but also Flemish artists such as Van Mander, Stellaert and Loots. Umbrian towns were totally dependent on the Church. In Todi, the construction of Santa Maria della Consolazione *(see pp132–3)*, worked on by

Baldassarre Peruzzi, Vignola and Ippolito Scalza, inaugurated a new concept of religious architecture. In 1569, on the plain below Assisi, work began on the great church of Santa Maria degli Angeli *(see p80)*, intended as a home for the Franciscan chapel of the Porziuncola. Designed by Galeazzo Alessi with Vignola as consultant, it was finished only in 1679.

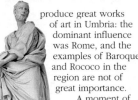

Statue in Santa Maria della Consolazione

Umbria's noble families, often important figures in administration and in the ranks of Roman power, built palazzi and villas in their native cities.

18TH–19TH CENTURIES

THE FOLLOWING centuries, dominated by papal rule right up to the unification of Italy in 1861, did not really

produce great works of art in Umbria: the dominant influence was Rome, and the examples of Baroque and Rococo in the region are not of great importance.

A moment of regional pride came with the brief period of splendour of Perugia's Accademia di Belle Arti, which championed the Neo-Classical style. It is certainly no coincidence that the artist Canova, who stayed at San Gemini (near Todi), took up contacts with the great families of Perugia.

The 19th century saw the cities of Umbria becoming stages on the set routes followed by travellers on the Grand Tour. Admiration for the art of the Middle Ages became the cult of the time and *medievalismo* took hold in Perugia and led to the restoration – sometimes rather ingenuously – of ancient buildings.

APPLIED ARTS

Along with most of Italy, Umbria has long been famous as a treasure trove of art, sculpture and architecture. However, it has also produced a great many master craftsmen of skill and stature. In the many museums in Umbria's towns, old and new, one can find pieces of rare beauty, in particular ceramics and textiles, worked by hand over the centuries. The production of these objects continues today, and no tourist in

Majolica jug, 16th century

Umbria should miss the opportunity of visiting one of the numerous handicrafts workshops in the region. Besides ceramics, for which Deruta *(see p83)* is particularly renowned, and fabrics, which are still woven by hand, look out for the embroidered tulle of Panicale (near Lake Trasimeno) and the delicate lace of Assisi, as well as painted stuccoes and woodcarving.

Antique fabric, manufactured in Todi in the 14th century

Architecture in Umbria

San Lorenzo di Arari in Orvieto

EVEN THOUGH the most significant impact on the towns of Umbria occurred during the centuries of the Middle Ages and the Renaissance, monuments from all periods of history are found in the region. From the time of the Etruscan city state to the era of Roman domination, from the rise of Romanesque architecture to the advent of Neo-Classicism, every people, every era, every architectural style and every artistic movement has left its traces, thanks to the work of the major artists of the time. The influence of the Roman Catholic church has been a constant.

A bas-relief, frequently used to decorate churches and palazzi

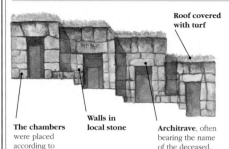

Roof covered with turf

The chambers were placed according to the terrain.

Walls in local stone

Architrave, often bearing the name of the deceased.

The necropolises are the most tangible sign of the Etruscan presence in Umbria. In general, they consisted of a series of tomb chambers lined up along cemetery roads. Inside, the deceased lay on a funeral bench.

ANTIQUITY

While the Umbri left few traces of the form of their cities, the imposing polygonal walls of Amelia and Spoleto owe their existence to this Italic people. The Etruscans left necropolises and tombs, such as those near Orvieto (Necropoli del Crocifisso del Tufo) or the extraordinary monumental burial site of the Ipogeo dei Volumni at Perugia. There are impressive Roman monuments such as the Temple of Minerva in Assisi, the theatres of Gubbio, Spoleto and Terni, the great cisterns of Amelia and Todi, and the city gates of Spello and Todi. Not forgetting the Via Flaminia, which still links Rome with the Adriatic coast, as it did 2,300 years ago.

THE MIDDLE AGES AND THE RENAISSANCE

After a period of Byzantine and Lombard domination, architecture was rejuvenated by the birth of the Romanesque style. Town squares lined with public buildings – a sign of temporal and communal power – were being built, as were cathedrals, a tangible and potent symbol of spiritual power.

The building of commercial towns in contact with outside markets brought about the arrival of the Gothic style during the 14th century. Especially fine examples of this style are Orvieto cathedral *(see pp136–7)* and the decoration in the Sala delle Arti Liberali e dei Pianeti in Palazzo Trinci in Foligno *(see p102)*, from the early years of the 15th century.

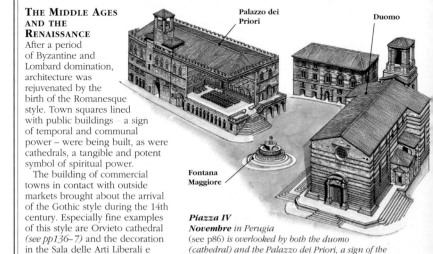

Palazzo dei Priori

Duomo

Fontana Maggiore

Piazza IV Novembre *in Perugia (see p86) is overlooked by both the duomo (cathedral) and the Palazzo dei Priori, a sign of the political power of the medieval commune. Between the two stands the Fontana Maggiore, decorated between 1275 and 1278 by Nicola Pisano and his son Giovanni.*

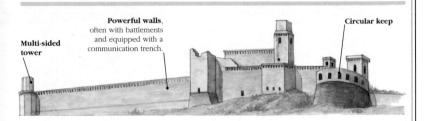

Multi-sided tower

Powerful walls, often with battlements and equipped with a communication trench.

Circular keep

The Rocca Maggiore at Assisi (see p79) *was rebuilt in 1356 on the foundations of a feudal fortification built by Frederick Barbarossa. Its restoration was the work of Cardinal Albornoz, the papal legate who studded central Italy with these strongholds of the faith.*

THE AGE OF THE FORTRESSES

The conquest of Umbrian towns by the papacy brought about profound changes in the urban layout. The new power, aiming to increase military control and to diminish the importance of the traditional social space of the town square, commissioned a series of imposing fortresses which, although they have been modified over the centuries, have come down to us today virtually intact. These include the fortresses of Orvieto (begun in 1364 and then rebuilt in 1450), Narni (built from 1367–78), Assisi (rebuilt in 1356) and Spoleto (built in 1359).

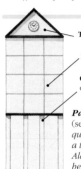

Tympanum in classical style

Mirrored windows

Colonnade inspired by the entrance to a classical temple.

Palazzo della Regione (see p90), *in the Fontivegge quarter of Perugia, was part of a town plan by the architect Aldo Rossi. From 1982 to 1989 he rebuilt this area of the regional capital in postmodern style, with classical references.*

MODERN ARCHITECTURE

Outside the encircling walls of Umbria's medieval towns, large and small, modern suburbs have developed, usually on the flat land just below the hilltop towns. Building styles have not always been particularly respectful of the artistic beauty of the old town, but there are some successful examples of modern architecture, such as the quarter of Fontivegge in Perugia. The countryside, too, has had to accept change. Many medieval groups of houses and farms have been converted for modern use, for example as hotels.

ROMANESQUE CHURCHES IN UMBRIA

Around the 11th century, when medieval society was developing and the Church was re-creating its own autonomy, a style of religious architecture developed which, with simple linear forms, attempted a direct link with local cultures. In the 19th century, this style was defined as "Romanesque", after its derivation from the Christian basilica of the Roman era. The Romanesque church presents a harmonious façade, featuring arches and one or more rose windows. From the three doorways access is gained to the three aisled interior, at the end of which is a presbytery, raised to allow the construction of a crypt. Examples of the style, since reworked, are San Lorenzo di Arari in Orvieto and the cathedrals of Spoleto, Assisi and Todi.

Three-mullioned window in a square frame

Large rose window (13th century)

San Michele (1195) in Bevagna has a beautiful doorway in which Romanesque elements and Roman finds are combined.

Literature in Umbria

AFTER THE FALL of the Roman empire, Umbria became a battleground for various peoples for the entire duration of the Middle Ages. Around the 13th century, when the principal Umbrian towns were asserting themselves, the use of the vernacular became widespread here and in Tuscany. The *Canticle* by St Francis of Assisi and Jacopone da Todi's *Laudi* were among the first great examples of literature in Italian. Unlike in Tuscany, Umbria did not develop its own literary school, and over the following centuries local authors became part of the more general development of Italian literature. Travellers and writers of all nationalities and all eras have, however, left memorable accounts of Umbria.

First page of the manuscript of the *Laudi* by Jacopone da Todi

EARLY WRITERS OF ITALIAN: ST FRANCIS AND JACOPONE DA TODI

TOWARDS THE END of his life, ill and suffering, Francis wrote the poem *Laudes Creaturarum*. It was around 1225 and he was living at the Porziuncola, not far from Assisi. His decision to write in vernacular Italian had a deep significance for the saint, since it enabled him to reach ordinary people and to distance himself from the more well-to-do classes, who used Latin. After Francis's death, his friars drew up the *Fioretti* ("little flowers", as his writings were known), signalling the birth of a school of religion and literature which chose to use the vernacular

as its expressive form and which saw in Francis its greatest forerunner.

Jacopo di Iacobello dei Benedetti (1236–1306), known as Jacopone da Todi *(see p132)*, was originally a rich merchant. After the death of his wife, he decided to devote himself to prayer, becoming a lay brother with a group of Franciscan Friars Minor called the "Spirituals". His ideals of penitence and rigour frequently caused him to clash with his own, less intransigent, brothers, the Friars Minor Conventuals, who adhered less strictly to the Franciscan Rule. These radical ideas also meant that he often risked being condemned for heresy by the Roman Catholic church. The latter half of Jacopone da Todi's life and his spiritual and intellectual journey are

Jacopone da Todi (1236–1306), one of the first writers in Italian

described in the *Laudi*, an extensive work in vernacular Italian which is considered one of the fundamental texts of early Italian literature. Despite the controversies, Jacopone left a message of peace at the end of his life.

THE CANTICLE OF ST FRANCIS

A hymn to the majesty and beauty of Creation, the *Canticle* of St Francis is one of the most famous pieces of Italian literature known to his fellow Italians. In the poem, Francis praises all the creations and creatures of God, from the stars to the sun, even Sister Death. "Praised be You my Lord with all Your creatures, / especially Sir Brother Sun, / Who is the day through whom You give us light. / And he is beautiful and radiant with great splendour, / Of You Most High, he bears the likeness. / Praised be You, my Lord, through Sister Moon and the stars, / In the heavens you have made them bright, precious and fair."

One of the many images of St Francis

Other important literary legacies from the Middle Ages are the missals and the choral books which formed part of the church treasury. These illuminated manuscripts reproduce fine Latin texts and images from the Life of Christ.

Franciscan missal from the end of the 13th century

WRITERS IN UMBRIA

SINCE THE TIME of the rise of the great mercantile cities, and thanks also to the strong attraction exercised by Assisi as the home of St Francis, Umbria has long been an important destination for Italian and foreign travellers. Dante and Goethe, Dumas and Gregorovius, Hawthorne and Carducci have all made interesting – and often curious – comments on this region of Italy.

IN THE WORDS OF THE TRAVELLERS

DANTE, IN THE 11th canto of *Paradiso* (Paradise), describes the geography of Perugia and then of Assisi: *"Intra Tupino e l'acqua che discende / dal colle eletto del Beato Ubaldo / fertile costa d'alto monte pende / onde Perugia sente freddo e caldo / da Porta Sole…".* ("Between the Topino and the water that falls from the hill chosen by the blessed Ubaldo hangs a fertile slope of the lofty mountain from

which Perugia feels cold and heat at Porta Sole.")

In the 16th century the writer Bartolomeo Fontana described his visit to Perugia: *"Perosa è città nobile, et magnifica posta in monte, non lungi da questa è il Lago Trasimeno hoggi detto Perugino famoso per la stragge di Flamminio consule Romanoe per la sua vettoria del Carthaginese Annibale."* ("Perugia is a noble city, in a magnificent hilltop setting, not far away is Lake Trasimeno now known as Perugino, famous for the slaughter of the Roman consul Flaminius and the victory of the Carthaginian Hannibal.")

Tobias Smollett, the author of *Travels through France and Italy* (1766), recounted in it his experience of various Umbrian cities, such as Foligno. "…the Fulginium of the antients is a small town, not unpleasant, lying in the midst of mulberry plantations, vineyards, and corn-fields, and built on both sides of the little river Topino. In choosing our beds at the inn, I perceived one chamber locked and desired it might be opened; upon which the cameriere declared with some reluctance, *'Bisogna dire a su' eccellenza; poco fa, che una bestia è morta in questa camera e non è ancora*

Tobias Smollett (1721–71), British novelist and visitor to Umbria

German writer Johann Wolfgang von Goethe (1749–1832)

lustrata' ('Your excellency must know that a filthy beast died lately in that chamber, and it is not yet purified and put in order'). When I enquired what beast it was, he replied, *'Un' eretico inglese'*. 'An English heretick.'"

Johann Wolfgang Goethe was a great lover of classical art and also an admirer of the pagan world. When he arrived in Assisi he did not go to the basilica of St Francis but wanted to see the ruins of the Temple of Minerva: "…I turned away in distaste from the enormous structure of the two churches on my left, which are built one on top of the other like a Babylonian tower, and are the resting place of St Francis … I asked a handsome boy the way to the Maria della Minerva, and he accompanied me up into the town …".

The American writer Nathaniel Hawthorne passed through Perugia during his "Italian year" in 1858. "The scene was livelier than any I have seen in Rome, the people appearing more vivacious, in this mountain air, than the populace of the eternal city, and the whole piazza babbling with a multitudinous voice. I noticed to-day, more than yesterday, the curious and picturesque architecture of the principal streets, especially that of the grand piazza."

Dante Alighieri (1265–1321)

UMBRIA
THROUGH THE YEAR

ALL YEAR ROUND in Umbria there are feast days, religious celebrations and pagan festivals linked to the farming year, including the harvest, or to popular and historical traditions of the ancient communes. Some of these events are famous worldwide, but every small village in Umbria has

Spoleto festival logo

its own festival or saint's day worthy of wider renown. Besides the traditional events that have taken place for decades or centuries, there is also a full calendar of cultural events, such as the Festival of Spoleto and Umbria Jazz, not to mention historical re-enactments, and cinema and theatre seasons.

SPRING

UMBRIA HAS no sea coast. As a result, the spring climate can be cool and windy. On higher ground, the snow may remain until March or April, while on the hills and high plains spring flowers emerge. The main religious events during this season are those that fall during the Easter period, but there also important feast days in May.

MARCH

Coloriamo i Cieli, Castiglione del Lago. Biennial kite festival.
Benedictine celebrations, Norcia *(20–21 Mar)*. Includes a torchlit procession and a crossbow competition.

APRIL

Antiques fair, Todi *(mid to late Apr)*. Held in Palazzo delle Arti.
Wine week, Montefalco *(Easter)*. Trade fair of DOC wines.

Opening of the Corsa all'Anello festival in Narni

Women in medieval costume at the Calendimaggio in Assisi

La Desolata, Perugia *(Holy Week)*. Staging of the Passion.
Tableaux Vivants, Città della Pieve *(Holy Week)*. Scenes from the Passion.
Processione del Cristo Morto, Assisi, Tuoro sul Trasimeno and Norcia *(Holy Week)*.
Via Crucis, Alviano and Amelia *(Good Friday)*.
Processione della Rinchinata, Bastia Umbra and Cannara *(Easter)*. Staging the meeting between Christ and the Madonna.
Corsa all'Anello, Narni *(late April to mid-May)*. Costumed knights spear a ring *(anello)* with a lance.

MAY

Cantamaggio, Terni *(May)*. Folk festival celebrating the advent of spring. Parade of floats with allegorical scenes.
Festa del Calendimaggio, Assisi *(first week)*. Three days

of fun, including a costumed re-enactment of medieval stories, in which two of the town's districts compete.
Corsa dei Ceri, Gubbio *(15 May)*. Three guilds challenge each other to carry towering candlesticks *(ceri)* on their shoulders up to the basilica of Sant'Ubaldo.
Palio della Balestra, Gubbio *(last Sun)*. In Piazza della Signoria, the crossbowmen of Gubbio and Sansepolcro (Tuscany) challenge each other in a Palio.
Festa di Santa Rita, Cascia *(21–22 May)*. A torchlit procession towards the Santa Rita basilica, then a historical procession with the saint's remains and the staging of scenes from her life.
Festa della Palombella, Orvieto *(Pentecost)*. Similar to the Scoppio del Carro in Florence, in which an artificial "dove" sets light to a cart of fireworks.

AVERAGE DAILY HOURS OF SUNSHINE

HOURS

10

8

4

2

0

Jan Feb Mar Apr May Jun Jul Aug Sep Oct Nov Dec

Sunshine
In summer the days are long and sunny, and it can become very hot in the towns. In September and October the days are still sunny, and often pleasantly warm, as they are also in the spring – perhaps the best time to visit Umbria.

SUMMER

U MBRIA CAN BE very hot and humid in July and August, so many summer events are held outside, and in the evening. Festivals take place in squares, parks and gardens, and attract locals and tourists alike.

JUNE

Festa della Fioritura, Castelluccio di Norcia. Ancient feast marking the return of flocks of sheep to the mountains.
Mercato delle Gaite, Bevagna *(second half of Jun)*. Medieval fair with splendid costumes and stalls.
Infiorata, Spello *(Corpus Christi)*. Procession along a flower strewn route. Floral carpet competition.
Procession, Orvieto *(Corpus Christi)*. Procession in historical costume.
Festa del Voto, Assisi *(22 Jun)*. Re-enactment of the

Floral decorations in the street during the Infiorata, Spello

Piazza IV Novembre in Perugia, crowded with jazz fans

expulsion of the Saracens.
Rockin' Umbria, Perugia and Umbertide *(last ten days of Jun)*. Rock music festival, with up-and-coming bands, as well as photography and comic exhibitions.
Biennale di Scultura, Gubbio. A biennial exhibition of works by contemporary Italian artists.
Festa delle Acque, Piediluco and at the Cascata delle Marmore *(late Jun)*. Processions of boats, canoe races and fireworks.

JULY

Festival di Spoleto *(end Jun–mid-Jul)*. A major international event dedicated to theatre, dance and music.
Umbria Jazz, Perugia *(mid-July)*. Theatres, gardens and squares are taken over by some of the world's great jazz artists.
Festival delle Nazioni, Città

di Castello. Chamber music festival.
Gubbio Festival *(Jul–Aug)*. Chamber and symphony music in the open air.
Palio delle Barche, Passignano sul Trasimeno *(last week in Jul)*. Town districts compete in a boat race, for which participants wear medieval costume.

Historical costume

AUGUST

Palio dei Terzieri, Città della Pieve *(mid-Jun)*. Archery competition and all manner of street entertainment, including acrobats and a procession featuring costumes derived from the works of Perugino.
Palio dei Quartieri, Nocera Umbra. Popular historical re-enactment in costume.
Palio di San Rufino, Assisi. Crossbow competition.
Rassegna internazionale del folklore, Castiglione del Lago. Folklore festival.

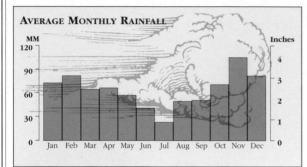

AVERAGE MONTHLY RAINFALL

Rainfall
Late autumn is the time of year when rainfall is at its heaviest. In winter heavy snowfalls are common in the Apennines, while storms may occur in spring and late summer.

The Joust of the Quintana in Foligno, September

AUTUMN

THE END OF THE SUMMER heralds the grape harvest, followed by the olive harvest. These are two very important occasions for the customs and culture of the region. Summer festivals and tourist events are usually over by this stage, and this is the start of a season of festivals linked to the gastronomy and history of the region.

SEPTEMBER

Cavalcata di Satriano, Nocera Umbra *(first Sun)*. Knights in medieval costume retrace the last journey of St Francis, from the hermitage at Nocera to his native Assisi.
Giostra della Quintana, Foligno *(second Sun)*. In this joust, competing knights attempt to spear a ring held by a wooden puppet. The streets are filled with historical processions.
Giochi delle Porte, Gualdo Tadino *(last week of Sep)*. Includes archery and catapult competitions, donkey and donkey cart races all around

the town. There are also historical re-enactments.
Festa dell'Uva *(end Sep)*, Montefalco. Celebration of the grape harvest.
Segni Barocchi, Foligno *(Sep–Oct)*. Musical and theatrical performances, all with a Baroque theme.

OCTOBER

Giostra dell'Arme, San Gemini *(late Sep–mid-Oct)*. Costumed knights from two town districts compete in a jousting tournament.
Palio dei Terzieri, Trevi *(1 Oct)*. Cart race and historical parade.
Festival Eurochocolate, Perugia *(mid–late Oct)*. Chocolate stands and superb chocolate sculptures fill the historic centre.
Festa di San Francesco, Assisi *(3–4 Oct)*. Important religious celebration on the anniversary of Francis's death.
Marcia per la Pace, Perugia to Assisi *(biennial)*. Groups and movements from around the world participate in an

international march for peace.
Rassegna Antiquaria, Perugia *(end Oct–early Nov)*. Antiques fair. Includes displays of antique textiles.
Ottobre Trevano, Trevi. Gastronomic feasts and historical re-enactments in costume.

NOVEMBER

Fiera dei Cavalli, Città di Castello *(third Sun of Nov)*. Cattle markets and horse fairs.
Wine Tasting, Torgiano *(late Nov)*. World-famous wine-tasting competition of Umbrian and other Italian wines.
Mostra del Tartufo, Città di Castello *(second weekend)*. See and taste white truffles and all sorts of other tasty woodland delicacies.
Festa dei Ceramisti, Deruta *(25 Nov)*. Festival for Deruta's older ceramicists, plus displays of ceramics.
Rassegna cinematografica di Assisi. Film festival dedicated to Italian cinema.

Flag waving display at the Giochi delle Porte in Gualdo Tadino

AVERAGE MONTHLY TEMPERATURE

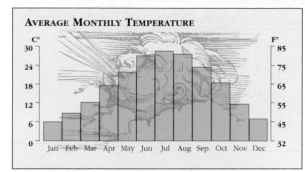

Temperature

The Umbrian climate is temperate, though temperatures are much cooler in the Apennines. Autumn and spring, when the days are not too hot, are the most pleasant seasons. The summer months are hot and humid, especially in the towns.

The Nativity in Città di Castello, one of Italy's most important

WINTER

THIS SEASON can be very cold and windy, and snow often falls at higher mountain altitudes. There are festivals celebrating the chestnut harvest, for instance, but Christmas is the focus of the season. At Christmas, living nativity scenes are staged, a popular tradition dating from the Middle Ages.

NATIONAL HOLIDAYS

New Year (1 Jan)
Epiphany (6 Jan)
Easter Sunday
Anniversary of Liberation (25 Apr)
Labour Day (1 May)
Festa della Repubblica (2 Jun)
Ferragosto (15 Aug)
All Saints (1 Nov)
Immaculate Conception (8 Dec)
Christmas (25 Dec)
Santo Stefano (26 Dec)

DECEMBER

Ri Fauni or Festa delle Campane (*9 Dec*). Commemorating the transporting of the Madonna of Nazareth to Loreto (9 December 1921).
World's largest Christmas tree, Gubbio (*from 7 Dec*). Lights transform Monte Ingino into a giant Christmas tree.
Living Nativity, Attigliano, Alviano, Acquasparta, Calvi, Giove, Monteleone, Petrignano, Lugnano in Teverina, Perugia and Rocca Sant'Angelo (*24 Dec*).
Christmas in Assisi. Concerts and formal celebrations in the basilica and other churches.
Monumental nativity, Città della Pieve (*Christmas to Epiphany*). This is displayed in the Palazzo della Corgna.

Norcia black truffles

JANUARY

Umbria Jazz Winter, Orvieto (*end Dec–early Jan*). Winter version of the Perugia jazz festival. Concerts and musical events.

FEBRUARY

Festa dell'Olivo and **Sagra della Bruschetta**, Spello (*Feb 5*). Olive and bruschetta festivals, including parades, feasts and traditional music.
Mascherata, San Leo di Bastia (*1st Sun of Carnival*). Masked procession around the village.
Festa di San Valentino, Terni (*Feb*). Events all month, but 14 Feb is the focus. Betrothed couples exchange vows of love in the basilica dedicated to St Valentine, one of Terni's first bishops.
Sagra del Tartufo Nero e dei Prodotti Tipici della Valnerina, Norcia (*Feb*). Tastings and sales of the area's famous produce, including truffles.

Gospel singing in Orvieto cathedral during Umbria Jazz Winter

THE HISTORY OF UMBRIA

WEDGED BETWEEN POWERFUL NEIGHBOURS *like Tuscany, Le Marche and Lazio (especially Rome), the territory of Umbria has been an area of conquest, transit and trade for millennia. Its regional identity today dates back to the creation of a unified Italy in the 19th century, although the towns and cities of Umbria nonetheless have many characteristics in common.*

The first populations date back to the Neolithic age – evidence remains of ceramics from the 6th and 5th millennia BC. Later, the Apennine civilization occupied Umbria's hills and mountains, and lived off agriculture and stock raising. They left behind decorated vases and tools of stone, bone and metal.

The golden age of prehistory in central Italy coincided with the development of the Villanovan culture in the 9th and 8th centuries BC. This people used iron for tools and arms, and had complex funerary rituals. The cities of many Italic peoples developed from the settlements of this era. They had a turbulent relationship with the emerging economic and military powers of the Etruscans and the Romans, and would manage to remain independent for only a few more centuries.

Until the Romans arrived, the Umbrian territory was divided into two areas of control: on the west bank of the Tiber was a series of rich Etruscan cities, while on the east bank the Umbri held control.

Black lacquer Etruscan vase, 3rd century BC

The little that is known about the Umbri comes from the famous Eugubine Tablets *(see p60)*. Discovered in 1444, these seven bronze slabs were written in the 2nd century BC in the Umbrian language, using the Etruscan and then the Latin alphabet. The text describes religious rites and also Gubbio's political system. Other cities founded by the Umbri include Todi, Assisi, Spello and Gualdo Tadino.

Confrontation between Rome and the Etruscans reached crisis point in 295 BC, when Roman legions defeated the Umbri, the Sannites, Gauls and Etruscans, opening up territory for conquest. The cities changed sides quickly, and the opening in 219 of the Via Flaminia from Rome to the Adriatic confirmed Rome's power. Rome suffered one of its most bitter defeats, however, on the shores of Lake Trasimeno. In 217 BC the Roman army clashed with Hannibal and the Carthaginians to the west of the lake. The Carthaginians laid a trap to surprise the enemy on the lake shore and Hannibal's army wiped out two-thirds of the Roman forces.

TIMELINE

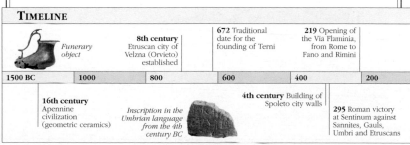

			672 Traditional date for the founding of Terni	219 Opening of the Via Flaminia, from Rome to Fano and Rimini	
Funerary object	**8th century** Etruscan city of Velzna (Orvieto) established				
1500 BC	**1000**	**800**	**600**	**400**	**200**
16th century Apennine civilization (geometric ceramics)		*Inscription in the Umbrian language from the 4th century BC*	**4th century** Building of Spoleto city walls	**295** Roman victory at Sentinum against Sannites, Gauls, Umbri and Etruscans	

◁ **Fortitude and Temperance**, Perugino (1448–1523), Collegio del Cambio in Perugia (detail)

Roman Umbria

**Emperor
Augustus**

A FTER THE DEFEAT OF the Etruscans and
the Italic peoples allied to the Umbri,
Rome consolidated its domination of
Umbria in the 1st century BC, when
Emperor Augustus created Region VI
(Umbria), which included all the cities
and municipal towns on the west bank of
the river Tiber. Region VII (Etruria) took
in territory and settlements on the east
bank of the river. The Romans, who were great civil
engineers, undertook a series of urban projects in
the 1st and 2nd centuries AD: including aqueducts,
cisterns, theatres and walls that would feature in the
lives of Umbrian towns for centuries. Via Flaminia and
Via Amerina would become the main communication
routes in the region for hundreds of years to come.

The Villa di Plinio (Pliny's
Villa) at San Giustino would
have been very grand at one
time. This shows one of many
hypothetical reconstructions.

*Lake Trasimeno was the scene
of a battle between the Romans
and Carthaginians (see
p93). Today, there is little to
be seen of the encounter:
just the names of a
river and a hill – Rio
Sanguineto (bloody river)
and Monte Sanguigno
(Mount Blood) – and several
ditches dug to cremate the
corpses of Hannibal's soldiers.*

ROMAN UMBRIA

This map shows the administrative shape of
Umbria under the Romans, as well as the
busy network of Roman roads planned and
built over the centuries. The Via Flaminia
was of particular importance to Umbria.
Construction began at the end of the 3rd
century BC, and a number of towns of
importance developed along its length,
among them Spoleto. The road maintained
its role in the centuries following Roman
domination.

Tuoro al Trasimeno

*LAKE
TRASIMENO*

VIA TIBERINA

Tifernum
Tiberinum (Città
di Castello)

Perusia
(Perugia)

REGION VII

VIA ORVIETANA

VIA CASSIA

VIA NOVA TRAIANA

Tuder (Todi)

VIA AMERINA

Volsinii Veteres
(Orvieto)

Paglia

River Tiber

Ameria (Amelia)

The site of Carsulae
(see p128) *is one of
the most important in
Umbria, and many of
the objects discovered
here now feature in
the museums of the
region. The site was
abandoned in 27 BC,
when commercial
traffic moved to the
eastern side of the Via
Flaminia.*

Via Amerina was
the second main
artery road.

**The baths at
Otricoli** were built
on the site of natural
springs. Baths were an
important feature of
Roman civilization.

Ocriculum
(Otricoli)

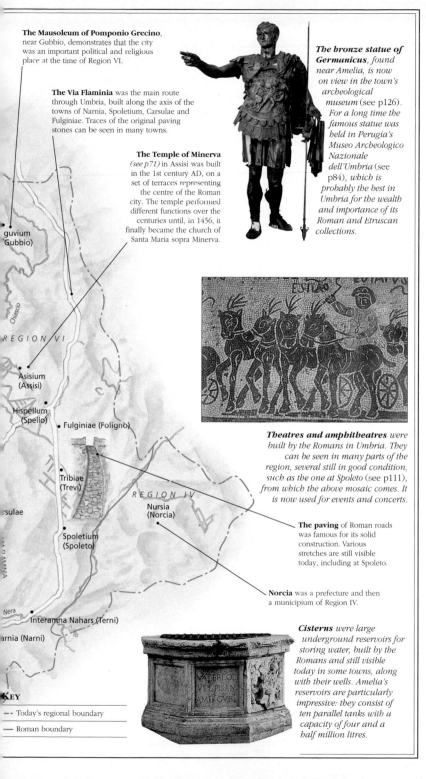

The Mausoleum of Pomponio Grecino, near Gubbio, demonstrates that the city was an important political and religious place at the time of Region VI.

The Via Flaminia was the main route through Umbria, built along the axis of the towns of Narnia, Spoletium, Carsulae and Fulginiae. Traces of the original paving stones can be seen in many towns.

The Temple of Minerva *(see p71)* in Assisi was built in the 1st century AD, on a set of terraces representing the centre of the Roman city. The temple performed different functions over the centuries until, in 1456, it finally became the church of Santa Maria sopra Minerva.

The bronze statue of Germanicus, found near Amelia, is now on view in the town's archeological museum (see p126). For a long time the famous statue was held in Perugia's Museo Archeologico Nazionale dell'Umbria (see p84), which is probably the best in Umbria for the wealth and importance of its Roman and Etruscan collections.

Theatres and amphitheatres were built by the Romans in Umbria. They can be seen in many parts of the region, several still in good condition, such as the one at Spoleto (see p111), from which the above mosaic comes. It is now used for events and concerts.

The paving of Roman roads was famous for its solid construction. Various stretches are still visible today, including at Spoleto.

Norcia was a prefecture and then a municipium of Region IV.

Cisterns were large underground reservoirs for storing water, built by the Romans and still visible today in some towns, along with their wells. Amelia's reservoirs are particularly impressive: they consist of ten parallel tanks with a capacity of four and a half million litres.

guvium
(Gubbio)

Chiascio

REGION VI

Asisium
(Assisi)

Hispellum
(Spello)

Fulginiae (Foligno)

Tribiae
(Trevi)

rsulae

REGION IV

Nursia
(Norcia)

Spoletium
(Spoleto)

Nera

Interamna Nahars (Terni)

arnia (Narni)

KEY

-- Today's regional boundary

— Roman boundary

THE LATE MIDDLE AGES

The ending of Roman rule in Umbria was a heavy blow to a region that depended on trade and agriculture. Communication routes ceased to be secure, apart from the road linking Rome with Amelia, Narni, Perugia and Gubbio. The townspeople had built houses on the plain in the quest for more space during the years of the *pax romana* (as can still be seen today in Gubbio), but they were forced to return to the hills to protect themselves from the aggressive barbarians – the Goths and Huns – coming from the north. The towns became crowded and unsanitary, plague and famine wrought havoc in many areas. The Umbrian population declined noticeably and the ordered farms of the Roman era rapidly became fragmented into numerous small plots of land. Feudal power held sway virtually everywhere, typically dominated by local families who ruled over small areas from a castle or a fortress. In 553, a narrow strip of Umbrian land passed into Byzantine hands, but of far greater significance was the arrival of the Lombards, who set up a principality that included much of Umbria. From the 570s onwards, the so-called Duchy of Spoleto developed into a political entity of some weight. When either historians or geographers referred to "Umbria" at this time, and indeed for centuries to come,

Frederick Barbarossa flanked by his sons Enrico il Severo and Frederick, 12th-century miniature

Lombard sword hilt

they generally meant the lands of the Duchy of Spoleto and therefore only the east bank of the Tiber. In the centuries prior to the year 1000, small monasteries and convents appeared all over the region, albeit scattered and often in inaccessible places. Under the Lombards, who adopted many of the customs of the local people, there was a flowering of art and architecture.

The end of the first millennium signalled a change in the tendency to build hill fortresses. During this phase, lower, flat ground gradually began to be reoccupied, as trade became more significant. New towns (which sometimes kept Roman elements in their names, such as Villa nova) were built, populated by ordinary peasants, now freed from their feudal obligations. This led to

TIMELINE

4th century Construction of the basilica of Santo Salvatore in Spoleto

553 End of the war with the Goths: part of Umbria comes under Byzantine domination

756 Pepin the Short gives Perugia and the Duchy of Spoleto to Pope Stephen II

300 d.C.	400	500	600	700	800

c.480 Birth of St Benedict (San Benedetto) in Norcia

St Benedict in a miniature

6th–7th centuries Invasion of the Lombards. The Duchy of Spoleto includes Terni, Foligno, Spello and Assisi.

the birth of early forms of self-government, which would later develop into the communes of the 11th and 12th centuries.

At the request of the papacy, the Franks (under Pepin the Short and then Charlemagne), drove the Lombards and the Byzantines out of Umbria. Charlemagne won the title of Holy Roman Emperor from the papacy in exchange for territory, but relations soured. When Barbarossa, Holy Roman Emperor, arrived in Italy in the 1150s, he destroyed Spoleto and a number of other towns.

Artisans and farm labourers at work in the era of the communes

THE RISE OF THE COMMUNES

Eventually, economic progress and demographic growth made it essential to expand the towns, too restricted now inside their old walls. In 1244 construction began of the new walls in Todi, and in 1296 Spoleto enlarged its city walls. The emphasis on ambitious public works, such as town halls and cathedrals, demonstrated a lively spirit of initiative on the part of the town populations. It was certainly no coincidence that they elected to adopt a form of autonomy in the 11th and 12th centuries, leading to the rise of the communes (see pp42–3). By 1111, Pope Pasquale II was complaining that Umbrian towns did not recognize the authority of the Church of Rome. In Umbria, meanwhile, the communes

flourished: Perugia's Palazzo dei Priori, Orvieto cathedral and the basilica in Assisi date from this time. In addition, the Franciscan influence started to spread from Assisi, encouraging the use of the Gothic style in new churches. The years of architectural, social and political triumph of these autonomous towns were, however, also years of constant battles for regional or local domination, and plagues and earthquakes badly affected the towns and countryside. The end of the era of the communes coincided with a push by the papacy to regain control. Between 1350 and 1370 the figure that the Umbrians feared most was Egidio Albornoz, cardinal and papal legate, creator of the great fortresses which were to watch over Umbrian towns on behalf of Rome for the next five centuries.

Montefalco, an example of a fortified city commune, in a painting by Benozzo Gozzoli (1420–1497)

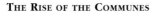

The Communes of Umbria

THE COMMUNES *(COMUNI)*, or independent city states, and their organizational structures spread rapidly throughout central Italy in the 11th–12th centuries. The independence of the communes – which were frequently at war with one another – developed at a time when central power was weakening. Despite the reaction of the papacy and of the Holy Roman Empire, the 12th century marked the rise of the commune, asserting the autonomy of the city state and enabling the arts and economy to flourish. The political master was no longer a feudal lord but an urban bourgeoisie growing rich through manufacturing and trade. Textile industries were established, as were the first banks (which later led to the creation of the great Italian banks of subsequent centuries). In the meantime, merchants from the communes developed trade relationships with the rest of Europe and the Mediterranean, and, thanks to the Crusades, with the Far East, too.

Palazzi Comunali (town halls), symbols of the communes, were built in Umbria during the 13th and 14th centuries. In many towns and cities, they are still the seat of the town hall.

The Torre del Popolo remains a landmark in Assisi's Piazza del Comune.

One of the first signs *of the birth of communal civilization was population growth, which required cities to increase available housing. City walls were enlarged and rebuilt in all the main town centres in Umbria, among them Spello, shown above.*

Increasingly imposing cathedrals *(left is the cathedral of Foligno) were often built facing the centres of temporal power. After centuries of fortified towns criss-crossed with narrow streets, the era of the commune saw the building of town squares that functioned as meeting places as well as centres of power.*

St Francis was the subject of a book by St Bonaventure, written in the same century that the saint died.

The Temple of Minerva, still visible in Assisi's Piazza del Comune, is clearly recognizable, even in this stylized rendering.

Population growth meant that urban centres were forced to expand upwards as well as outwards. This is how multi-storey houses and porticoes arose.

The town fountain was a celebration of the wealth of a city – the years when the communes flourished signalled the return of water supplies to many towns. After centuries of abandonment, ancient aqueducts were restored and rebuilt. This is the famous Fontana Maggiore in Perugia (see p87).

HOMAGE OF A SIMPLE MAN

St Bonaventure, a 13th-century Franciscan monk, tells the story that one day, in Assisi, Francis met "a simple man". Inspired by God, the man laid his own cloak down before the saint. This episode begins the story of the life of St Francis in the cycle of frescoes in the basilica in Assisi. The work is of great importance because, with great attention to detail and careful observation, the artist has created a perfect picture of the medieval centre of Assisi at the end of the 13th century. A picture that is not so different from that visible in Piazza del Comune today.

Clashes and battles between the Umbrian communes were continual. Some cities had troops of soldiers, such as the crossbowmen, that formed exclusive companies. They are commemorated today in numerous historical processions.

The citizen in the era of the communes, like the one present in this scene, was expected to maintain a dignified demeanour in public squares: swords should never be unsheathed. Crimes committed in this place were severely punished.

Impressive fortresses, like the one at Spoleto, pictured here, dominate Umbrian towns. They were built by the papacy, from the end of the 14th century, in order to consolidate the power of the Church. The construction of such strongholds, often under the watchful eye of Cardinal Albornoz, heralded the end of communal power.

Perugia, as depicted in a fresco by Benedetto Bonfigli in the mid-15th century

THE CENTURIES OF DECLINE

The conquest of Umbria by the papacy coincided with the effects of the great plague that had devastated Europe in 1348.

At the end of the 15th century the term Umbria began to appear in the works of scholars and academics: the clergyman Innocenzo Malvasia, in his *Italia Illustrata* drawn up for Pope Sixtus V, defined Umbria as the land of the Duchy of Spoleto, while he described the remainder of the region as being part of Etruria, and Gualdo and Gubbio as dependencies of the Duchy of Urbino.

Following centuries of development, 16th-century Umbria found itself in a tricky situation. The cities, peripheral dominions of the state gravitating around Rome, were declining, while craftsmen and industries were diminishing in number and quality.

The heads of the great aristocratic families abandoned the cities and returned to the land and agriculture.

TOWN AND COUNTRYSIDE

A fundamental instrument in the development of the new Umbrian economy was the "mezzadria", or sharecropping system, and the gradual colonization of the hills and plains, on partly reclaimed land in some cases. One very noticeable effect of the agricultural revival was the gradual de-population of the cities. The historian Cipriano Piccolpasso wrote of Assisi: "...it is a badly composed city, with many derelict and unoccupied houses next to inhabited ones, so that it seems more like the residue of a city than a completed one...". The move to the country was not the only factor to alter the appearance of the cities: during the 16th and 17th centuries, nobles invested some of the profits from their farms in town projects.

Politically, the 17th century saw important new

Urban VIII, pope from 1623 to 1644

developments: in 1624 the della Rovere family ceded the Duchy of Urbino to the pope, and the following year Pope Urban VIII put the University of Perugia under episcopal control.

FROM PAPAL RULE TO THE UNIFICATION OF ITALY

By now an agricultural, rural region, Umbria became one of Rome's "bread baskets" and a major producer

TIMELINE

1416–24 Braccio da Montone becomes lord of Perugia

1472 In Foligno, 300 copies of the *Divine Comedy* are printed: the first book published in Italian in Italy.

Paul III, pope from 1534 to 1549

1400	1500	1600	1700

1444 The Eugubine Tablets are discovered

1508 Building begins on Santa Maria della Consolazione, near Todi

1540 Perugia comes under the papal rule of Paul III

1656–1701 The population of Umbria falls from 317,000 to 280,000

Perugia's Rocca Paolina, destroyed on 14 September 1860

MODERN UMBRIA

Following a plebiscite, the province of Umbria was created in 1861, as part of a unified Kingdom of Italy. It included all the current provinces (plus Rieti), with a population of 500,000. The economic situation in the closing decades of the 19th century was, however, woeful: agriculture was languishing and farmers were increasingly forced into seasonal migration towards the Maremma and the countryside around Rome. Even so, the industrial revolution did not leave Umbria behind: in 1866 the railway line that links Rome, Terni and Foligno was completed, and between 1875 and 1887 arms factories and the Terni steelworks (the first – and only – really major employer in the region) were founded. In 1881 the population of Umbria numbered 611,000, in 1911 it was 767,000.

of olive oil. Mills multiplied, as did the frequency of country fairs, which took the place of town markets in the economy of the countryside.

With the end of the 18th century came the Napoleonic revolution. As part of the Roman Republic created in 1798, Umbria was divided into the two departments of Trasimeno and Clitunno. In the imperial era the division was dissolved, and Umbria became a single territory with Spoleto as its capital. This confirmation of a common identity would be returned to without much alteration by the unified state after 1860.

In line with the Romantic movement elsewhere, the 19th century saw a rise in interest in the Middle Ages. The discovery of the remains of St Francis (1818) and Santa Chiara (1850) caused a sensation. In 1859, a great popular uprising in Perugia against the papal troops resulted in a brutal massacre, which became known as the "Stragi di Perugia". In September 1860 soldiers entered the town, and the local population immediately set about destroying the Rocca Paolina fortress, a much detested symbol of the power of the Roman Catholic church.

World War II saw the bombing of Umbria's industries, and recovery in the postwar period was slow. The development of light industry, cottage industries and especially tourism has helped boost the region's fortunes, though the earthquakes that strike periodically have affected certain areas of Umbria badly. The worst happened in 1979, in Valnerina, but the quake that struck Assisi, Foligno and Nocera Umbra in 1997 received broader coverage around the world because of the damage done to the art-packed St Francis basilica.

Portale Reale, Orvieto, dedicated to the website "Umbria 2000"

| 1859 Uprising in Perugia and sacking by the papal troops | 1861 The Province of Perugia is established as part of the Kingdom of Italy | 1958 First Festival dei Due Mondi in Spoleto |
| | | 1997 26 September: an earthquake devastates Umbria |

1800	1900	2000
1798 During Napoleonic domination Umbria is divided into two departments: Trasimeno and Clitunno	1923 Rieti becomes part of Lazio 1875 The steelworks of Terni built	*Website logo* 1999 December: launch of the tourist information website "Umbria 2000"

UMBRIA
AREA BY AREA

Umbria at a Glance

T HE REGION OF UMBRIA is not particularly large, but it
has numerous towns, villages, parks and other
places of great interest. Northern Umbria includes the
upper valley of the River Tiber (Alta Val Tiberina), the
Apennine regional parks (Monte Subasio and Monte
Cucco), the medieval towns of Perugia, Assisi and
Gubbio and the great expanse of Lake Trasimeno.
The southern half of the region revolves around the
towns of Todi, Narni, Terni and Orvieto, on the border
with Tuscany, within the area once occupied by the
Etruscans. Completing this picture of southern Umbria
are the great mountains of the Monti Sibillini national
park and the Valnerina (the valley of the Nera River),
with its famous waterfalls, the Cascata delle Marmore.

**NORTHERN
UMBRIA**
(pp50–95)

Città della Pieve

Città della Pieve

*Famous as the birthplace of the artist
Perugino (some of his works are here),
this small town near the Tuscan border
is a good departure point for visiting the
area south of Lake Trasimeno.*

0 kilometres   15

0 miles   15

Todi

Todi

*Perched on a hill above
the Tiber, Todi was for
centuries a border town
between the land of the
Etruscans and territory
occupied by the Umbri.
It has a lovely historic
quarter, centred around
Piazza del Popolo.*

◁ **The Abbey of San Pietro in Valle (11th century), near Spoleto**

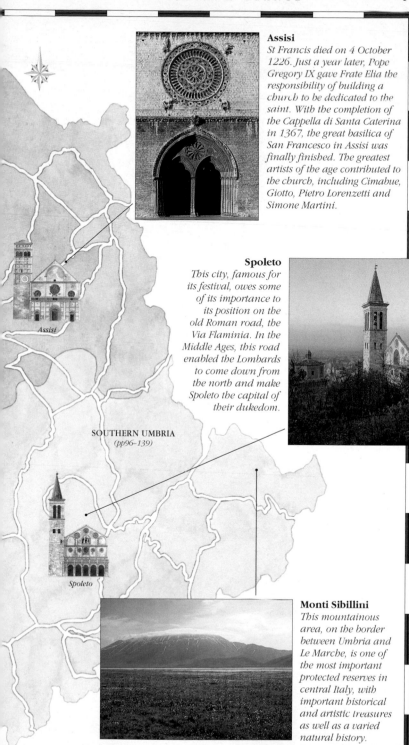

Assisi

St Francis died on 4 October 1226. Just a year later, Pope Gregory IX gave Frate Elia the responsibility of building a church to be dedicated to the saint. With the completion of the Cappella di Santa Caterina in 1367, the great basilica of San Francesco in Assisi was finally finished. The greatest artists of the age contributed to the church, including Cimabue, Giotto, Pietro Lorenzetti and Simone Martini.

Spoleto

This city, famous for its festival, owes some of its importance to its position on the old Roman road, the Via Flaminia. In the Middle Ages, this road enabled the Lombards to come down from the north and make Spoleto the capital of their dukedom.

SOUTHERN UMBRIA
(pp96–139)

Assisi

Spoleto

Monti Sibillini

This mountainous area, on the border between Umbria and Le Marche, is one of the most important protected reserves in central Italy, with important historical and artistic treasures as well as a varied natural history.

NORTHERN UMBRIA

NORTHERN UMBRIA CONSISTS OF *three distinct geographical areas: the first is the Alta Val Tiberina (the Upper Tiber Valley), the second is the area around Lake Trasimeno, and the third is the easterly Apennine region around Gubbio and the Via Flaminia. These three regions, laden with history and culture, meet at northern Umbria's two most important towns, Perugia and Assisi.*

Perugia is the capital of the region and one of the main cities in central Italy, both culturally and economically. Assisi is visited every year by thousands of tourists and pilgrims, who come to retrace the steps of St Francis and admire the fresco cycles in the basilica.

The three aforementioned areas have differing histories. The Alta Val Tiberina, as well as delineating the border between the Etruscans (to the west) and the Umbri (to the east), has long been of commercial importance, with its direct lines of communication with the north. The entire area of Lake Trasimeno, on the other hand, has always been of great strategic and military significance, as can still be seen today from the many fortifications scattered around the lake. The lake shore was the setting for one of the battles of the Second Punic Wars (217 BC), which culminated in the victory of Hannibal over the Romans. To the east, in contrast, hermitages that were refuges for entire populations in the time of barbaric invasions cling to the Appenines. Northern Umbria's fortunes became allied to those of the rest of the region with the ending of the Duchy of Spoleto.

Despite the bombardments of World War II and the earthquake of 1997, which struck the area along the border with Le Marche, splendid testimony remains to the region's history, including Etruscan and Roman buildings and finds. The legacy of the Middle Ages and the Renaissance can be seen in churches, palazzi, town halls and castles, as well as in works by the great artists of the day, among them Perugino, a native of Città della Pieve.

The varied and well-preserved landscape of the northern region includes two national parks, Monte Cucco and Monte Subasio, where the "song of nature" that so struck St Francis of Assisi can still be sensed.

A patchwork of ordered fields carpeting the hillsides of northern Umbria

◁ **Looking down over Gubbio rooftops and the Palazzo dei Consoli**

Exploring Northern Umbria

Città di Castello is the first main town on the road into Umbria from neighbouring Emilia-Romagna, along the old trade route which then continues down through the Upper Tiber Valley. At Umbertide, a road heads off eastwards to Gubbio and beyond to the Via Flaminia, which skirts the Apennines on its route south towards Assisi. West of Assisi lies the province of Perugia and the regional capital itself. Further west again, bordering Tuscany, is Lake Trasimeno and the homeland of Perugino.

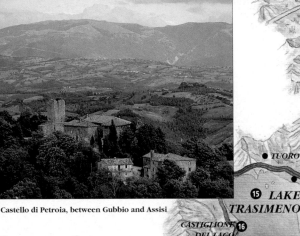

Castello di Petroia, between Gubbio and Assisi

Sights at a Glance

Sansepolcro

CITTÀ DI CASTELLO **1**

MONTON

UMBERTIDE **3**

416

TUORO

PASSIGNANO

15 LAKE TRASIMENO

MAGIONE

CASTIGLIONE DEL LAGO **16**

18 SOUTHERN TRASIMENO

Tresa

17

CITTÀ DELLA PIEVE

Nestore

Nestore

220

71

Orvieto

0 kilometres   10

0 miles   10

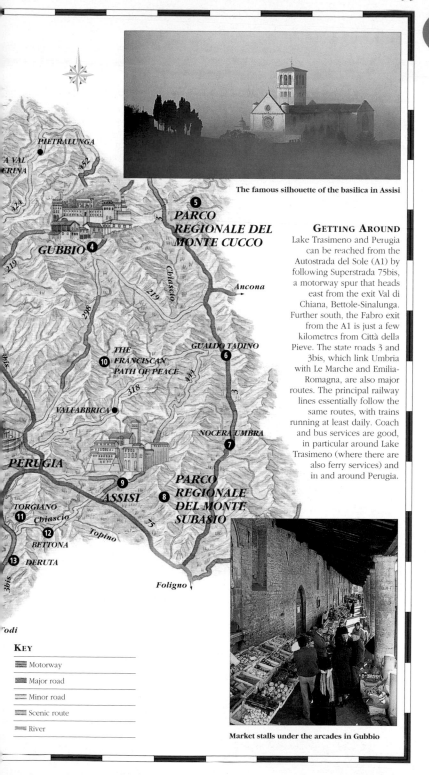

The famous silhouette of the basilica in Assisi

PIETRALUNGA

A VAL
ERINA

PARCO
REGIONALE DEL
MONTE CUCCO ⑤

GUBBIO ④

Chiascio

Ancona

GUALDO TADINO ⑥

THE
FRANCISCAN
PATH OF PEACE ⑩

318

VALFABBRICA

NOCERA UMBRA ⑦

PERUGIA

⑨
ASSISI ⑧

PARCO
REGIONALE
DEL MONTE
SUBASIO

TORGIANO
⑪ Chiascio
⑫
BETTONA
⑬ DERUTA

Topino

Foligno

odi

GETTING AROUND

Lake Trasimeno and Perugia can be reached from the Autostrada del Sole (A1) by following Superstrada 75bis, a motorway spur that heads east from the exit Val di Chiana, Bettole-Sinalunga. Further south, the Fabro exit from the A1 is just a few kilometres from Città della Pieve. The state roads 3 and 3bis, which link Umbria with Le Marche and Emilia-Romagna, are also major routes. The principal railway lines essentially follow the same routes, with trains running at least daily. Coach and bus services are good, in particular around Lake Trasimeno (where there are also ferry services) and in and around Perugia.

KEY

▬	Motorway
▬	Major road
▬	Minor road
▬	Scenic route
▬	River

Market stalls under the arcades in Gubbio

Città di Castello ❶

THE TOWN THAT IS TODAY the most important centre in the Upper Tiber Valley, the gateway to Umbria for anyone approaching from the north, was originally a settlement of the ancient Umbri.

Decoration on the Palazzo del Podestà

Situated as it was between Le Marche and Tuscany, and not far from Emilia-Romagna, the town was in a perfect position as far as trade was concerned. It became a commune in the Middle Ages, when it was in almost perpetual conflict with the nearby city-states. Even so, the former "Civitas Castelli" grew in power and riches, thanks to the flourishing commercial activity, including printing, which is still an important part of the city's economic fabric today. Following a period of rule by nobles installed by the Church, Città di Castello was completely redesigned under the rule of the Vitelli family, in the 16th century, as can be seen by the various palazzi bearing its name.

Exploring Città di Castello

The town is built on the right bank of the River Tiber, at the northernmost edge of Umbria. The architecture displays Tuscan influences, thanks to the work of the Florentine architects Antonio da Sangallo and Giorgio Vasari, brought in by the Vitelli family in the 16th century.

The tour described here begins in Piazza Gabriotti. Visitors are advised to leave their cars in the car park in Viale Nazario Sauro and then take the escalator up to the piazza. The monuments seen at the beginning of the tour date from the period prior to that of the Vitelli.

⛪ Duomo
Piazza Gabriotti. ◯ *daily.*
It is immediately apparent that the cathedral exterior has undergone more than one remodelling. The round bell tower formed part of the original 11th-century building, but the body of the church reveals two successive rebuildings, in the 14th and then the 15th–16th centuries. The unfinished Baroque façade dates from 1632–46. The interior has a single nave and

contains a wooden choir and a *Resurrection* by Rosso Fiorentino (1529), in the chapel on the right-hand side. In the **Museo del Duomo**, objects on display map the evolution of the church in the Middle Ages.

🏛 Museo del Duomo
Piazza Gabriotti. ☎ 075 855 4705.
◯ Apr–Sep: 9:30am–1pm, 2:30–7pm. Oct–Mar: 10am–1pm, 2:30–6:30pm; ⬤ *Mon (except in Aug).* ✎

⛪ Palazzo Comunale
Piazza Gabriotti.
In the same piazza (as was typical in a medieval town) is the Palazzo Comunale, or town hall. This 14th-century building is the work of Angelo da Orvieto and shows how the Florentine influence on the town's architecture

Paliotto, c.1144, Museo del Duomo

pre-dates the arrival of the Vitelli family: in particular, the use of rusticated stone echoes the style of the Palazzo Vecchio in Florence.

In front of the palazzo, on the other side of the piazza, stands the **Torre Civica**, also 14th-century and once called "del Vescovo" (the bishop's), because it stood next to the bishop's palace (Palazzo Vescovile). From the top of the tower (open daily, entrance fee), there are good views over the town and the surrounding countryside.

The 14th-century Torre Civica

⛪ Palazzo del Podestà
Corso Cavour.
From the east of the piazza runs Corso Cavour, home to the Palazzo del Podestà. The façade facing the street dates from the same era as the Palazzo Comunale, and it may be that the original design was also by Angelo da Orvieto. The eastern side is Baroque and gives on to Piazza Matteotti, where **Palazzo Vitelli "in piazza"** stands.

⛪ San Francesco
Via D. Albizzini. ◯ *daily.*
The street which cuts the city in half from north to south is made up of Via XX Settembre, Via Angeloni and Corso Vittorio Emanuele. Halfway along Via Angeloni, near the corner of Via Albizzini, stands the church of St Francis, of 13th-century origin, to which the famous Florentine painter and architect Giorgio Vasari contributed in the 1500s. He was responsible for the Cappella Vitelli as well as an altar with a *Coronation of the Virgin* (1564).

⛪ Palazzo Vitelli a Porta Sant'Egidio
Piazza Garibaldi.
A short distance from San Francesco is this Vitelli palace (1540), one of many that the family had built in the town in an effort to impose some stylistic unity. The façade is

THE WORK OF ALBERTO BURRI

Alberto Burri, a major figure in 20th-century Italian art and known all over the world, was born in Città di Castello in 1915 (he died in Nice in 1995). A doctor by profession, he turned to art during World War II. His work, part of the Informal Art movement, is often large-scale and makes use of innovative materials: particularly famous is the *Cretto* at Gibellina Vecchia, in Sicily, a huge carpet of white cement covering the ruins left by the earthquake of 1968. Città di Castello is home to a good collection of his work – in Palazzo Albizzini and in the former tobacco drying house (Ex Seccatoi del Tabacco).

Collezioni Burri 075 855 46 49.
Palazzo Albizzini Via Albizzini.
Ex Seccatoi del Tabacco Via Pierucci.
9am–12:30pm, 2:30–6pm Tue–Sat; 10:30am–12:30pm, 3–6pm Sun & public hols; Nov–Mar: opening hours may vary.

Great Iron Sextant, 1982, on show in Città di Castello

symmetrical and there is a pretty garden inside.

San Domenico
Largo Monsignor Muzi. daily.
Between Piazza Garibaldi and the Pinacoteca is the church of San Domenico, the largest in the town. It was built by the Dominicans in the 15th century and later reworked, although the façade remains unfinished. Frescoes from the 15th century line the nave.

Pinacoteca Comunale
Via della Cannoniera 22.
075 852 0656.
Apr–Oct: 10am–1pm, 2:30–6:30pm; Nov–Mar: 10am–12:30pm, 3–6:30pm.
Mon.
The Pinacoteca, one of the region's top art galleries, is housed in the **Palazzo Vitelli alla Cannoniera**, the

Coronation of the Virgin, detail, Ghirlandaio workshop

most notable of the various Vitelli palazzi. It was built by Antonio da Sangallo (1521–32) with the assistance of Vasari, who was responsible for part of the frescoed friezes.

Among the many works of value are an *Enthroned Madonna and Child* by the Maestro di Città di Castello (early 14th century); a *Martyrdom of St Sebastian* by Luca Signorelli (1497– 98), a *Gonfalone della Santissima Trinità* by Raphael (1499); and a *Coronation of the Virgin* attributed to the workshop of Ghirlandaio (early 1500s). There is, also, a remarkable *Assumption of the Virgin* in terracotta from the workshop of Andrea della Robbia (early 16th century).

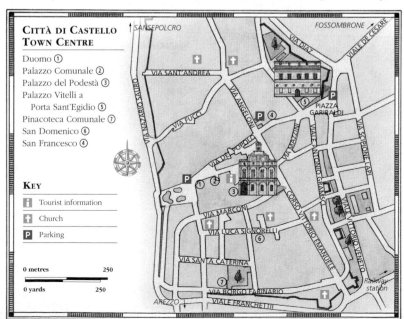

CITTÀ DI CASTELLO TOWN CENTRE

Duomo ①
Palazzo Comunale ②
Palazzo del Podestà ③
Palazzo Vitelli a Porta Sant'Egidio ⑤
Pinacoteca Comunale ⑦
San Domenico ⑥
San Francesco ④

KEY

Tourist information

Church

Parking

0 metres 250
0 yards 250

View of the verdant Upper Tiber Valley, from the medieval village of Montone

Montone ❷

Perugia. **Road Map** C2.
🏛 1,500. 🚉 Umbertide, 13 km
(8 miles), Perugia–Sansepolcro line.
🚌 ℹ Piazza Fortebraccio.
🖥 www.montone.info

Montone, 10 km (6 miles)
from Città di Castello, is
built on two hill tops on the
left bank of the Tiber, and is
the first town of historical
interest on the road running
south through the Upper
Tiber Valley. Founded as a
fortified site in the Middle
Ages (probably in the 11th
century), Montone is still
enclosed within a powerful
circle of walls. These are
pierced by three gates: Porta
del Verziere, Porta di Borgo
Vecchio and Porta del Monte;
the names correspond to the
districts into which the castle
was once divided.

Montone was the birthplace
of Braccio Fortebraccio,
better known as Braccio da
Montone (1368–1424), who

became perhaps Umbria's
greatest condottiere (leader
of a mercenary army). He
created a genuine state, with
Perugia as its capital.

The medieval village is
beautifully preserved and,
furthermore, offers superb
views. There are several
buildings of interest. On the
road leading up to the centre
of Montone from the south is
the church of the **Madonna
delle Grazie** (16th century),
as well as the oldest church
in the village, the Romanesque
Pieve di San Gregorio,
dating from the 11th century.

Beyond the walls, it is
worth visiting the Gothic
church of **San Francesco**
(14th century), at the top of
the village. Along with the
attached monastery, this is
now home to the **Museo
Comunale**. The fine doorway
is made of inlaid wood
(1519). Inside, the single-nave
building contains several
valuable works of art by
Bartolomeo Caporali. Above

the votive altar are frescoes of
the Fortebraccio family and
also a painting depicting the
Madonna del Soccorso.

The church, which also
contains a splendid wooden
choir dating from the 16th
century, once housed a
Madonna in Gloria by Luca
Signorelli. This is now in the
National Gallery in London.
The former monastery houses
an ethnographic museum.

Students of Italian history
should consider visiting the
Archivio Storico Comunale,
one of the most important
historical archives in Umbria,
with papal bulls and other
important documents. It is
housed in the former convent
of Santa Caterina, at the
southern end of the village.

🏛 **Museo Comunale**
Ex Convento di San Francesco.
📞 075 930 6535.
🕐 Apr–Sep: 10:30am–1pm,
3:30–6pm Fri–Sun; Oct–Mar:
10:30am–1pm, 3–5:30pm
Sat & Sun. 🈳

Environs: The countryside
around Montone offers plenty
of opportunities for walking,
particularly along the
course of the **Torrente Carpina**,
which skirts the village to the
east and joins the Tiber at
Umbertide. On its banks,
4 km (2 miles) northwest of
Montone, is the splendid
Rocca d'Aries, a fortress with
Byzantine origins. It was
renovated in the Renaissance
era and restored in the 1990s,
and is now open for concerts
and exhibitions. It offers
marvellous views over the
Valle del Carpina.

A narrow, paved street in the heart of Montone

Umbertide ❸

Perugia. **Road Map** C2.
🏛 *15,000* 🚆 *Perugia–Sansepolcro
line.* 🚌 ℹ️ *I.A.T. Alta Valle del
Tevere, Piazza Caduti del Lavoro,
075 941 7099.*
🌐 *www.comune.umbertide.it*

Oⁿᵉ ᵒᶠ ᵗʰᵉ principal centres of the Upper Tiber Valley, Umbertide is of ancient origin, dating back to the 6th century BC, and was probably founded by the Etruscans. The town, skirted to the west by the Tiber, frequently found itself at the centre of wars and suffered the resulting destruction and sackings. In 1863, the town's traditional name of Fratta was replaced by the name Umbertide in honour of the sons of Umberto Ranieri, who rebuilt the city after the devastation caused by the Lombard invasions of 790 AD.

Much more recently, the centre of the old town was badly damaged by bombardments during World War II (1944). Even so, many important buildings survive. Two of these overlook the vast Piazza Mazzini, northwest of the town centre: **La Rocca** (1385), a fortress inserted into the walls and Umbertide's main landmark, and the church of **Santa Maria della Reggia**, begun in the second half of the 16th century and built on an octagonal plan. The design was by Galeazzo Alessi and Giulio Danti. Inside, among the canvases

The square and circular towers of the Rocca of Umbertide

that decorate the tambour (the wall below the dome), note the one above the organ, an *Ascension to Heaven* by Pomarancio (1578).

Other important works to be found in the town's churches include a fresco by Pinturicchio (1504), in the lunette of the doorway to the church of **Santa Maria della Pietà** (north of the old town, outside the walls) and, in particular, a *Deposition* by Luca Signorelli in the Baroque church of **Santa Croce**, in the southern (and oldest) part of the town, in Piazza San Francesco. Due to the importance of the Signorelli painting – it is the only one by the Cortona artist still to be found in its original setting – the church is now a museum. In the same square are two other churches: San Francesco (13th–14th centuries) and San Bernardino (18th century).

The octagonal Santa
Maria della Reggia

🏛 **Santa Croce Museum**
Piazza San Francesco.
📞 *075 942 0147.* ⏰ *Jun–Sep:
10:30am–1pm, 4–9:30pm Fri–Sun;
Oct–May: 10:30am–1pm, 3–5:30pm.*
♿

Environs: The countryside around Umbertide is scattered with fortifications, lasting evidence of the region's great strategic military importance. Along the road to Preggio, 15 km (9 miles) southwest of Umbertide, is the **Rocca di Preggio**, one of the principal strongholds in the area, dating from the 10th century. Also of note along this route are the castles of **Romeggio** and **Polgeto**.

A short distance east of Umbertide, towards Gubbio, look out for the privately-owned **Castello di Civitella Ranieri** (15th century), which is one of the most complete and best preserved examples of military architecture in the area. Nearby, but higher up, is the splendid **Castello di Serra Partucci**.

Just north of Umbertide, along the Città di Castello road, you can see the tall tower of another castle, the **Castello di Montalto**.

A couple of kilometres south of town, along the River Tiber, a road climbs up to the **Badia Monte Corona**, a Romanesque abbey with a beautiful underground crypt. Climbing still higher, you reach the 16th-century hermitage and pretty village of **San Giuliana**, set in a panoramic position, and restored to its medieval appearance.

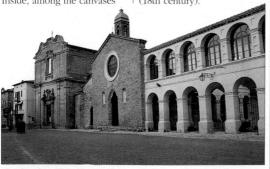

The churches of Santa Croce and San Francesco in Umbertide

Gubbio ❹

THE SIGHT OF GUBBIO, built from local stone at the foot of Monte Ingino, is one of the most famous images of medieval Umbria. Founded by the Umbri, the town holds the famous Eugubine Tablets, seven bronze slabs that survived from the ancient city of Iguvium; they were engraved in the 2nd century BC with text in the local language describing rites and sacred sites. Under the Romans the town spread onto the plain, but after the Lombards invaded the people returned to the slopes, where they could defend themselves more effectively. A walled city, including the monumental Palazzo dei Consoli, was built here in the Middle Ages. At the end of the 14th century, the city, by now powerful and rich, passed to the Montefeltro of Urbino. In 1624 Gubbio, like the Duchy of Urbino, came under papal rule.

The well-preserved 1st-century arcades of the Roman theatre

Exploring Gubbio

The easiest route into Gubbio is by the road from the south, which also provides a chance to admire the town as a whole, as it spreads out in horizontal swathes against the slopes of Monte Ingino. Before climbing up to explore one of the best preserved medieval cities in the world, take a look at the ruins of the Roman city, which, during the stability of the *pax romana*, developed on the flat land below the slopes.

⋔ Roman Ruins

Via del Teatro Romano.
The first Roman monument that you see as you arrive in Gubbio from the south is a mausoleum, a monumental tomb of which the burial chamber has survived with its barrel vault. Further on, not far from Piazza Quaranta Martiri, are the ruins of the Roman theatre (Teatro Romano), which dates from the 1st century. It could accommodate around 6,000 spectators, and was faced in squared and rusticated blocks. Among other works uncovered over the last two centuries of excavations are some beautiful mosaics.

▦ Piazza Quaranta Martiri

This broad square is the principal point of arrival in Gubbio, as well as the best place to leave a car. It is dedicated to the 40 local people, randomly chosen, who were massacred by the Germans in 1944. The lowest point in Gubbio, the piazza is a good place from which to gaze upwards to admire the full extent of the town.

Gubbio's finest church, **San Francesco**, dominates the piazza. Its construction was begun in the mid-1200s and continued at least until the end of that century (though the façade was never finished). Inside are three aisles without a transept. There is a fresco cycle by Ottaviano Nelli in the apse chapel on the left (*Scenes from the Life of Mary*, c.1408–13). The frescoes in the central apse, by an unknown artist, can be dated to around 1275, but they are badly damaged.

On the opposite side of the piazza is the **Antico Ospedale** (Old Hospital) of Santa Maria della Misericordia, a 14th-century building, with a long portico in front, surmounted by a loggia, added in the 17th century by the wool merchants' guild, which used the premises for some of its processing. Nearby stands the church of **Santa Maria dei Laici**, dating back to 1313 and now restored.

⌂ San Giovanni Battista

Via della Repubblica. ◯ *daily.*
From Piazza Quaranta Martiri the steep Via della Repubblica leads to the base of the great structure supporting Piazza Grande (*see p61*). Heading up this street, you enter the oldest part of the medieval city, where the first cathedral, dedicated to San Mariano, is believed to have stood. What is now the church dedicated to San Giovanni Battista (St John the Baptist) probably occupies the site of the old cathedral.

This church, built in the 13th and 14th centuries, has a Gothic façade with a Romanesque bell tower. The Gothic style continues inside, with characteristic coupled

Gubbio, clinging to the lower slopes of Monte Ingino

The church of San Giovanni Battista, with Palazzo dei Consoli behind

VISITORS' CHECKLIST

Perugia. **Road Map** D2.
🚶 32,000. 🚉 Fossato di Vico,
20 km (12 miles), Roma–Ancona
line, 892021. 🚌 🛈 Piazza
Oderisi 6, 075 922 0693.
📅 Corsa dei Ceri, 15 May; Palio
della Balestra, last Sun in May.

columns and great arches in stone. The single-nave church culminates in a squared apse.

🛈 San Domenico

Piazza G. Bruno. ◻ daily.
Returning to Piazza Quaranta Martiri, turn into Via Cavour to enter the old quarter of San Martino, which is built on both sides of the river Camignano.

At the heart of this district, in Piazza Bruno, is the church of San Domenico, which was built by the Dominicans in the 14th century on the site of a 12th-century church dedicated to San Martino. The appearance of the interior dates primarily from a period of restoration during the 18th century, but 16th-century frescoes from the Gubbio school remain; there is also a fine lectern decorated with inlaid wood.

🚌 Via Gabrielli

This street, lined with medieval houses, runs north from Piazza Bruno to Porta Metauro. Near the end is the small but impressive **Palazzo del Capitano del Popolo**, whose façade curves in line with the road. Adorned with a series of small Gothic windows, the palazzo is a typical Gubbio construction from the late 13th century. Nearby is the park attached to the **Palazzo Ranghiaschi Brancaleoni**. Laid out in the mid-1800s, the garden extends south along the slopes of Monte Ingino as far as the Palazzo Ducale. There is a Neo-Classical temple here.

Sculpture on the tower of Palazzo Ranghiaschi Brancaleoni

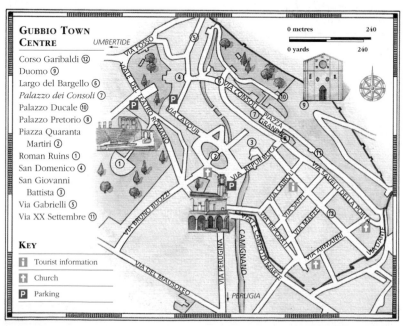

GUBBIO TOWN CENTRE

UMBERTIDE

Corso Garibaldi ⑫
Duomo ⑨
Largo del Bargello ⑥
Palazzo dei Consoli ⑦
Palazzo Ducale ⑩
Palazzo Pretorio ⑧
Piazza Quaranta Martiri ②
Roman Ruins ①
San Domenico ④
San Giovanni Battista ③
Via Gabrielli ⑤
Via XX Settembre ⑪

KEY

🛈 Tourist information

🛐 Church

🅿 Parking

0 metres 240
0 yards 240

↓ PERUGIA

Gubbio: Palazzo dei Consoli

Ceramic plate,
Museo Civico

THIS SUPERB BUILDING, begun in 1332, lords it over Piazza Grande and is supported on the west side by an impressive row of arched buttresses. The entrance doorway, approached by a fan-shaped flight of steps, is a masterly example of the Gothic style and is decorated with a lunette representing the *Madonna and saints John the Baptist and Ubaldo*, patron saint of the city. The palazzo houses the Museo Civico and an art gallery. From the loggia there are fine views over the city and countryside around.

VISITORS' CHECKLIST

Piazza Grande. **[** 075 927 4298.
◻ 10am–1pm, 3–6pm (Oct–Mar: 2–5pm) daily. ● public hols. 🏛

Madonna and Child
This fresco by Mello da Gubbio from 1340–50 is one of the works on display in the Pinacoteca Civica (art gallery) on the first floor.

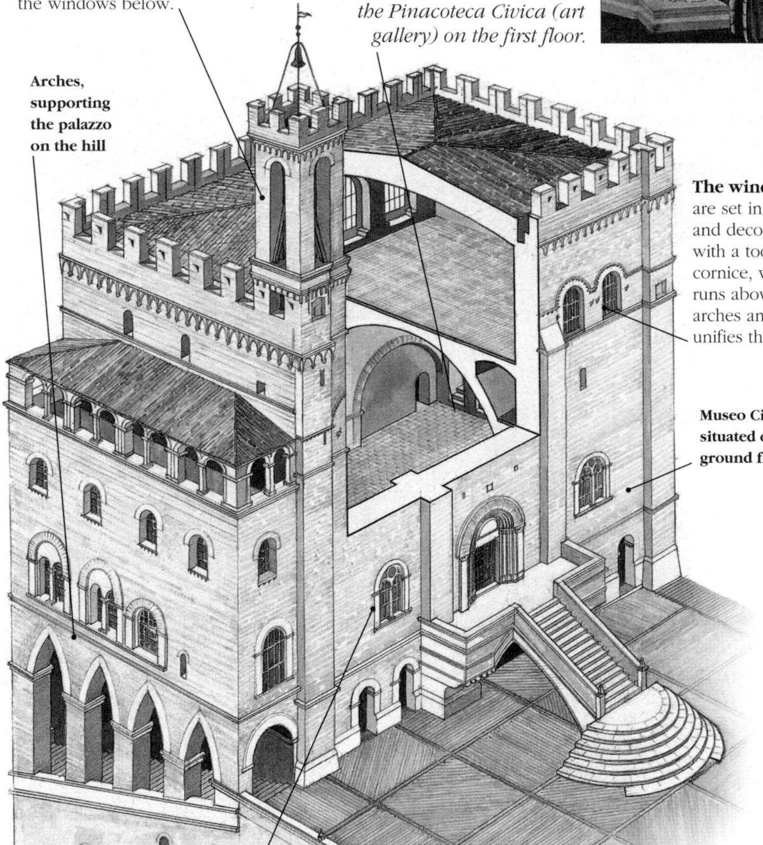

The tower is crowned with battlements and has four apertures echoing the form of the windows below.

Arches, supporting the palazzo on the hill

The windows are set in pairs and decorated with a toothed cornice, which runs above the arches and unifies them.

Museo Civico, situated on the ground floor

In the Sala dell'Arengo, a magnificent room which occupies the entire floor area of the building, popular assemblies were held in the 14th century. Today fragments and stone tablets are displayed here.

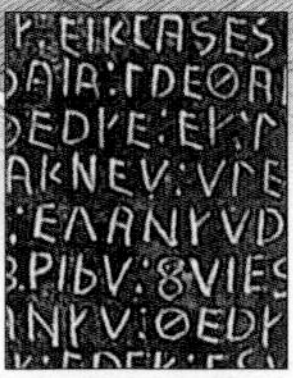

Eugubine Tablets
These inscriptions in the old Umbrian language are on display in the Museo Civico. They provide crucial evidence of life in the region before the Roman conquest.

The Fontana dei Matti in Largo del Bargello

🏛 Largo del Bargello

About halfway along Via dei Consoli, which connects the San Martino quarter and Piazza Grande, the street broadens out to form Largo del Bargello, the centre of the ancient quarter of San Giuliano. In front of the 14th-century palazzo, after which the square is named, is the small **Fontana dei Matti**: tradition has it that in order to be defined as mad (*matto*), people had to run around the fountain three times bathing themselves in the water.

🏛 Piazza Grande

Via dei Consoli follows the route of the old Umbrian fortifications before suddenly opening out into Piazza Grande. Quite apart from the importance of the buildings

found here, the square is an extremely impressive piece of engineering; it is, in fact, an artificial space supported by walls and embankments.

In front of the more famous and much larger Palazzo dei Consoli is **Palazzo Pretorio** (closed to the public), which was erected in the mid-14th century and designed by the same architect, Gattapone. On the last Sunday in May the traditional Palio della Balestra (involving the crossbowmen of Gubbio and Sansepolcro, over the border in Tuscany), takes place between the two buildings.

🏛 Duomo
Via Galeotti. ◷ *daily.*

From Piazza Grande, Via Galeotti climbs in a series of steps to the cathedral. This was founded in 1229 and enlarged around a century later. The façade has an entrance with an ogival arch and an oculus with bas-reliefs which belonged to the previous church on the site. Inside, the single nave is covered by a very high and distinctive stone "wagon vault", a local speciality. There are many frescoes and other paintings, as well as some fine stained-glass windows.

🏛 Palazzo Ducale
Via Federico di Montefeltro.
📞 *075 927 5872.* ◷ *9am–7pm.*
♿ *Wed.* 🎫

The Palazzo Ducale stands right in front of the cathedral. Locally known as the Corte Nuova, it was built by the Montefeltro family after they had taken possession of the town. Recently restored, the palazzo has an interesting archaeological area under-ground (where it is possible to see traces of the piazza that was here before the palazzo was built) as well as rooms used for temporary exhibitions.

🏛 Via XX Settembre

From Piazza Grande, Via XX Settembre leads past palazzi and churches to the quarter of Sant'Andrea and the **Porta Romana**. This medieval town gate, with its high tower, houses a collection of majolica pottery and other pieces in various materials, as well as weaponry, maps and so on. Nearby, outside the walls, is the church of **Sant'Agostino**, which retains traces of frescoes dating back to the church's foundation (1294), as well as several works dating from the 14th century.

The medieval Porta Romana

A short walk east of the church is the terminal for the funicular up to the **Basilica di Sant'Ubaldo**, which lies high above the town on Monte Ingino. The ride takes eight minutes and offers lovely views on the way; there is also a path, if you prefer to go up on foot.

🏛 Corso Garibaldi

This street runs parallel with the quarter of Sant'Andrea and is the main thoroughfare through the San Pietro quarter, the busy centre of Gubbio. The narrow streets retain a village atmosphere and are lined with shops. On Corso Garibaldi itself look out for the churches of **Santissima Trinità** and of **San Pietro**, of 13th-century origin and built close to a large monastery complex.

THE FESTA DEI CERI

The Corsa dei Ceri (candle race), considered within Umbria almost as great a spectacle as Siena's Palio, takes place every year on 15 May. The finishing line is the hilltop basilica of Sant'Ubaldo. The "candles" in question, three in all, are heavy wooden and papier mâché structures in the form of superimposed prisms, 10 m (33 ft) high and 200 kg (440 lb) in weight. They bear the effigies of Sant'Ubaldo, St George and St Anthony Abbot, patron saints of masons and stonecutters, craftsmen and peasants respectively. The first drum roll is heard at dawn, but the *ceri* are not brought out until noon. The actual race, which attracts huge crowds, takes place in the evening.

The heavy wooden "candles", carried aloft over the crowd

Parco Regionale del Monte Cucco ❺

ON THE BORDER WITH THE neighbouring region of Le Marche, Monte Cucco is one of the most fascinating peaks in central Italy. Below ground are miles and miles of galleries and caverns, which form one of the most impressive cave systems in Italy: the Grotta di Monte Cucco. The higher altitudes can be reached from the village of Costacciaro, and the windswept terrain attracts devoted fans of hang-gliding. Within the park, which is centred around the village of Sigillo, various hiking trails have been marked out. There are also facilities for various open-air sports. Besides paragliding, the park can arrange exploration of the Forra di Riofreddo gorge (for experts only), and there are also mountain bike trails and tracks for runners. Many paleontological and archaeological finds have been discovered in the park, as well as ancient Roman settlements.

La Valdorbia

URBINO

Aiale

Ponte Calcara

360

Scheggia

GUBBIO

Campitello

Costa San Savino

Caprile

Costacciaro

Scirca

Scheggia

From this village of Roman origin it is possible to enter and explore the northern part of the park, with its Benedictine abbeys – in particular, Sant'Emiliano at Isola Fossara and the Hermitage of San Girolamo a Pascelupo.

Costacciaro

Unlike the other villages that surround the park, which are almost all of Roman origin, Costacciaro was built in 1250 by the citizens of Gubbio as a fortified town.

At Scirca, ruins of a large Roman settlement have been uncovered. In the village, the old church of Santa Maria Assunta is decorated with frescoes by Matteo da Gualdo.

THE "NATIVES" OF MONTE CUCCO

Besides all kinds of opportunities for sport, the Parco Regionale del Monte Cucco is also one of the best places in the Apennines for observing wildlife. In fact, as well as being home to typically Apennine species (such **Wildcat** as deer, wild boar, porcupines and martens), the park also harbours other species that are increasingly rare in Central Italy, including the wolf, wildcat and golden eagle. Among other birds that can be seen in the park are partridges, quails, eagle owls and kingfishers. Crayfish can also be found in the rivers.

Golden eagle

0 kilometres 1

0 miles   1

The Badia di Sitria is an abbey with an interesting Romanesque church (Santa Maria) with a single nave and a barrel vault. The crypt is held up at the centre by a Roman column with a Corinthian capital.

The Forra di Riofreddo is a deep, narrow gorge, which can only be tackled by experienced climbers. It was formed after many centuries of erosion by streams coming down from the mountain top.

Summit of Monte Cucco

At 1,566m (5,136ft), Monte Cucco is one of the highest peaks in Umbria. It can be reached fairly easily along the scenic Via del Ranco, which leads out of Sigillo.

Grotta di Monte Cucco

This cave can be reached on foot from the car park just beyond Val di Ranco. The cave reaches the record depth of 922m (3,024 ft) and the water that gathers within the mountain emerges, after a lengthy subterranean journey, at the Scirca spring near Sigillo.

Sigillo

Home to the park administration, this village has visible Roman origins, in the bridges on the Via Flaminia and over the Scirca torrent. Of note are the church of Sant'Agostino, in the heart of the village, and Sant'Anna, near the cemetery, with frescoes by Matteo da Gualdo.

Gualdo Tadino

Perugia. **Road Map** D3.
🏛 15,000. 🚉 Foligno–Ancona
line. 🚌 Piazza Orti Mavarelli.
🛈 Via Calai 39, 075 912 172.

THE TOWN OF Gualdo Tadino, of ancient Umbrian and Roman origins, endured a tormented history of defeats, destruction and emigration until the 12th century, when it was resettled on its present site. The name is a combination of the Roman name *Tadinum* and the Lombard word *wald*, meaning forest.

As a commune, the village took shape in the Middle Ages, but was heavily modified over the course of the centuries and today bears only a few traces of its centuries-old history. Gualdo suffered terrible damage during the 1997 earthquake, but has now been almost totally restored. The town is still, as it was in the Middle Ages and later centuries, one of the principal centres of majolica manufacture in Umbria.

The only ancient gate to survive in Gualdo is that of San Benedetto, on the eastern side: from here, Corso Italia (which becomes Corso Piave) cuts through the whole of the historic centre. Walking along this street, you reach Piazza XX Settembre, home to the churches of **San Donato** (12th century) and **Santa Maria dei Raccomandati** (13th century) . The latter contains a fine triptych by Matteo da Gualdo of the *Madonna with Child and saints Sebastian and Roch*, but is closed to the public.

Further along, on Corso Piave, is the church of **San Francesco**, built by the Franciscans in the 13th and 14th centuries. It has a beautiful façade, with an elegant Gothic doorway, and inside are many frescoes, most of which are the work of Matteo da Gualdo (1435–

Fresco on a palazzo in the centre of Gualdo

1507), the best-known artist native to Gualdo Tadino whose works can also be seen in Assisi and Spoleto. The fresco on the first pilaster on the left, of *St Anne, the Virgin and Child*, is said to be the oldest work by the artist.

You soon arrive at the central **Piazza Martiri della Libertà**, better known to the residents of Gualdo as Piazza Grande, and where the town's most important buildings are found. Lording it over the space is the **Palazzo Comunale**. The original, 12th-century palazzo was rebuilt after a terrible earthquake in 1751, so what is seen now is its 18th-century form. Most of the town's medieval buildings collapsed during the same earthquake, and the **Palazzo del Podestà** (13th century), in front of the Palazzo Comunale, was also badly damaged. An international ceramics exhibition and competition is held annually in the Palazzo del Podestà, which brings dozens of ceramic workers back to Gualdo, a centre for the manufacture of lustreware.

The cathedral of **San Benedetto** stands on the eastern side of Piazza Martiri. The façade, dating from the 13th century but carefully restored after the earthquake, has three doors – one for each of the aisles inside – and a beautiful rose window. The interior was

Detail of a fountain

entirely rebuilt in the 19th century, and has 20th-century frescoes. Outside, to the left, stands a lovely Renaissance fountain. The only building that remained intact after the earthquake, and that is still visible in the piazza today, is the **Torre Civica**.

In common with many other villages in this part of Umbria, Gualdo Tadino has a fortress at the top of the hill. The origins of the **Rocca Flea** date back to the 10th century, when the construction of fortifications began on the site of a church, of which several frescoes have recently been uncovered. Today, the sizeable fortress has more than 40 rooms – the result of a series of enlargements and restoration work carried out over the centuries. In particular, the buildings show the influence of Frederick II, who restored and made improvements to the castle during the 13th century, and also of the Perugians, who made changes in the following century. The Rocca, due to reopen after several years of closure, houses a **Pinacoteca** (art gallery), a ceramics gallery and also a collection of archeological finds. The former has on display detached frescoes by Matteo da Gualdo as well as works by Jacopo Palma, Antonio da Fabriano and Niccolò Alunno.

🏛 Rocca Flea

Piazza della Rocca. 📞 075 912 072.
🕐 Jun–Sep: 10:30am–1pm, 3:30–7pm Tue–Sun; Oct–May: 10:30am–1pm, 3:30-6pm Thu–Sun.

The fortified bulk of Rocca Flea, guarding the town

ENVIRONS: About 7 km (4 miles) north of Gualdo Tadino is **Fossato di Vico**, a town that is divided into two parts: Fossato Basso, the largely modern town along the road, and Fossato Alto, the remnants of a major medieval settlement perched on a rocky spur. It is worth stopping off along the road between the two parts, at the church of San Benedetto, in order to see the frescoes by Matteo da Gualdo.

In the heart of Fossato Basso are covered walkways and the Cappella della Piaggiola, with frescoes by Ottaviano Nelli and his school (early 15th century).

Porta Vecchia, ancient entrance to the old centre of Nocera Umbra

Nocera Umbra **7**

Perugia. **Road Map** D3. 🏠 6,000.
🚉 *Nocera Scalo, 3 km (2 miles), Rome–Ancona line.* ℹ️ *APT to open in Piazza Caprera. For information, call the Comune (0742 834 011).*
🌐 *www.umbria2000.it* 🎪 *Palio del Quartiere, first Tue in Aug.*

THE COLLAPSE of the Torre di Nocera Umbra during the earthquake of 1997 has become one of the enduring symbolic images of that tragic natural disaster. The town has been hit by earthquakes on a number of occasions, but perhaps never before with such ferocity. The structural damage affected the whole of the historic centre, formerly one of the best-preserved in the region. Even now, only a small number of inhabitants have returned. Yet Nocera

Nocera Umbra, devastated by the 1997 earthquake but being rebuilt

Umbra is a hive of activity – houses are being rebuilt, while historic buildings are gradually being restored. The symbolic tower has already been reconstructed.

High on a rocky outcrop that looms over fertile valleys drained by the Topino and Caldognola rivers, Nocera Umbra has always occupied a strategically significant location, thanks partly to the town's position on the border of Le Marche and to its proximity to the Adriatic Sea. Originally an ancient Umbrian town (called *Nuokria*), it was an important settlement under both the Romans and the Lombards. The waters that gush from the many springs in the area are known for their curative properties.

You can enter the historic centre (which closes at 7pm) through Porta Vecchia, a gate in the medieval walls. From here, Corso Vittorio leads to Piazza Caprera, the heart of the old town.

Most of the important buildings in Nocera Umbra, are still closed for obvious reasons, including the **Duomo**, on the top of the hill. The former church of **San Francesco**, now an art gallery, is open, however. It is also worth going as far as the western walls to the church of **San Filippo**, a Neo-Gothic structure from the late 19th century. This marks the start of the Portici di San Filippo, a covered walkway within the walls, which is punctuated at intervals by apertures and arrow-slits that enable visitors to admire the views.

ENVIRONS: The peak of **Monte Pennino** (1,571 m/5,155 ft), on the Le Marche border, is reachable from Nocera Umbra by car along 20 km (12 miles) of tortuous road (asphalted, apart from the last stretch). This mountain, as well as being a very scenic place to visit, has facilities for hiking and skiing.

THE WATERS OF NOCERA

The therapeutic quality of the mineral water springs in the Nocera area has been known since the 16th century; in the 18th century the water was used as a benchmark for measuring the purity of other waters. However, it wasn't until the 20th century that the spring

The modern spa at Bagni di Nocera

waters began to be exploited for economic and industrial use, through the building of bottling plants and spas. The two main springs are at Bagni di Nocera and at Schiagni (Fonte del Cacciatore). Their curative powers derive from the combination of a water that is particularly pure and mineral-rich in itself, and the clay typical of this terrain.

Parco Regionale del Monte Subasio 🔞

IN OUTLINE, Monte Subasio (1,290 m/4,230 ft) has a distinctively rounded form. It rises, isolated, between the historic centres of Assisi, Spello and Nocera Umbra and, since 1995, has formed the southern margin of a 7,442-ha (18,390-acre) regional park. As well as its own natural beauty, Monte Subasio offers superb views across to the high Appenines in the east. The park also includes many places of historic and religious significance. Subasio's distinctive rose-coloured stone was used to build much of Assisi, which lies right on the fringes of the park. The mountain was regarded as a sacred place in the 10th century BC, and its importance endured during the life of St Francis, who perhaps drew inspiration from these magical and mystical surroundings.

Monte Subasio
The summit of Monte Subasio is easily reached and seems to offer a view of the whole of Umbria. To the southeast are the sink-holes known as "mortaro grande" and "mortaro piccolo", cavities which were once used for collecting ice.

The northern road leaves Assisi near Cà Piombino, base for the park administration. Before winding its way south towards Spello, the road goes through the small historic centres of Armenzano, San Giovanni and Collepino.

I Prati degli Stazzi, on the road between the Eremo delle Carceri and the peak, offer fine views over Assisi. In May, the fields are carpeted in flowers.

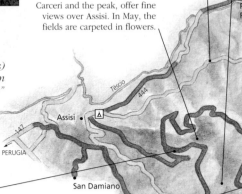

Eremo delle Carceri
Around 4km (2 miles) from Assisi, this small and peaceful hermitage is surrounded by dense woodland. The name (Hermitage of the Prisons) derives from the fact that Franciscan friars used to "lock themselves away" here in order to pray: there is still a 15th-century church here, as well as a cave where St Francis would go to rest. Beyond the hermitage is a bridge that leads to a wood containing a series of caves and hermitages used in the Middle Ages by the devout and by friars.

Road to the summit
Between Assisi and Spello the road retraces the route of an ancient cart track. A lovely scenic road, it leads almost to the peak of Monte Subasio. On the descent towards Spello, the road passes the sanctuary of the Madonna della Spella.

0 kilometres 2

0 miles 2

KEY

‖ Minor road

▬ Scenic route

🅰 Campsite

Rocca di Postignano
Within the park is the ancient fortification of Rocca Postignano, as well as several churches that were built on the site of places where hermits once prayed.

VISITORS' CHECKLIST

Perugia. **Road Map** C2.
FS *Santa Maria degli Angeli, Assisi, Foligno–Terontola line, 892021.* Assisi–Eremo delle Carceri, 800 512 141.
i *Cà Piombino, Assisi, 075 815 181.* **FAX** *075 815 307.*
@ *parco.monte.subasio@parks.it*

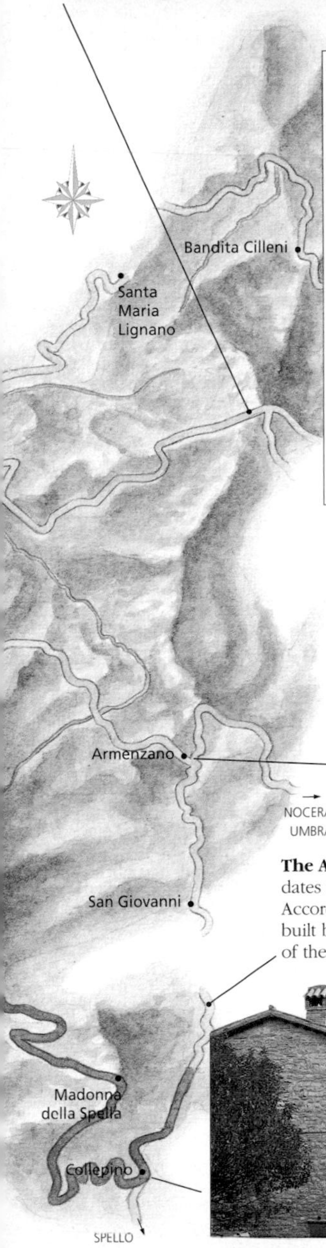

WILDLIFE ON MONTE SUBASIO

The slopes of the mountain are today covered with three different kinds of vegetation. Olive trees are grown on land stretching from Assisi as far as Spello. Other areas support mixed woodland, including oak, black hornbeam, ash, maple, beech and holm oak. Forests of

A pair of porcupines

resiniferous trees, the result of replanting, characterize the third type of vegetation, along with meadow pasture. This range of natural habitats does not support a wide variety of wildlife, however, despite a ban on hunting lasting several decades: the golden eagle has not been seen since the 1960s. Current wildlife sightings include the partridge, wood pigeon, magpie, jay, wildcat, squirrel, porcupine, badger, wolf, weasel, stone marten and wild boar. Birds of prey seen here include the buzzard and goshawk.

Bandita Cilleni

Santa Maria Lignano

Castello di Armenzano
During the Middle Ages, this place was fortified because it occupied a strategic position. Today, the village offers peace and fine views.

Armenzano

→ NOCERA UMBRA

The Abbey of San Silvestro
dates from the 11th century. According to tradition, it was built by San Romualdo, founder of the Camaldolese order.

San Giovanni

Collepino
About 10 km (6 miles) from the peak of Monte Subasio, this walled medieval village stands isolated near the source of the river Chiona.

Madonna della Spella

Collepino

SPELLO

Assisi ❾

View of the Basilica di San Francesco

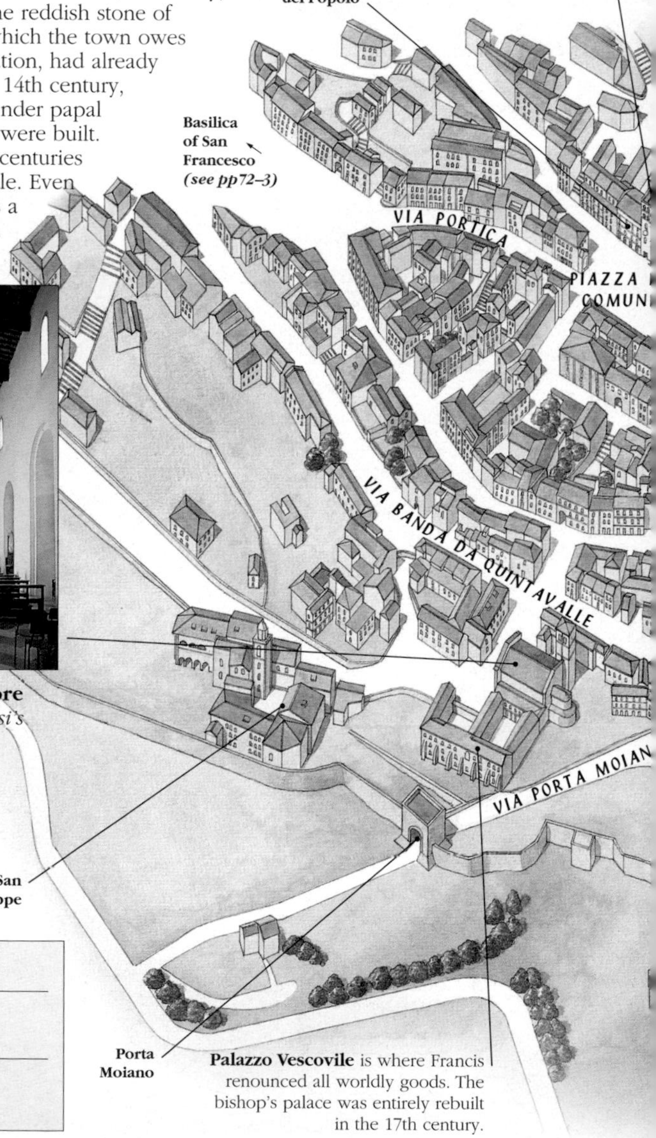

EVEN WITHOUT THE CHURCHES, extraordinary frescoes and associations with St Francis, it would be worth coming to Assisi simply to witness a sunset. As the sun sinks, the medieval centre of Assisi, one of the best-preserved in the world, is bathed in a warm glow. Founded by the Umbrians, Assisi was prominent during the Roman era, but the town achieved greatest fame and importance during the era of the communes in the Middle Ages. By the time the basilica of San Francesco was founded in the 13th century, Assisi, built using the reddish stone of Monte Subasio to which the town owes its distinctive coloration, had already taken shape. In the 14th century, when Assisi came under papal rule, two fortresses were built. Over the following centuries the city changed little. Even today, the town has a timeless fascination.

Palazzo del Capitano del Popolo

Temple of Minerva

Basilica of San Francesco (see pp72–3)

VIA PORTICA

PIAZZA COMUNE

VIA BANDA DA QUINTAVALLE

Santa Maria Maggiore
This church was Assisi's first cathedral. Its Romanesque origins are clear from its formal simplicity.

Monastery of San Giuseppe

VIA PORTA MOIAN

STAR SIGHTS

★ Duomo (San Rufino)

★ Basilica di Santa Chiara

Porta Moiano

Palazzo Vescovile is where Francis renounced all worldly goods. The bishop's palace was entirely rebuilt in the 17th century.

Piazza del Comune
This square has always been the heart of Assisi. Around the piazza are the Temple of Minerva (1st century BC), Palazzo del Capitano del Popolo (13th century), the Torre del Popolo (13th–14th century) and Palazzo dei Priori (14th century).

VISITORS' CHECKLIST

Perugia. **Road Map** D4.
🏠 25,000. **FS** *Assisi (Piazza Matteotti); Santa Maria degli Angeli (Piazza Garibaldi), Foligno-Terontola line, 892021*
📞 800 512 141. 🛈 *Piazza del Comune 12, 075 812 534.*
🎪 *Calendimaggio, 4–6 May.*

Santa Maria delle Rose

★ **Duomo**
The present building was begun in the 12th century. The beautiful Romanesque façade with its rose windows dates from this time. It was here that saints Francis and Clare were baptized, and perhaps Emperor Frederick II, too.

VIA SANTA MARIA DELLE ROSE

VIA SAN RUFINO

VIA SAN GABRIELE DELL'ADDOLORATA

CORSO MAZZINI

At the base of the cathedral apse and bell tower, courses of Roman blocks are visible.

The Chiesa Nuova (17th century) was built where the house of the father of St Francis, Pietro di Bernardone, is thought to have stood.

PIAZZA SANTA CHIARA

Porta Nuova

The convent alongside the basilica still contains the crypt of the ancient little church of San Giorgio, in the cloister.

★ **Basilica di Santa Chiara**
This church was built shortly after the Basilica di San Francesco. As well as the remains of St Clare, it contains prized works of art and the famous Byzantine Crucifix of San Damiano.

Exploring Assisi

Duomo, detail of the façade

THE DRAW OF ASSISI's famous basilica can be overpowering, but there is much else to explore in the town. Motorists would do best to leave their car in the huge car park in Largo Properzio, just outside the walls, and to enter the historic centre through Porta Nuova, on the southeastern side of town. From here, Via Borgo Aretino leads to Assisi's first great building, the basilica of Santa Chiara. This lies in the heart of a medieval quarter, which is linked by steep streets to the upper town, dating from Roman times and home to the duomo and Piazza del Comune. From this central piazza, continue along Via Seminario and Via San Francesco, lined with medieval buildings, to reach the great basilica of St Francis *(see pp72–3)*.

Baptismal font in the cathedral of San Rufino

The door and rose window of the basilica of Santa Chiara

🏛 Santa Chiara
Piazza Santa Chiara.
[075 812 282.
○ 6:30am–noon, 2–7pm (6pm in winter).

Assisi's second great church was begun in 1257, and consecrated eight years later by Pope Clement IV: the body of St Clare (declared a saint in 1255), founder of the order of the Poor Clares, was buried here in 1260.

The façade has a simple doorway with a rose window above, while the side that faces the street is supported by three vast buttresses. The church is distinctive because of the use of alternating layers of white and red stone, as seen in some Tuscan churches.

The interior is in the form of a Latin cross, simple and spare. In the right transept there is a cycle of frescoes

depicting *Scenes from the Life of St Clare*, by an unknown artist called the Master of Santa Chiara (late 13th century). Other interesting frescoes, from the 14th century, can be found on the left wall, while on the right, in the Oratorio delle Reliquie, there is the late 12th-century wooden Crucifix of San Damiano. According to the hagiography, this is the crucifix that famously spoke to Francis in San Damiano, asking him to "repair his church" *(see p80)*.

🏛 Duomo (San Rufino)
Piazza San Rufino.
[075 816 016, 075 812 283.
○ summer: 8am–1pm, 3–7pm daily; winter: 8am–1pm, 2–6pm (Holy Week 7am–7pm).

From Santa Chiara, a climb up stepped streets leads to the duomo, built on a Roman religious site in around 1029 by archbishop Ugone, and then rebuilt in the 12th–13th centuries. The church was consecrated in 1253, the year

construction was completed, by Pope Innocent IV.

Less well known than the other basilicas of Assisi, the cathedral is worth a visit just for its splendid façade, a masterpiece of Umbrian Romanesque. It is divided into three horizontal sections. At ground level are three doors decorated with lions, with bas-relief lunettes; above, divided from the lower level by a band of sculpted corbels, are three rose windows with symbols of the evangelists. At the top is a triangular tympanum with a Gothic arch. To one side, rising above the scene, is the bell tower, part of the 11th-century church and with double-mullioned windows.

The interior, laid out on a rectangular plan, dates from the 16th century. It still has the old baptismal font where both St Francis and St Clare were baptized, a wooden choir dating from the 16th century and the underground Franciscan oratory, where the

View of Assisi, with its walls and fortifications, from Monte Subasio

saint would withdraw before preaching to the crowd. The Cappella del Sacramento, by Giacomo Giorgetti, is a Baroque composition on the theme of the Eucharist.

Adjacent to the church is the **Museo della Cattedrale** (cathedral museum), which contains pieces from the original church, a series of frescoes from the Oratorio di San Rufinuccio and paintings from various churches in Assisi. To the left of the church are the ruins of a Roman theatre and, a little further north, those of an amphitheatre. In the church courtyard a plaque shows the site of the house where St Clare was born.

🕎 Piazza del Comune

From the cathedral, heading along Via di San Rufino, you reach the square that has always been the true heart of the city. It was created in its current form in the 13th century. The main focus of the piazza is the **Temple of Minerva**, built in the 1st century BC on a set of terraces that once marked the centre of the town. This beautifully preserved Roman temple has changed function at various times over the centuries: first a church, then a group of shops, then seat of the town hall until, in 1456, it finally became a church again, with the name of Santa Maria sopra Minerva.

On the left of the temple portico is the **Palazzo del Capitano del Popolo**, built in the 13th century and extensively restored in the

The late Renaissance façade of the Chiesa Nuova

20th century. At the foot of the bell tower (Torre del Popolo), you can see the 14th-century measures for bricks, tiles and fabrics then in use in Assisi, set into the wall. On the opposite side of the piazza is the **Palazzo dei Priori**, begun in 1275 and completed in the late 15th century. On the right is the Arco della Volta Pinta, with 16th-century frescoes. The Fonte di Piazza, at the far end of the square, is an 18th-century fountain built on the foundations of a 13th-century water basin.

A brief descent through the Arco dei Priori leads to the 17th-century **Chiesa Nuova**, which was commissioned by Philip III of Spain to mark the spot where St Francis was said to have been born.

🏛 Temple of Minerva
Piazza del Comune.
📞 075 812 268.
🕐 7:15am–7pm Mon–Sat; 8:15am–7pm Sun & public hols.
🔵 2–5.15pm Tue, Fri.
🔒 Chiesa Nuova
Piazzetta Chiesa Nuova.
📞 075 812 339.
🕐 6:30am–noon, 2:30–6pm (5pm in winter).

🏛 Museo and Foro Romano
Via Portica.
📞 075 813 053.
🕐 mid-Mar–mid-Oct: 10am–1pm, 2–6pm daily; mid-Oct–mid-Mar: 10am–1pm, 2–5pm. 📷

On the corner of Piazza del Comune, beyond the Arco del Seminario – the ancient limit of the walled city in the Roman era – is a museum of Roman finds. From the museum, visitors can gain access to the ruins of what may have been the Roman forum, beneath the Piazza del Comune.

🔒 Via San Francesco

Heading towards the Basilica di San Francesco, you cover the whole length of Via del Seminario, which becomes Via San Francesco. Along the way you pass the **Palazzo Giacobetti** (17th century)

The Loggia dei Maestri Comacini, on Via San Francesco

and, opposite, the delightful **Oratorio dei Pellegrini** (15th century), once part of a pilgrim's hospice, followed by the arches of the Portico del Monte Frumentario, part of a 13th-century hospital.

Next comes the Palazzo Vallemani, which is temporary home of the **Pinacoteca Comunale**; the art gallery's most important work is probably the *Madonna in Maestà* (Giotto school), found near the entrance.

A little further along is the **Loggia dei Maestri Comacini**, a 13th-century palazzetto which, according to tradition, was the seat of the Lombard rulers; it is adorned with 15th-century coats of arms. Nearby, the steep Vicolo di Sant'Andrea climbs up to the Piazza di Santa Margherita, from where there are classic views towards the Basilica di San Francesco. It is especially moving at sunset or at dawn.

Madonna in Maestà

🔒 Oratorio dei Pellegrini
Via San Francesco. 📞 075 812 267.
🕐 10am–noon, 4–6pm Tue–Sat.
🏛 Pinacoteca Comunale
Palazzo Vallemani, Via San Francesco 10. 📞 075 812 033.
🕐 mid-Mar–mid-Oct: 10am–1pm, 2–6pm daily; mid-Oct–mid-Mar: 10am–1pm, 2–5pm. 📷

Assisi: Basilica di San Francesco

The rose window above the door

ST FRANCIS DIED on 4 October 1226. Just 18 months later Frate Elia, Vicar-General of the Franciscan Order, was charged by Pope Gregory IX with building a church dedicated to the saint. After the laying of the first stone, the Lower Church was the first part to take shape; the Upper Church was eventually built on top of it. The basilica was consecrated by Pope Innocent IV in 1253, though the chapel of Santa Caterina, the final stage in the basilica's construction, was not completed until 1367. Some of the greatest artists of the age, including Cimabue and Giotto, left their mark on the building. On 26 September 1997, a severe earthquake badly damaged the church: part of the vault collapsed and cracks appeared in the transept. Just two years later, however, the basilica re-opened for visits and worship, the culmination of an exceptional feat of restoration.

The walls of the transept are decorated with an outstanding cycle of frescoes painted by Cimabue and his assistants. The *Crucifixion* in the left transept is superb.

The wooden choir, situated in the apse and on the sides next to the crossing, is an example of Gothic Renaissance engraving and inlaid wood, the work of Domenico Indovini.

★ **Quattro Vele**
The celebrated allegorical frescoes of the Quattro Vele (vault above the altar), in the Lower Church, represent The Three Virtues of St Francis. *Long attributed to Giotto, they are now thought to be the work of one of his assistants. A detail of the* Allegory of Obedience *is shown here.*

The Tomb of St Francis, in the crypt, was discovered only in 1818. The exact location had never been revealed for fear that someone might want to seize such a precious relic. The remains of the saint were transferred here in 1230, before the basilica was finished.

★ **Frescoes in the Crossing**
The left side of the crossing was decorated by Pietro Lorenzetti in 1515–20. This is one of two portraits of the Madonna and Child.

Frescoes in the Nave

The vault in the nave is decorated with frescoes by various masters, one of whom may have been the young Giotto. The vault in the first bay represents the Four Doctors of the Church working in their studies, each with an assistant. St Augustine is shown here.

The façade is an example of Italian Gothic. It has a double rose window in Cosmatesque style and a double door.

Interior of the Upper Church

The bright, soaring, single-nave upper church is typical of Franciscan monastic architecture. It takes the forms of French Gothic but simplifies them and adds local elements. It was intended to symbolize the asceticism and spirituality that characterized the life of St Francis.

Entrance to the Upper Church

Entrance to the Lower Church

The Cappella di San Martino, the first on the left in the Lower Church, was decorated by Simone Martini (1312–1320). His frescoes, depicting several saints and a cycle illustrating the *Life of St Martin*, are true masterpieces.

★ **Life of St Francis**

The frescoes on the lower walls of the nave (1290s), long thought to be by Giotto and his assistants, are now attributed by most specialists to a superb unknown artist, often referred to as the Maestro di San Francesco.

STAR FEATURES

★ **Quattro Vele**

★ **Frescoes in the Crossing**

★ **Life of St Francis**

Assisi: The Frescoes in the Basilica

Apotheosis of St Francis, Giotto, detail

IT WAS NOT WITHOUT controversy that Frate Elia erected such a grandiose building to hold the relics of a saint who had preached poverty. It appears that two buildings, one above the other, were envisaged from the very beginning, although the exact date of the commencement of work on the Upper Church is not known. The Lower Church, both smaller and simpler, was to function as the saint's burial place and to accommodate pilgrims, while the Upper Church was for regular worship. The speed with which the work was carried out evidently did not allow for much sculptural decoration, and the vast plain walls seemed designed for impressive cycles of frescoes, on which the greatest painters of the age could work. Together they created one of the finest and most loved monuments in the history of Western art.

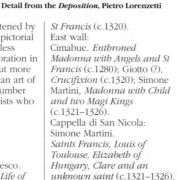

Detail from the *Deposition*, Pietro Lorenzetti

LOWER CHURCH

Austere and rather gloomy, the Lower Church shows the influence of the Romanesque style. The solemnity is lightened by the wonderfully rich pictorial decoration, which is less famous than the decoration in the Upper Church, but more representative of Italian art of the time, given the number and quality of the artists who worked here.

MAIN FRESCOES IN THE LOWER CHURCH
Walls
Maestro di San Francesco.
Left: *Stories from the Life of St Francis*; Right: *Scenes from the Passion* (c.1260, much damaged, only half visible).
Quattro Vele (vault above the altar)
Maestro delle Vele.
Apotheosis of St Francis; Allegory of Obedience; Allegory of Poverty; Allegory of Chastity (c.1315–1320).
Right Transept
Vaults:
Workshop of Giotto.
Infancy and Adolescence of Jesus (c.1315–1320).
West and north walls:
Workshop of Giotto.
Posthumous Miracles of St Francis (c.1320).
East wall:
Cimabue. *Enthroned Madonna with Angels and St Francis* (c.1280); Giotto (?), *Crucifixion* (c.1320); Simone Martini, *Madonna with Child and two Magi Kings* (c.1321–1326).
Cappella di San Nicola:
Simone Martini.
Saints Francis, Louis of Toulouse, Elizabeth of Hungary, Clare and an unknown saint (c.1321–1326).

Left Transept
Entirely frescoed by Pietro Lorenzetti and workshop (c.1315–1320).
Barrel vault:
Entry into Jerusalem; the Last Supper; Washing of the Feet; Expulsion from the Temple; Ascent to Calvary; Flagellation; Crucifixion.
South wall:
Descent from the Cross; Deposition; Descent into Limbo; Resurrection.
East wall:
Crucifixion; Madonna and Child; St Francis and St John the Evangelist.
West wall:
Death of Judas; St Francis receives the stigmata.
Cappella di San Giovanni Battista:
Madonna with Child and Sts Francis and John the Baptist.
Cappella di San Martino di Tours (first on the left)
Entirely frescoed by Simone Martini (c.1321–26).
Figures of saints and cycle of frescoes depicting the *Life of St Martin.*

UPPER CHURCH

The Upper Church is as airy and light as the Lower Church is low and dark. Its pictorial decoration is divided substantially into two main blocks: the frescoes of the apse, transept and the crossing, by Cimabue and his school, and those of the nave and vaults, where the life of St Francis and episodes from the Old and New Testament are portrayed in one of the world's great masterpieces.

Madonna and Child, Pietro Lorenzetti, detail, Lower Church

◁ **The interior of the Upper Church, Basilica di San Francesco, Assisi (pre-1997 earthquake)**

FRESCOES IN THE APSE AND THE TRANSEPTS

Cimabue and his school (1280).

Left Transept
Crucifixion; Scenes from the Apocalypse; Michael and the Angels.

Main Apse
Scenes from the Life of the Virgin Mary.

Right Transept
The Apostles.

Crossing
The Evangelists.

Detail, *Dream of the Throne*, from the Life of St Francis cycle

FRESCOES IN THE NAVE

Scenes from the Life of St Francis, either by Giotto or the Maestro di San Francesco; the upper register and vaults by Cimabue and others.

Detail from *Miracle of the Spring*, 14th scene, Giotto cycle

KEY TO FRESCOES IN THE NAVE AND VAULTS

OLD TESTAMENT

1 Creation of the World
2 Creation of Adam
3 Creation of Eve
4 Original sin
5 Expulsion from Paradise
6 The labours of Adam and Eve
7 Cain and Abel
8 Cain kills Abel
9 Noah builds the Ark
10 Boarding the Ark
11 Sacrifice of Isaac
12 Abraham and the three angels
13 Isaac blessing Jacob
14 Esau before Isaac
15 Joseph thrown into the well by his brothers
16 Joseph forgives his brothers

NEW TESTAMENT

17 Annunciation
18 Visitation
19 Nativity
20 Adoration of the Magi
21 Presentation at the Temple
22 Flight into Egypt
23 Christ among the Doctors
24 Baptism of Christ
25 Marriage at Cana
26 Resurrection of Lazarus
27 Capture of Christ
28 Flagellation
29 Ascent to Golgotha
30 Crucifixion
31 Lament over the dead Christ
32 Maries at the Sepulchre

LIFE OF ST FRANCIS

I Francis honoured in the piazza
II Gift of the Cloak
III Dream of Arms
IV Prayer in San Damiano
V Renounces worldly goods
VI Dream of Innocent I
VII Approval of the Order
VIII Apparition in Chariot of Fire
IX Dream of the Throne
X Expulsion of Demons from Arezzo
XI Francis before the Sultan
XII Francis in ecstasy
XIII Celebration of Christmas
XIV Miracle of the Spring
XV Preaching to the birds
XVI Death of the Knight
XVII Prayer before Honorius III
XVIII Apparition in Arles
XIX Francis receives the stigmata
XX Death of Francis
XXI Apparition of the saint
XXII Girolamo accepts the truth of the stigmata
XXIII Poor Clares mourn the saint
XXIV Canonization
XXV Dream of Gregory IX
XXVI Healing of the man from Ilerda
XXVII Revival of the devout woman
XXVIII Liberation of Pietro di Alife

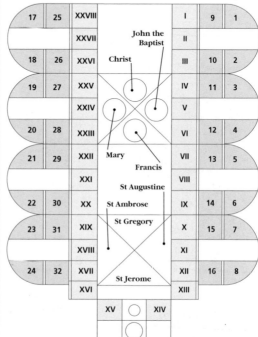

Monastic Orders

ANYONE VISITING Umbria, and in particular Assisi, will be aware immediately of the many convents and monasteries belonging to different religious orders, direct descendants of the ministry of St Francis and St Clare. Monastic orders in Europe were born officially in the 6th century, with the drawing up of St Benedict's Rule. Reforms to the Benedictine Order instigated at Cluny in the 10th century gave a great boost to the monastic movement, as did the

Franciscan arms

development of the Cistercian Order two centuries later. St Francis (1182–1226) broke new ground by reacting against the luxury and seclusion of old-fashioned monasticism, with its great abbeys, and instead invited his followers to live a life of poverty and renunciation, ministering to the urban poor. It was very hard to apply such a severe precept to a group, even of monks, which led to the the birth of other Franciscan orders. Three exist today.

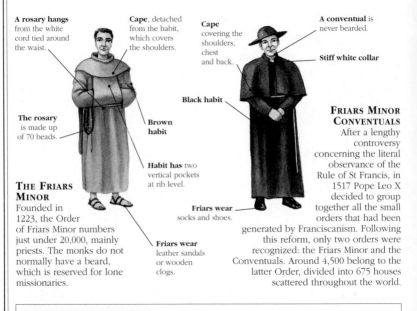

A rosary hangs from the white cord tied around the waist.

Cape, detached from the habit, which covers the shoulders.

Cape covering the shoulders, chest and back.

A conventual is never bearded.

Stiff white collar

Black habit

The rosary is made up of 70 beads.

Brown habit

Habit has two vertical pockets at rib level.

THE FRIARS MINOR

Founded in 1223, the Order of Friars Minor numbers just under 20,000, mainly priests. The monks do not normally have a beard, which is reserved for lone missionaries.

Friars wear socks and shoes.

Friars wear leather sandals or wooden clogs.

FRIARS MINOR CONVENTUALS

After a lengthy controversy concerning the literal observance of the Rule of St Francis, in 1517 Pope Leo X decided to group together all the small orders that had been generated by Franciscanism. Following this reform, only two orders were recognized: the Friars Minor and the Conventuals. Around 4,500 belong to the latter Order, divided into 675 houses scattered throughout the world.

The cloister of the convent of San Damiano

POOR CLARES, FRANCISCAN NUNS AND CAPUCHIN NUNS

The origin of the Order of Poor Clares (Clarisse) dates back to when St Clare (Santa Chiara) took the veil, celebrated by St Francis in 1212 at Santa Maria degli Angeli *(see p80)*, when Clare was just a teenager. Having entered a traditional Benedictine convent, she left with a group of sisters and went to the church of San Damiano *(see p80)*, where she decided to follow in the footsteps of St Francis by establishing a female Franciscan order. The Rule of the Poor Clares was drawn up in 1224 by Francis himself and was observed with rigour by St Clare. Over time, the severity of the original Rule was slightly relaxed. In the 15th century, the establishment of the Reformed Franciscan Order of nuns signalled a return to the earlier, stricter observance, and in 1525 a female branch of the Capuchin Order was founded. The three orders survive to this day.

Robe of St Francis
The nature of the robe that is traditionally regarded as the first one worn by St Francis obeys his own rules of poverty and is in keeping with the description that history provides of the saint's renunciation of worldly goods.

The Capuchin
always has a beard, once unkempt, but today less neglected.

Pointed hood

There are two pockets within the sleeves.

Brown habit

CAPUCHIN FRIARS

Seeking a return to the rigour of the traditional Rule of St Francis, in 1525 Matteo da Bascio founded the first house of the Capuchins at Camerino. The Order spread throughout Italy as well as abroad, but its members suffered persecution because of the character of the Friars' rule, which was considered to be too rigid and extreme. Currently, around 11,000 belong to this Franciscan Order (including 70 bishops, 7,300 priests and 3,500 lay members).

Exterior view of San Pietro showing its clean lines

San Pietro

Piazza San Pietro. (075 812 311.
○ summer: 8am–7pm; winter: 8am–6pm.

It is just a short walk from Basilica di San Francesco along Via Frate Elia to the church of San Pietro, which was founded, along with the adjacent monastery, by the Benedictines in the 10th century. The existing church dates from the same period as the basilica of St Francis, and was consecrated in 1254.

The striking Romanesque-Gothic façade was originally decorated with a pediment, taken down in the 19th century. The interior, mainly Romanesque, contains no works of art of note. Its distinguishing features are its sober simplicity and the height of its nave.

Santa Maria Maggiore

Piazza del Vescovado.
🏠 075 813 085.
○ Easter–mid-Nov: 8:30am–7pm; mid-Nov–Easter: 8:30am–5pm.

Walking east from San Pietro, you eventually emerge into Piazza del Vescovado. This

square was an important site in the Middle Ages, shown by the presence of the Palazzo Vescovile (Bishop's Palace) and the church of Santa Maria Maggiore, the city cathedral until 1020. The church was probably founded in the 10th century, but was rebuilt in Romanesque form around 1163. From the crypt, which is original, there is access to what is supposed to be the House of Propertius (Casa di Properzio) – "supposed" since the origins of the great Roman poet (c.50–16 BC) are anything but clear. In fact, at least three Umbrian cities – Assisi, Spello and Bevagna – have claimed to be the poet's birthplace.

Rocca Maggiore

(075 813 053. ○ 10am–sunset daily.

This well-preserved fortress stands at the northern edge of the city, reached by walking up Via di Porta Perlici from Piazza San Rufino. The panorama, overlooking the Valle del Tescio, the Valle Umbra and Assisi itself, with the façade of the duomo in the foreground, more than compensates for the effort of the climb.

The fortress was built in the 12th century and was used by duke Corrado di Urslingen (tutor to the future emperor Frederick II). It was destroyed and rebuilt more than once, including by Cardinal Albornoz in 1367, from which period most of what is now visible dates. Later additions include the polygonal tower (1458) and the round tower by the entrance (1553–58).

The fortress of the Rocca Maggiore, on the skyline above Assisi

San Damiano, its formal simplicity suited to such a mystical place

🏛 Sanctuary of San Damiano

Via Padre Antonio Giorgi.
📞 075 812 273. ⬚ summer:
10am–noon, 2–6pm (winter: 4:30pm);
Vespers at 7pm and 5pm respectively.

From Porta Nuova, a walk of
around 15 minutes leads to
the Franciscan church of San
Damiano, one of the most
significant places in the life
of St Francis. It was here that,
in 1205, the saint said he
heard the words: "Francis, go
and repair my church which
is falling down". According
to the great chronicler of
Francis' life, Tommaso da
Celano, the words were
spoken by the Crucifix which
is now in Basilica di Santa
Chiara (see p 70). The building
indicated by the crucifix was
that of the church of San
Damiano. Francis himself,
together with a few faithful
followers, undertook the
restoration.

St Francis brought St Clare
to San Damiano; she and her
first followers congregated
here, and founded the
convent in which St Francis
composed his Canticle of the
Creatures (1225). Today, the
convent is run by the Order
of the Frati Minori Osservanti
(Friars Minor).

Besides the spiritual value
of the place, the sanctuary is
worth a visit from both an
architectural and artistic point
of view, especially for the old
convent rooms: the Oratorio
di Santa Chiara, the cloister
with frescoes by Eusebio da
San Giorgio (1507) and the
refectory. A good part of the
13th-century structure of the
building can still be seen.

🏛 Santa Maria degli Angeli-Porziuncola

Santa Maria degli Angeli.
📞 075 805 11.
⬚ summer: 6:15am–12:30pm,
2–7:45pm; winter: 6:15am–7:45pm

Another place which was
dear to Francis and where he
discovered his spiritual side is
at the bottom of the hill
(through Porta San
Pietro). Built at the
end of the 16th
century, the church
of Santa Maria degli
Angeli (the seventh
largest church in
the world) was,
in fact, designed
to accommodate
the buildings of
the 11th-century
Porziuncola ("the little
portion"), the small chapel
where St Francis lived and
which was the centre of the
early Franciscan Order. In
1569, Pope Pius IV laid the
first stone of the vast Santa
Maria, constructed to receive
the hordes of pilgrims wishing
to visit places associated with
Francis. The project was
given to Galeazzo Alessi, and
work was concluded more
than a century later with the
building of the
great cupola

The little oratory of the Porziuncola

(1667) and one of the two
bell towers. Inside the vast
church, beneath the dome, is
the old oratory, known as the
Cappella della Porziuncola;
on the right is the Cappella
del Transito, the old infirmary
cell where the saint died on
4 October 1226; the door is
original. This chapel contains
a majolica statue of St Francis
by Andrea della Robbia. Also
of note is the Cappella del
Roseto (chapel of the rose
garden), with early 16th-
century frescoes by Tiberio
d'Assisi. The chapel takes
its name from a legend,
according to which St Francis
rolled naked on the roses in
the garden (to mortify his
body), only to find that all the
thorns immediately vanished.

In the convent there is a
small museum, with a painted
Crucifix by Giunta Pisano
(mid-13th century) and a
St Francis by an unknown
artist who, thanks to
this portrait, later
passed into history
as the Maestro di
San Francesco.

ENVIRONS: About 5
km (3 miles) south
of Assisi, on the
road to Foligno,
is the imposing
**Santuario di
Rivotorto**, built in 1854 in
Neo-Gothic style on the site
of a stone hut where the first
community of Franciscan
friars made their home for a
brief spell, in 1209; St Francis
wrote the first set of rules for
his Order here. On the façade
are the symbols of the Basilica
di San Francesco.

🏛 Santuario di Rivotorto

Rivotorto di Assisi, 5 km (3 miles).
📞 075 806 5432.
⬚ 6:45am–12:30pm,
2:30–7pm daily.

***Crucifixion*, 1561, fresco by Dono Doni in the duomo of San Rufino**

The Franciscan Path of Peace

The logo of Umbria Mistica

THERE ARE MANY TRAILS in the Umbrian hills, among them this one, established in the Jubilee year (2000). It retraces the journey taken by St Francis in 1206. Along the way, the saint decided to abandon his lay life and discovered the force of his spiritual conversion. The route, which is reasonably easy to walk, links Assisi and Gubbio and not only follows the physical paths trodden by Francis, but also recaptures the future saint's spiritual journey.

VISITORS' CHECKLIST

Piazza del Comune 12, Assisi, 075 812 534.
www.sentierofrancescano.org
Length: c.40 km (25 miles).
Time needed: Two days.
Stopping-off points: Assisi, Valfabbrica, Gubbio. Lodgings at Vallingegno abbey, 075 920 158.

Gubbio ⑦
Just before the town is the "Vittorina", the church dedicated to Santa Maria della Vittoria, where it is said that Francis tamed the wolf. In Gubbio, the trail ends at the church of San Francesco.

Abbey of Vallingegno ⑥
Another notable spiritual stopping place is the abbey dedicated to San Verecondo, a Benedictine centre from the 11th century, still in good condition. The church, cloister and crypt can be visited.

UMBERTIDE

Ponte d'Assisi

Castiglione

Santa Maria di Colonnata

Mengara

298

Chiascio

219

Biscina

Church of Caprignone ⑤
Foremost among all the churches that Francis built, stone by stone, during his life, this simple church sums up the austerity of the order and marks the start of the history of the Franciscan movement.

Pieve di Coccorano ④
This is one of many chapels that Francis must have encountered on his journey, giving him the chance to stop and pray. The countryside here is particularly beautiful and tranquil.

318

318

Abbey of Valfabbrica ③
This may well have been the place where Francis stayed before continuing to Gubbio. Only the little church of Santa Maria remains today, with frescoes of the Umbrian school.

Pieve San Nicolò ②
After a hilly journey from Assisi, you reach this village, which marks the divide between Assisi and Valfabbrica. Both towns can be seen from here, and, when the weather is good, you can even see as far as Gubbio.

Pianello

Rocca Sant'Angelo

Palazzo

Assisi ①
The trail starts from Porta San Giacomo, probably the gate through which Francis passed when he left Assisi. It is near the Basilica di San Francesco, where the body of the saint now lies.

KEY

▬▬ Tour route

═══ Other roads

PERUGIA

147

SPELLO

| 0 kilometres | 3 |
| 0 miles | 3 |

Vineyards belonging to the Lungarotti family, near Torgiano

Torgiano ⓫

Perugia. **Road Map** C4.
🏠 *5,000.* 🚉 *Perugia and Assisi stations, 5 km (3 miles) and 8 km (5 miles), Foligno–Terontola line.* 🚌
🛈 *Piazza Baglioni 1, 075 988 6037.*

T HE SMALL TOWN of Torgiano, 15 km (9 miles) south of Perugia (just east of the main road 3bis), occupies a lovely position at the confluence of the Tiber and Chiascio rivers. Inhabited since the Roman era, it was rebuilt during the Middle Ages as a fortified site to guard over the territory of Perugia – as the Torre Baglioni (probably 13th century) still bears witness.

Torgiano is not an especially remarkable town in itself, and yet it is famous for the now historic production of wine, acknowledged in the town's coat of arms and recorded in the excellent **Museo del Vino**. Housed in the 17th-century Palazzo Baglioni, this is a private museum owned by the Lungarotti family, probably the best-known wine producers in Umbria; the Rubesco di Torgiano is one of Italy's best red wines.

The 19 rooms illustrate the history of oenology and vine-growing since antiquity: on display, with good notes and explanations (including in English), are the tools used for the production of wine over the centuries, as well as old books and printed material relating to wine. There is also a valuable collection of majolica pieces,

among them a plate by Maestro Giorgio da Gubbio (1528) and a tondo with Bacchus attributed to Girolamo della Robbia.

Next door to the museum is the **Osteria del Museo**, where it is possible to taste and buy wines from the **Cantine Lungarotti** (open to the public by appointment).

In an additional demonstration of the high esteem in which local agricultural products are held, the Lungarotti Foundation has recently added a **Museo dell'Olio e dell'Olivo**, where displays relating to olives and oil are housed in attractively restored medieval dwellings.

🏛 **Museo del Vino and Osteria**
Corso Vittorio Emanuele 31/33.
📞 *075 988 0200 or 075 988 0069.*
🖥 *www.lungarotti.it*
@ *fondlung@lungarotti.it*
🕙 *summer: 9am–1pm, 3–7pm (winter: 6pm).*
⬤ *25 Dec.* 🎫
🍷 **Cantine Giorgio Lungarotti**
📞 *075 988 0348.*
🏛 **Museo dell'Olivo e dell'Olio**
Via Garibaldi 10.
📞 *075 988 03 00.*
🕙 *summer: 10am–1pm, 3–7pm (winter: 6pm).*
⬤ *25 Dec.* 🎫

Bettona ⓬

Perugia. **Road Map** C4.
🏠 *3,700.* 🚉 *Perugia and Assisi stations, 7 km (4 miles) and 4 km (2 miles), Foligno–Terontola line.*
🚌 🛈 *Comune: 075 988 571 or 075 986 9115.*

I T IS WORTH TAKING the time to travel the 6 km (4 miles) along the Assisi road from Torgiano, in order to visit the village of Bettona. Apart from offering lovely views over the surrounding countryside, Bettona is unusual historically: it is among the extremely rare centres of culture of Etruscan origin found to the east of the River Tiber. Evidence of Etruscan beginnings is clear from the huge blocks of stone set into the medieval walls. Significant sections of the walls remain, dating from the 4th century BC and typically Etruscan in design. The best example is the 40-m (131-ft) section at the northwestern corner; the other sections are of medieval origin, but rest on an Etruscan base. You can do a complete circuit of the outer ring of the walls, which is worth doing for the views alone.

St Anthony, by Perugino

Bettona has largely kept its medieval feel. It is home to works of art which some have attributed to the school of Perugino, while others believe they are the work of the master himself. The first is a processional banner with a *Madonna and Child and St Anne*. Until recently, it was kept with other important works in the church of Santa Maria Maggiore, erected in the 13th

The old walls of Bettona, with typical stonework

century but later rebuilt. Today, the work is on display in the **Pinacoteca Comunale**, a good art collection housed in the Palazzo del Podestà, on Piazza Cavour. The gallery also has a *St Anthony of Padua* by Perugino, an *Adoration of the Shepherds* by Dono Doni (a masterpiece from 1543, once kept in the church of San Crispolto), and other works of importance by Jacopo Siculo, Niccolò Alunno, Tiberio d'Assisi and Fiorenzo di Lorenzo.

🏛 Pinacoteca Comunale

Palazzo del Podestà, Piazza Cavour 3.
📞 075 987 306. ⏰ Mar–May,
Sep–Oct: 2–6pm daily; Jun–Jul:
3–7pm daily; Aug: 3–7:30pm daily.
Nov–Feb: 10:30am–1pm, 2:30–5pm
Tue–Sun. 🖼

A work by Niccolò Alunno, in the Pinacoteca in Bettona

Deruta ⓭

Perugia. **Road Map** C4.
🏛 7,900. 🚌 🛈 Pro Deruta, Piazza
dei Consoli 4, 075 971 1559.

HEADING OUT of Torgiano along road 3bis, you soon reach Deruta, just 6 km (4 miles) south. On a knoll overlooking the Tiber valley, Deruta has been inhabited since Neolithic times, and still bears traces of its history in part of the walls and in the three arches that give access to the old centre. The name of the town may derive from the fact that it has been destroyed ("distrutta") several times over the centuries.

The heart of Deruta is Piazza dei Consoli where, as in most medieval settlements, all the chief religious and civic monuments stand. **Palazzo dei Consoli**, seat of the town hall and also

---

THE CERAMICS OF THE TIBER

Decorating a plate by hand

Umbria is famous all over the world for its ceramic production. Between the 15th and 16th centuries some extraordinary ceramicists emerged, including the locally born Giacomo Mancini and Francesco Urbini. Even today, ceramics manufacture is one of the most important aspects of the local economy for many towns along the Val Tiberina, and particularly in Deruta, which is full of workshops where craftsmen can be seen at work. It is not just by chance that the vast majority of the main production centres for ceramics should have emerged and are still found along the Tiber: this is due to the fact that there is a greater availability of clay, malleable and at the same time fire-resistant, in the area, as well as the silica needed for the glazes.

---

the Pinacoteca (art gallery), is here, as well as the Romanesque-Gothic church of **San Francesco**.

Housed in the former monastery of San Francesco, next door to the church, is the **Museo Regionale della Ceramica**, which highlights the importance of ceramics in Deruta. The production of jars, plates and other everyday items started in the Middle Ages and is now well documented in perhaps the most important museum of its kind in the region. On the ground floor, room 5 is of most interest, with pieces of ancient pottery; on the first floor are fragments from the floor in the church of San Francesco. On the second floor are more valuable pieces, among them a series of Renaissance plates including one depicting the myth of Pyramus and Thisbe, from the late 16th century.

Pottery is also the main attraction at the church of the **Madonna di Bagno** (1657), 2 km (1 mile) south of Deruta. Its walls are covered in old *ex votos* made of Deruta pottery.

A typical example of Deruta ceramics

🏛 Museo Regionale della Ceramica

Largo San Francesco.
📞 075 971 10 00. ⏰
Apr–Jun: 10:30am–1pm, 3–6pm daily;
Jul–Sep: 10am–1pm, 3:30–7pm daily;
Oct–Mar: 10:30am–1pm, 2:30–5pm
Wed–Mon.

⛪ Madonna di Bagno

SS E45, exit Casalina, 075 973 455.
⏰ 9:30am–12:30pm, 2:30–5:30pm
Tue–Sun.

The fertile Umbrian countryside near Deruta

Perugia ⓮

NOW WITH ALMOST 160,000 INHABITANTS, Perugia has always been the largest city in Umbria. The historic centre of the city has a medieval appearance but is based on an Etruscan layout. The old city occupies a strategic position on a hill dominating the Tiber valley, while the modern city, with flourishing clothing and food industries, developed down below. The Etruscans settled *Perusia* in the 5th century BC or earlier, and it was conquered by the Romans in 309 BC. Perugia saw its greatest splendour in the 13th and 14th centuries, after which civil strife undermined the city's stability; it came under the jurisdiction of the papacy in 1531. Modern Perugia has a distinctly young, cosmopolitan and artistic population and outlook, that set it apart from other cities in the region. It has a thriving University for Foreigners, and hosts Italy's top jazz festival, Umbria Jazz.

Porta Marzia, set into the eastern bastion of the Rocca

Exploring Perugia

Visitors arriving by car are advised to leave their vehicle in the underground car park at Piazzale Partigiani, and from here to take the escalators, which take about ten minutes to reach the historic centre, passing by the ruins of the Rocca Paolina and emerging in Piazza Italia.

🏰 Rocca Paolina and Porta Marzia

Built in 1543 and virtually destroyed in 1860, this fortress is a symbol of papal domination over Perugia. It was built on the orders of Pope Paul III Farnese, who sacked the city in 1540 and annexed it to the Church.

Embossed bronze plate

Construction of the Rocca was entrusted to Antonio da Sangallo, the great exponent of military architecture of the age. To make way for the fortress, many other buildings were razed. This only served to increase the hatred of the people of Perugia towards the Rocca Paolina, which was destroyed as soon as the city gained independence from the pope in the mid-1800s. The Perugians filled the gap created with Piazza Italia.

Parts of the fortress survive, including the Porta Marzia, an astonishing Etruscan archway which Sangallo liked so much that he incorporated it into the wall of his own building. Beneath the archway is the entrance to the bizarre Via Baglioni Sotterranea, a medieval street once buried beneath the Rocca Paolina.

🏛 Museo Archeologico Nazionale dell'Umbria

Piazza G. Bruno. 📞 *075 572 7141.* ☐ *2:30–7:30pm Mon, 8:30am–7:30pm Tue–Sun.* ♿ ♿

Heading away from the centre along Corso Cavour you reach the church of San Domenico and its attached monastery, now home to a Museo Archeologico. This is built around two main collections: that of the old Museo Preistorico and the antiquities collection of Filippo Frigeri.

Numerous finds are kept here, including from the Etruscan and Roman eras. Among the most prized items are the many embossed bronze plates and, in particular, the famous *Cippus Perusinus*, an Etruscan boundary stone which bears one of the longest inscriptions in Etruscan ever found.

🏛 San Domenico

Piazza G. Bruno. 📞 *075 572 7141.* ☐ *8:30am–7:30pm daily.* ♿ ♿ ♿ *Sat, Sun am; 075 573 1635.*

This huge church was built in the 14th century, to a design

reminiscent of the Florentine churches of Santa Croce and Santa Maria Novella. It was rebuilt in the Baroque style in the 17th century, but was never finished. Inside, note in particular the Cappella del Rosario, with statues by Agostino di Duccio (second half of the 15th century), and also the wonderful stained-glass window (1411), the second largest in Italy after the one in Milan cathedral.

Detail from the polyptych, San Pietro

🏠 San Pietro

Borgo XX Giugno.
◻ 8am–noon, 4pm–dusk, daily.

Further along Via Cavour, beyond Porta San Pietro (14th–15th centuries, built with some help from Agostino di Duccio), you reach one of the oldest religious buildings in Perugia, the Benedictine church of San Pietro. The church was founded in the 10th century, but there is some

VISITORS' CHECKLIST

Road Map C3, 🏙 158,000.
🚊 Cortona–Foligno line, 892021. 🚌 800 512 141
🛈 Piazza IV Novembre, 075 573 6458.

evidence to suggest that, in this slightly elevated site, there were underground passages used for burial by the Etruscans and the Romans and, later, a building from the early Christian era (6th century AD).

San Pietro is strikingly original, particularly in its wonderfully sumptuous decoration, which is more reminiscent of the Venetian than the local tradition. There are also numerous works of art by several notable artists, including Perugino, Guercino, Guido Reni and Sassoferrato.

An impressive amount of the original Romanesque church survives, including the partially frescoed façade. The exuberant decoration inside is late Renaissance, and includes cycles of large paintings reminiscent of those done by Tintoretto. There is also a painted coffered ceiling and wonderful wooden choir stalls, the work of various artists in the 16th century. The vault is frescoed with *Stories from the Old Testament*. In the sacristy are five small canvases by Perugino depicting the saints.

0 metres 200

0 Yards 200

San Michele Arcangelo ↑

VIA PASCOLI

PIAZZA FORTEBRACCIO ⑪

VIALE SANT'ANTONIO

VIA PINTURICCHIO

VIA CESARE BATTISTI

VIA RAFFAELLO ⑩

PIAZZA CAVALLOTTI ⑦ ⑧ PIAZZA DANTI

VIA BONTEMPI

PIAZZA IV NOVEMBRE

I PRIORI

④ ⑤
⑥ ⑨

VANNUCCI

PIAZZA MATTEOTTI

VIA XIV SETTEMBRE

PIAZZA DELLA REPUBBLICA

CORSO VANNUCCI

VIA BAGLIONI

VIA XIV SETTEMBRE

VIA TANCREDI RIPA DI MEANA

VIA DELLA CUPA

PIAZZA ITALIA

VIALE INDIPENDENZA

CORSO CAVOUR

②
③

Piazzale Partigiani ↓

🚊

San Pietro ↘

The 16th-century entrance to the church of San Pietro

Perugia: Palazzo dei Priori

Piazza iv novembre is home to two of the most important monuments in Perugia, the Palazzo dei Priori and the Fontana Maggiore. The imposing palazzo, topped by crenellations, was built to hold the town council's administrative offices, and was constructed in stages between 1293 and 1443, during an era of great splendour in the city. Though somber outside, this is one of the most impressive medieval buildings in Italy, with truly gorgeous interiors. The palazzo is, in fact, composed of several buildings which face onto either Corso Vannucci or the piazza. These house four separate visitors' attractions, including the splendid Galleria Nazionale dell'Umbria *(see pp88–9)*.

Il Collegio della Mercanzia is a room on the ground floor of the palazzo which was placed at the disposal of the Merchants' Guild in 1390, for meetings. The ceiling and walls are lined with inlaid wood and date from the middle of the 15th century.

Belfry

The Guild of Money-Changers acquired the right to establish its headquarters in the Palazzo dei Priori between 1452 and 1457.

The Arco dei Priori marks the start of Via dei Priori, which, it is said, flowed with rivers of blood as a result of civil strife during the Middle Ages.

★ **Collegio del Cambio**
In the Sala dell'Udienza of the Collegio del Cambio (1452–57), where money-changers operated, there is a cycle of frescoes by Perugino, painted from 1496 to 1500. The iconography brings together religious themes and figures with secular ones, a hallmark of Renaissance Humanism.

★ **Portale delle Arti**
Framed by rounded arches, the doorway dates from 1346 and is adorned with sculptures and reliefs representing vices and virtues, as well as symbolic animals.

★ **Sala dei Notari**
The lawyers' meeting hall, with its magnificent vaulting, is one of the oldest parts of the palazzo, dating from the late 1290s. The rich decoration includes frescoes by local artists, dating from the same period.

STAR FEATURES

★ **Collegio del Cambio**

★ **Portale delle Arti**

★ **Sala dei Notari**

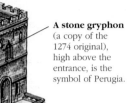

A stone gryphon
(a copy of the
1274 original),
high above the
entrance, is the
symbol of Perugia.

**The fan-shaped
flight of steps**
in Piazza IV
Novembre leads
up to the Sala
dei Notari.

Fontana Maggiore
*This is a superb piece
of work, featuring many
exquisite bas-reliefs and
sculptures by Nicola and
Giovanni Pisano.*

THE FONTANA MAGGIORE

Built from 1275 to 1270, and recently restored, this fountain was designed by a monk called Fra Bevignate, and decorated by Nicola Pisano and his son Giovanni. It is both a magnificent architectural creation (one of Italy's top Romanesque monuments) and a complex feat of hydraulic engineering. It was thanks to the engineer Boninsegna da Venezia that waters from a new aqueduct from Monte Pacciano converged here.

The fountain is built on three levels: two polygonal basins in marble, one above the other, with 25 and 24 sides respectively, and a third basin in bronze. The series of bas-reliefs is

Detail of the fountain

exceptional: on the lower basin are three consecutive cycles depicting episodes from the Old Testament, the Liberal Arts and the Labours of the Months. On the upper basin are 24 sculptures representing biblical figures (David, Moses, Solomon, Salome), saints, mythological figures or allegories from the history of the city, as well as the Perugian *condottiere* Ermanno di Sassoferrato, Capitano del Popolo in 1278.

Stylistically, all kinds of influences converge in the reliefs (including classical, Byzantine and medieval), making it difficult to attribute individual panels to one or other of the two artists.

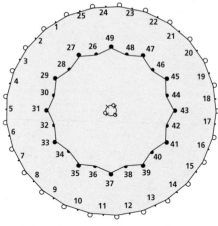

Lower Basin		
1 Temptation / Expulsion from Paradise	**15** August / Woman	**31** Rome
2 Samson and the Lion/ Samson and Delilah	**16** September / Woman	**32** Theology
	17 October / Man	**33** St Paul
3 Lion / Puppy	**18** November / Man	**34** Cleric of St Laurence
4 David / Goliath	**19** December / Man	**35** St Laurence
5 Romulus / Remus	**20** Lion / Gryphon	**36** Chiusi
6 She-wolf / Mother of Romulus and Remus	**21** Grammar / Dialectics	**37** Perugia
	22 Rhetoric / Arithmetic	**38** Lake Trasimeno
7 Wolf and Crane / Wolf and Lamb	**23** Geometry / Music	**39** Sant'Ercolano
	24 Astronomy / Philosophy	**40** The Traitor Cleric
8 January / Woman	**25** Eagle / Eagle	**41** St Benedict
9 February / Man		**42** John the Baptist
10 March / Man	**Upper Basin**	**43** Solomon
11 April / Woman	**26** Melchizedek	**44** David
12 May / Woman	**27** Ermanno di Sassoferrato	**45** Salome
13 June / Man		**46** Moses
14 July / Man	**28** Victory	**47** Matteo da Correggio
	29 St Peter	**48** Archangel Michael
	30 Roman church	**49** Euliste (founder of Perugia)

Perugia: Galleria Nazionale dell'Umbria

THIS IS THE MOST IMPORTANT museum not only in Perugia but in Umbria as a whole, featuring works of art dating from the 13th to 19th centuries. Created partly out of Napoleon's seizure of works of art held by religious orders, the gallery was established in 1863. It was moved to the Palazzo dei Priori in 1879, and has been state-owned since 1918. The 23 rooms, mostly grouped to cover various eras from the 13th to 16th centuries, include the 15th-century Cappella dei Priori, which features some splendid Perugian scenes. While the emphasis is clearly on Umbrian art, Sienese masters are dominant in the early rooms.

Flagellation (1480–85)
This fine work by Francesco di Giorgio Martini (1439–1502), in room 22, is a rare sculptural work by this Sienese painter-architect. The animation of the figures and the rough modelling create unusual lighting effects.

San Domenico Altarpiece (1437)
This work by Fra Angelico (1395–1455) is one of the major Renaissance masterpieces in the museum, and is displayed in the same room (8) as another great work from the same era from the artist: the Guidalotti Polyptych *(1447).*

Room 6 is dedicated to the International Gothic style, of which Gentile da Fabriano (1370–1427) was one of the major Italian exponents.

Room 5 contains the *San Francesco al Prato Polyptych* (1403) by Taddeo di Bartolo (1362–1422).

Room 15 displays many works by Perugino (1450–1523), such as the *Adoration of the Magi*, as well as the *Santa Maria dei Fossi Altarpiece* (1496) by Pinturicchio (1454–1513). There are also splendid works from the Umbrian school.

Room 3, one of four rooms devoted to the 13th and 14th centuries, contains an exquisite wooden crucifix – a full-height *Deposition* dating from 1236.

Room 2 has a *Madonna and Child with Angels* by Duccio di Buoninsegna (c.1305).

★ St Anthony Polyptych (1459–68)
In this work by Piero della Francesca, on show in room 4, innovative use of perspective blends in with a structure and colours that are still medieval.

STAR FEATURES

★ Donna alla Fonte

★ St Anthony Polyptych

KEY

- ▢ 13th and 14th centuries
- ▢ Late Gothic period
- ▢ Early Renaissance
- ▢ 15th century
- ▢ Treasury and the lesser arts
- ▢ Cappella dei Priori
- ▢ Second Renaissance

Room 1 contains a
Byzantine-influenced
Crucifix (1272), the
work of Maestro di
San Francesco.

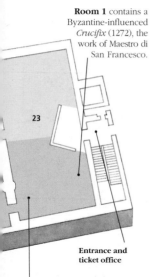

23

**Entrance and
ticket office**

★ *Donna alla Fonte* (1278–81)
*In room 1 there are five statues,
originally part of a public
fountain and including the
Donna alla Fonte, by the great
Tuscan sculptor Arnolfo di
Cambio (1240–1302).*

The duomo's Gothic doorway, the unfinished pulpit and papal statue

✠ Duomo

Piazza Danti. ☎ 075 572 3968.
○ 8:30am–noon, 4pm–dusk daily. ♿
The duomo, dedicated to San
Lorenzo, was built on the site
of a 10th-century basilica. The
first stone of the new building
was laid in 1345, but the
Black Death (1348) delayed
progress for many years, with
work starting again properly
only in 1437. Even then, the
façade was left unfinished.

The façade, which gives
onto Piazza Danti, is
undoubtedly of
much less interest
than the left-hand
side of the duomo,
which overlooks
Piazza IV Novembre.
This is covered in
distinctive pink and
white marble, and
features an impressive
monumental Gothic
doorway, designed
by Galeazzo Alessi
in 1568. In a niche
above the doorway is a cross,
beneath which the Perugians
symbolically laid down the
keys to the city following
their defeat by Pope Paul III
Farnese in the Salt War of
1540. In contrast, a statue of
Pope Julius III, sculpted by
Vincenzo Danti in 1555, to
the left of the doorway, was
commissioned by the people
of Perugia to celebrate the
pope who had restored some
communal liberty to the city.
On the right is an unfinished,
15th-century pulpit, from
which St Bernardino of Siena

**Detail from the
cathedral**

preached to vast crowds of
Perugians in the 1420s. The
saint was so popular with
Perugians that they built a
church in his honour *(see p91)*.

Also on the side of the
duomo that overlooks the
piazza is a loggia with an
arched portico, built for
Braccio Fortebraccio, the
celebrated condottiere from
Montone, in 1423.

The interior is bare and
solemn, and is fairly unusual
in Italy, being more
reminiscent of the
great churches of
northern Europe.
The most curious
thing inside is the
Virgin's "wedding
ring", housed in
the Cappella del
Sant'Anello and
said to change
colour according to
who wears it. On
the left, just past
the entrance, is the
Cappella di San Bernardino
da Siena, home to one of the
two major works of art in the
building, a *Descent from the
Cross* by Federico Barocci,
dated 1567–69. The other
work of art is a masterpiece
by Luca Signorelli, *Enthroned
Madonna with Saints*, which
was painted in 1484 and has
been beautifully restored to
show off its original brilliance.

Another restored feature
worth seeing is the choir,
featuring inlaid wooden stalls:
the work of Domenico del
Tasso and Giuliano da Maiano.

POSTMODERN PERUGIA

The quarter of Fontivegge is in the new part of Perugia, southwest of the historic centre, near the railway station. It stands out from the other quarters of the modern city because it was designed as a completely new district between 1982 and 1989 by the architect Aldo Rossi and his colleagues. It is one of the most successful examples of postmodern architecture in Italy, featuring buildings that are both futuristic and full of classical references (see in

particular the Palazzo della Regione, in Piazza Nuova), and also include elements from the past; a 17th-century fountain and a chimney from the old Perugina factory have both been incorporated into the new architectural context.

View of the Fontivegge quarter

⋔ Etruscan Well

Piazza Danti 18. **⦗** 075 573 3669.
◯ 10am–1.30pm, 2.30–6.30pm
(Nov–Mar: 5pm). **◓** Tue, except in
Apr & Aug. 📷

The Etruscan Well (Pozzo Etrusco), which is located in the basement of Palazzo Bourbon-Sorbello next to the cathedral façade in Piazza Danti, is an astonishing feat of engineering: it was capable of providing a constant supply of water to the entire city. The well (the bottom of which is accessible) is partially covered in vast blocks of travertine, from which the original cover was also made. You can still see the furrows left by the ropes that the Etruscans used to pull the buckets of water to the surface.

Behind Piazza Danti is the district of Rione di Porta Sole, where the Rocca del Sole fortress was built in 1372. It was the largest fortification of its time, but was destroyed shortly after its completion.

⊞ Piazza Matteotti

This long square, which runs parallel to Corso Vannucci, is home to two notable 15th-century buildings. The first is **Palazzo del Capitano del Popolo** (1472–82), designed by the Lombard architects Gasparino di Antonio and Leone di Matteo, and the seat of the judiciary in the era of

**Justice,
detail**

the communes. Its traditional medieval town hall design has been embellished with Renaissance elements. The palazzo was originally built on three floors, but the third was demolished following the earthquake of 1741. Behind the porticoes alongside the palazzo is a 1930s' covered market, from where you can see the piazza foundations.

The other 15th-century building of note is **Palazzo dell'Università Vecchia**, mostly from the same era as the Palazzo del Capitano del Popolo (the same Gasparino di Antonio collaborated in its construction); the building was made the seat of the university by Pope Sixtus IV in 1483.

⋔ San Severo

Piazza Raffaello. **⦗** 075 573 3864.
◯ 10am–1.30pm, 2.30–6.30pm
(Nov–Mar: 5pm). **◓** Tue, except in
Apr & Aug. 📷 ♿

Following the narrow streets up through the Porta Sole quarter, you reach the church of San Severo, famous as the home of one of Raphael's earliest frescoes (1507–1508), of the *Holy Trinity and Saints.* Perugino finished the work in 1521, adding the saints lower down on the same wall. Also look out for the 16th-century terracotta group of a Madonna and Child by an unknown Tuscan sculptor.

The church is of ancient origin: it certainly existed in the 11th century, and the site was probably used for sacred buildings before that. Its current appearance dates from the mid-18th century.

⋔ Arch of Augustus

Piazza Fortebraccio.

A scenic descent signals the end of the Porta Sole quarter, marked by the splendid 3rd-century BC Arch of Augustus (Arco di Augusto). This civic gate is also known as the Etruscan Arch since it was, in fact, of Etruscan origin, and was later modified by the Romans. The still-legible inscription, "Augusta Perusia", was placed here by Octavius Caesar (later Emperor Augustus); having destroyed and then rebuilt the city, he renamed it after himself.

Façade of the Oratorio di San Bernardino

♙ Oratorio di San Bernardino

Piazza San Francesco al Prato.
⦗ 075 573 3957. **◯** 8am–noon,
4pm–dusk daily.

Passing under the Arco dei Priori, part of the palazzo of the same name (*see pp86–7*), and heading down Via dei Priori, you cross what was once a main road through medieval Perugia. Beyond the city walls, the street widens into a piazza with the church of **San Francesco al Prato**, built in the mid-13th century on a particularly subsidence-prone piece of ground; it is now partially ruined. To the left of the church is the small and elegant **Oratorio di San Bernardino** (1452), whose fine multicoloured bas-reliefs on the façade make it a masterpiece of the Umbrian Renaissance. The sculptures, by Agostino di Duccio, are remarkable for the realism of the undulating lines and of the drapery.

Inside, in the first chapel on the left, are a 15th-century gonfalon (banner) showing the Madonna sheltering Perugia from the plague, by Benedetto Bonfigli, and the tomb of Braccio Fortebraccio da Montone. The altar was made from an ancient early Christian sarcophagus.

⛪ Borgo Sant'Angelo

Corso Garibaldi, running north from Piazza Fortebraccio, is the principal medieval street, along which the area of Borgo Sant'Angelo developed. Now the seat of Perugia's university, this district grew up around an Augustinian monastery and has the city's most important monastic

The early Christian church of Sant'Angelo

buildings, including the monastery of San Benedetto, the former hospital of the Collegio della Mercanzia, the convent of Santa Caterina and the monastery of Beata Colomba. It is in this last monastery that, according to popular tradition, St Francis met St Dominic in 1220.

At the end of the road, in the shelter of the walls and in a pretty setting, is the circular church of **San Michele Arcangelo (Sant'Angelo)**, whose origins date back to the late 5th century. Thanks to excellent restoration work, which included the removal of Baroque additions, major parts of the original church are now visible, along with a 14th-century Gothic doorway. The interior is rich with frescoes, also 14th century.

🏛 San Michele Arcangelo

Via Sant'Angelo, Corso Garibaldi.
☎ 075 572 2624.
🕐 10am–noon, 4–6pm daily.

ENVIRONS: Around 7 km (4 miles) southeast of the city, along road 75bis, is one of the most interesting burial sites among many in the area: the **Ipogeo dei Volumni**. Built into the side of a hill, it consists of a great tomb chamber where, in the 2nd century BC, the nobles of the Etruscan Velimna family were buried. Their Latin name of Volumni gives its name to their mausoleum.

A festival stage just before a concert

UMBRIA JAZZ

First held in 1973, Umbria Jazz is – the experts say – Europe's top jazz festival. After the first concerts, held in different towns throughout the region, the event went into crisis and was suspended. The festival was then transferred to Perugia, where it now takes place every July, and enjoys a fame and success second only to the famous Montreal festival. Concerts take place in different venues: from fields and open-air sites (where events are generally free) to the Morlacchi and Pavone theatres, for which audiences buy tickets. Every evening, stretched out on the grass, thousands of young people listen to music for free: a flashback to a time when Umbria Jazz was briefly the setting for mass youth gatherings. Historic open-air venues include the Giardini del Frontone, used since 1984 for the jazz festival's most important evening concerts. The gardens have hosted some of the most historic events, from Stan Getz to the get-together between John Scofield and Pat Metheny, from Bobby McFerrin to Phil Woods and Dizzy Gillespie hugging each other in the rain. As well as the main festival there are other events, including a jazz festival at Orvieto (Umbria Jazz Winter), and a gospel and soul festival (at Terni, at Easter).

Since 1937, another annual event has been staged in Perugia: the Sagra Musicale Umbra, a festival of sacred music, draws artists from all over the world in September.

Inside the burial chamber of the Ipogeo dei Volumni

Lake Trasimeno ⑮

THE FOURTH LARGEST LAKE in Italy, Lake Trasimeno covers an area of 126 sq km (48 sq miles). The perimeter is almost 60 km (37 miles) long, and the lake lies at the fortified heart of medieval Umbria. No matter where you gaze among the low hills that surround the lake, you will inevitably catch sight of a castle, a tower or a fortified village. In fact, Lake Trasimeno has been the scene of battles since antiquity, and it was on these shores that Hannibal defeated the Romans on 21 June 217 BC. Although the water levels rise and fall, and the lake periodically floods the surrounding land, the area has always been inhabited. Over the centuries villages grew up on the shores of the lake, and the islands became home to monasteries and convents, later active fishing communities.

★ **Isola Maggiore**
Briefly a refuge for St Francis, this island is inhabited by fishermen who still stretch out their nets to dry between the churches of Sant'Angelo and San Salvatore.

Tuoro sul Trasimeno
Near the town are the battle sites where the Carthaginians fought the Romans. A historical-archaeological trail of the battle has been created, with maps and information points along the route. There is a modern sculpture park, the Campo del Sole, at Lido di Tuoro.

Vernazzano

Terontola

• Borghetto

Ferretto

B O S C O
DEL
FERRETTO

• Piana

Castiglione
del Lago

Pucciarelli

Panicarola

STAR SIGHTS

★ **Isola Maggiore**

★ **Isola Polvese**

Borghetto is a small village among olive groves, with a 16th-century parish church, San Martino.

0 kilometres   5

0 miles   5

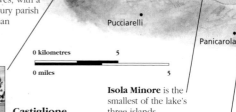

**Castiglione
del Lago**
This is the main town on the shores of Lake Trasimeno, a departure point for ferries (see p94).

Isola Minore is the smallest of the lake's three islands.

The southern shores are characterized, more so than the others, by marshy terrain, fringed with reed beds.

Passignano sul Trasimeno
This town of Etruscan origin is built on a chalk promontory. The most important monument in the town is the church of San Cristoforo, with 15th-century frescoes.

VISITORS' CHECKLIST

Perugia. **Road Map** B3.
FS *Castiglione del Lago, Tuoro, Magione, Cortona–Foligno line.*
C *892021.* **Oct–Mar:** *from Castiglione del Lago & Passignano to Isola Maggiore; Apr–Sep: from Castiglione del Lago, Passignano & Tuoro to Isola Maggiore, from San Feliciano to Isola Polvese.*
C *075 506 781 or 800 512 141.*
W *www.apmperugia.it*
Tuoro sul Trasimeno **i** *Via Ritorta 1, 075 825 220.* **Isola Maggiore** **i** *Piazza della Repubblica, 075 843 859.*
Passignano sul Trasimeno
i *Piazza Trento e Trieste 6, 075 827 635.*

Magione is a town in the hills behind the most populated stretch of shore, and the most developed in terms of tourism. There is a castle here, the Castello dei Cavalieri di Malta, and, at nearby San Feliciano, a Museo della Pesca (Museum of Fishing).

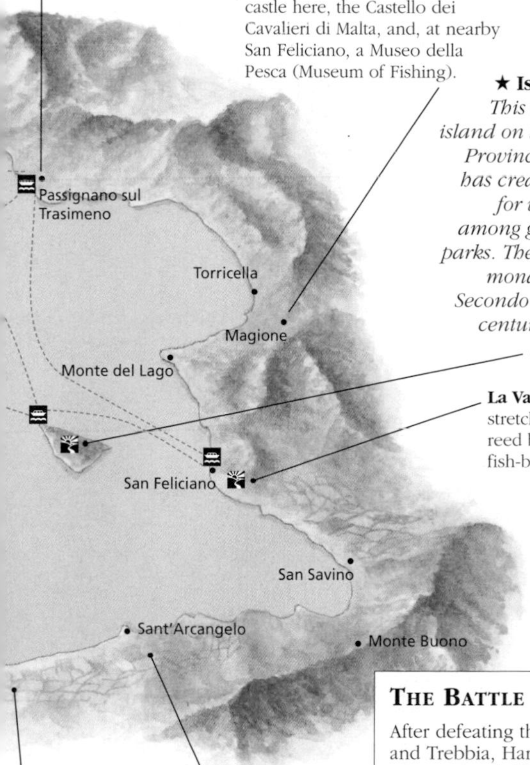

★ Isola Polvese
This is the largest island on the lake. The Province of Perugia has created an oasis for wildlife here, among gardens and parks. The ruins of the monastery of San Secondo and a 15th-century castle can also be seen.

La Valle is the name given to this stretch of lake, where there are vast reed beds and an area of protected fish-breeding grounds.

Passignano sul Trasimeno

Torricella

Magione

Monte del Lago

San Feliciano

San Savino

Sant'Arcangelo

Monte Buono

KEY

Ferry embarkation point

Place of natural beauty

---- Ferry route

The Badia di Sant'Arcangelo, in a lovely setting by the lake, is a castle of medieval origin with a Romanesque church.

The Castello di Montalera is one of many fortified sites along the lake shore. It was at one time the property of the Baglioni family.

THE BATTLE OF LAKE TRASIMENO
After defeating the Romans at the battles of Ticino and Trebbia, Hannibal was informed that his adversaries, led by Caius Flaminius, were directing part of the Roman army towards Lake Trasimeno. The Carthaginian leader distributed his men around the surrounding hills and then, on 21 June 217 BC, aided by foggy weather, he gave the order to attack the enemy forces. Trapped between the lake and the hills, the Roman soldiers suffered a crushing defeat: Hannibal lost 1,500 men, compared with the Romans' 15,000.

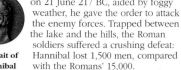

Portrait of Hannibal

View across Lake Trasimeno from Castiglione

Castiglione del Lago 🔟

Perugia. **Road Map** B3.
🏛 14,000. 🚆 Florence–Rome line.
🚌 ℹ Piazza Mazzini 10, 075 965
2484. 🎪 Festa degli Aquiloni, Mar.

THE TOWN OF Castiglione del Lago occupies a promontory which dominates the western shore of Lake Trasimeno, and which, during floods, used to be cut off from the surrounding area, in effect becoming an island.

The area was fortified by both the Etruscans and the Romans because of its strategic position. Fought over by Perugia and by the Tuscans, the site was often destroyed and rebuilt. It was following the reconstruction ordered by Frederick II Hohenstaufen in the 13th century that the place acquired the name Castello del Leone, from which its current name derives.

In the 16th century, the village was given by the papacy to the della Corgna family, who built the town's most important building, the **Palazzo della Corgna**. It may have been designed by Galeazzo Alessi and the frescoes were done by Pomarancio.

Linked to the palazzo by a covered walkway, backing on to the lake and with a fine view, is the **Rocca del Leone**, an interesting example of medieval military architecture. In the 16th century it was considered to be one of the most impregnable fortresses in Italy. From the palazzo,

the street leads towards the real heart of the town, which is centred around Piazza Mazzini. Here, the church of **Santa Maria Maddalena** is worth a visit: the building is Neo-Classical, built by Giovanni Caproni from 1836, but houses a 16th-century altarpiece (*Madonna and Child, St Anthony Abbot and St Mary Magdalene*). This was formerly identified as a youthful work by Raphael, but is now known to be by Eusebio da San Giorgio, one of Perugino's circle.

🏛 Palazzo della Corgna and Rocca del Leone
Piazza Gramsci.
📞 075 965 8210.
🕐 Apr: 9:30am–1pm, 3:30–7pm; May–Aug: 10.30am–1:30pm, 4:30–8pm; Sept & Oct: 10:30am–1:30pm, 3:30–7pm; Nov–Mar: 9:30am–4:30pm daily. 🏛
ℹ **Santa Maria Maddalena**
Via Vittorio Emanuele.
📞 075 951 159.

Città della Pieve 🔟

Perugia. **Road Map** A4.
🏛 7,000. 🚆 Chiusi–Chianciano, 10 km (6 miles), Florence–Rome line. 🚌
ℹ Piazza Matteotti, 0578 299 375.
🌐 www.cittadellapieve.org
🎪 Palio dei Terzieri, Aug.

THE FAME OF Città della Pieve, on the Tuscan border, is due primarily to the fact that it was the birthplace of the great Renaissance painter Pietro Vannucci. Known as Perugino (1450–1523) and famous in his own right, he also taught the young Raphael. Città della Pieve is worth a visit all because it houses several major works by Perugino.

***Adoration of the Magi,* Perugino, detail**

Città della Pieve, an Etruscan colony of Chiusi (in nearby Tuscany), and later Roman, suffered frequently from barbarian invasions. It finally developed as a fortified town in about 1000, around the church of Santi Gervasio e Protasio. The distinctive red coloration is due to the use of bricks – there was no stone available locally.

Città della Pieve is known for its very narrow streets, including what some claim to be the narrowest in Italy – vicolo Baciadonne, which is just 80 cm (31 inches) wide.

Fresco by Pomarancio, Palazzo Della Corgna

The central Piazza del Plebiscito is home to **Palazzo della Corgna** (with 16th-century frescoes by Pomarancio), the Biblioteca Comunale (library) and, most importantly, the cathedral of **Santi Gervasio e Protasio**. This was rebuilt on the site of the original parish church, perhaps in the 8th century, and then remodelled and restored at intervals between the 12th and 17th centuries. Inside, among various precious works of art (by Domenico Alfani, Giannicola di Paolo and Pomarancio), there are two paintings by Perugino – a *Baptism of Christ* and a *Madonna and Child and Saints Peter, Paul, Gervasio and Protasio*.

In the church of **Santa Maria dei Servi** (currently closed for restoration), just south of the centre, there were once some spendid frescoes by Perugino; only a *Deposition* survives, dating from 1517. You will find a far more beautiful fresco by Perugino in the church of **Santa Maria dei Bianchi**, in Corso Vannucci, just off Piazza del Plebiscito. This depicts the *Adoration of the Magi (1504)*, and is perhaps the best of all the works by Perugino found in his native city; the scene includes the view from Città della Pieve towards Lake Trasimeno, as well as a party of elegant Renaissance figures.

Southern Lake Trasimeno ⑱

Self portrait by Perugino

IN THE MOUNTAINS which rise to the south of Lake Trasimeno lies a series of villages where art and history have always played an important role. The painter Pietro Vannucci, better known as Perugino, was born and worked here. This tour partly retraces the steps of the great artist and partly seeks out small medieval hill towns, among the great treasures of Umbria.

VISITORS' CHECKLIST

🚩 *Piazza Mazzini 10, Castiglione del Lago, 075 965 2484.*
Length of tour: *55 km (34 miles).* **Time needed:** *one day.*
Stopping-off points: *in villages along the route.*

Panicale ②
This fortified town is perched on a rocky spur. Perugino's *Martyrdom of St Sebastian* (1505) can be seen in the church of San Sebastiano.

Corciano ⑤
Almost intact 13th-century walls, protected by tall towers and a castle, extend for a kilometre around this pretty village. Corciano has both Etruscan and Roman origins, as do other villages on this tour.

Paciano ①
Encircled by walls and in a lovely hilly setting of woods and olive groves, this is one of the best-preserved of the medieval villages in the area.

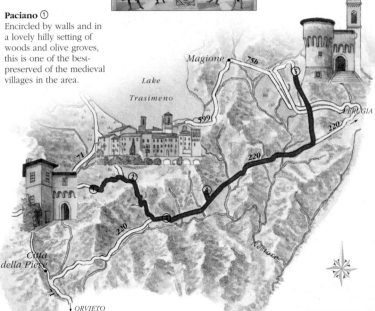

Lake Trasimeno

Magione

PERUGIA

Città della Pieve

↓ ORVIETO

Tavernelle ③
Just north of this village is the Santuario della Madonna di Mongiovino, a 16th-century church with frescoes from the same period.

Fontignano ④
This medieval village, built on a hillside, was where Perugino died in 1523. He left his last work of art here: a *Madonna and Child* in the church of the Annunziata.

KEY

■■ Tour route

⋯⋯ Other roads

0 kilometres 5

0 miles 5

SOUTHERN UMBRIA

THE COUNTRYSIDE OF SOUTHERN UMBRIA *is very hilly, rising to the peaks of the Monti Sibillini towards the eastern fringes. Rocks and water are constant features of the landscape, as at the spectacular Cascata delle Marmore and the springs of Clitunno. Most of the towns are medieval in appearance, but were once part of the Etruscan world. Even the language spoken has affinities with Tuscan.*

In the past, this part of the region was dominated by the Duchy of Spoleto, whose lands were regarded by geographers as the real heart of Umbria until the 16th century. Also part of this territory, culturally and politically, were Todi, of ancient Italic and Etruscan origin, and the Roman town of Narni, while Orvieto was viewed as an independent commune.

Despite the vicissitudes of history, here, as in the rest of Umbria, the sense of local identity derived from a long-standing communal spirit is strong and heartfelt. Every town has its own artistic and historical treasures, and each cherishes and takes pride in its own ancient past, manifested in numerous feast days and secular festivals. Southern Umbria's cultural calendar, which includes the Festival di Spoleto and events in Orvieto and Terni, is varied and popular, and draws people from all over the world.

Hills, and especially water, feature large in the natural landscape of southern Umbria. The River Tiber forms the Lago di Corbara, while the River Nera flows along the edge of the splendid valley known as the Valnerina. In the west, pale tufa soil and the high ridges of Orvieto signal the land of the Etruscans. The wilder peaks of the Apennines, on the other hand, occupy the south-eastern corner of the region. Here, Cascia, Piediluco and Norcia are the last towns before the steep rise towards the windswept plateaux of Castelluccio, just a stone's throw from Le Marche and Lazio.

The cultural and gastronomic traditions of this corner of Italy, although similar in many ways to those of the neighbouring regions, are still quite individual, successfully uniting flavours and ideas from different areas. Norcia, in the Valnerina, is a byword for good food all over Italy.

Detail of the *Coronation of the Virgin*, by Filippo Lippi (1467), apse of Spoleto cathedral

◁ **The dazzling and colourful façade of Orvieto's cathedral**

Exploring Southern Umbria

O RVIETO, TODI, TERNI, SPOLETO: a string of historical towns unravels from east to west in Southern Umbria. In between is fertile countryside, with farmhouses and cultivated fields, and important stretches of river, including the lower course of the River Tiber and the River Nera. There are also thermal springs and archaeological areas, as well as nature reserves, chief of which is the spectacular national park of the Monti Sibillini, superb territory for walking, mountain-biking and hang-gliding.

Tourists on horseback in the centre of Spello

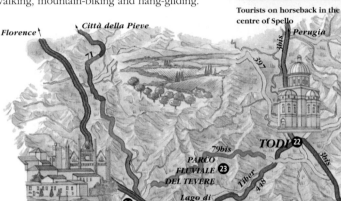

GETTING AROUND

The Autostrada del Sole (A1) motorway skirts the western side of Southern Umbria, with exits at Orvieto and at Orte, from where Superstrada 204 runs east towards Terni. The other two principal artery routes are, as for Northern Umbria, state roads 3 and 3bis, which serve Spoleto and Todi respectively and divide the region from north to south. The main railway line connects Rome to Ancona, passing through various Umbrian towns en route. There is a local line linking Perugia and Terni. Most smaller villages are linked by road.

SIGHTS AT A GLANCE

Classic agricultural landscape near Orvieto

Perugia

Nocera Umbra

Camerino

③ ALTOPIANO DI COLFIORITO

75

① SPELLO

3

77

② FOLIGNO

BEVAGNA

⑤ MONTEFALCO

⑥ TREVI

⑦ FONTI DEL CLITUNNO

3

PARCO NAZIONALE DEI MONTI SIBILLINI ⑧

395

⑨ SPOLETO

418

⑩ SAN PIETRO IN VALLE

Tissino

320

396

⑪ NORCIA

Teramo

⑫ CASCIA

209

Nera

3

471

Rieti

TERNI ⑬

⑯ PARCO FLUVIALE DEL NERA

0 kilometres		10
0 miles		10

KEY

▬	Motorway
▬	Main road
▬	Minor road
▬	Scenic route
▬	River

The medieval village of Campello Alto, near Fonti di Clitunno

Spello ❶

SPELLO LIES ON A HILLSIDE in the shadow of Monte Subasio and is built, like nearby Assisi, out of the same pink stone. A settlement founded here by the Umbri grew in size under the Romans, when it was known as Hispellum. The town walls, pierced by six gates, were built in the Augustan era. Later, the town was sacked by the Lombards, who made it part of the Duchy of Spoleto, and then, in 1238, crushed again by Frederick II. In 1389, by now a papal possession, Spello was given to the Baglioni family as a feudal estate. They ruled until the mid-16th century, after which Spello followed the fortunes of the rest of the region. The evident reminders of the town's past make it a fascinating place today.

🏛 Pinacoteca Civica
Piazza Matteotti 10.
Closed for restoration: call 0742 300 039 for the latest information.
Since 1994 the civic art gallery has been housed in the Palazzo dei Canonici (15th century), to the right of Santa Maria Maggiore. Among the varied works in the collection, one highlight is a splendid *Wooden Madonna* dating from around 1240, brightly coloured and yet serene and stately. Also of note are several polyptyches of the 14th and 15th centuries and other significant works of the local school.

Dispute in the Temple, detail

Porta Consolare, one of the Roman gateways to the town

Exploring Spello

From Piazza Kennedy, access to the walled town is through Porta Consolare, a well-preserved Roman gateway. Heading north into the centre, Piazza della Repubblica marks the real centre of Spello.

🔒 Santa Maria Maggiore
Piazza Matteotti.
Completed in 1285, this fine church is the most important monument in Spello. Its façade was reconstructed, using the original materials, in the 17th century.

The single-nave church owes its fame to the presence of the Cappella Baglioni, where there is a series of frescoes by Pinturicchio, perhaps the finest ever done by the artist. Painted from 1500–1501, the frescoes depict the *Four Sibyls* (on the vault) and *Scenes from the Life of Christ* (on the walls). The most important frescoes are an *Annunciation* (under which hangs a self-portrait of Pinturicchio), an *Adoration of the Magi* and a *Dispute in the Temple*. The floor of the chapel was made of majolica tiles from Deruta. More Pinturicchio frescoes can be found in the Cappella del Sacramento, reached from the left transept. In the right transept is the Cappella del Sepolcro, which at one time housed the town art gallery. Also of interest are a pulpit in sandstone and a tabernacle on the high altar.

🔒 Sant'Andrea
Via Cavour.
Near the Pinacoteca, the church of Sant'Andrea (13th century) has a rather gloomy interior; and yet in the right transept is a superb fresco by Pinturicchio of the *Madonna and Child with Saints*. In the left transept look out for the mummified body of Andrea Caccioli, one of the first followers of St Francis.

🏛 Piazza della Repubblica
In this not particularly notable square at the end of Via Cavour the most interesting building is the 13th-century **Palazzo Comunale** (now restored), which contains the Library and the Town Archive.
Heading north along Via Garibaldi, you pass **Palazzo Cruciani**, seat of the town council, and then the 12th-century church of **San Lorenzo**, an architectural hotch-potch. Of interest inside is the carved wooden pulpit, the work of Francesco Costantini (1600).

🔒 Porta Venere
Via Torri di Properzio.
A short detour west from Piazza della Repubblica takes you to Porta Venere, a Roman gateway flanked by two imposing 12-sided towers dating from the Middle Ages. The gate, heavily restored over the centuries, dates from

View of the town of Spello, on a hillside above the Valle Umbra

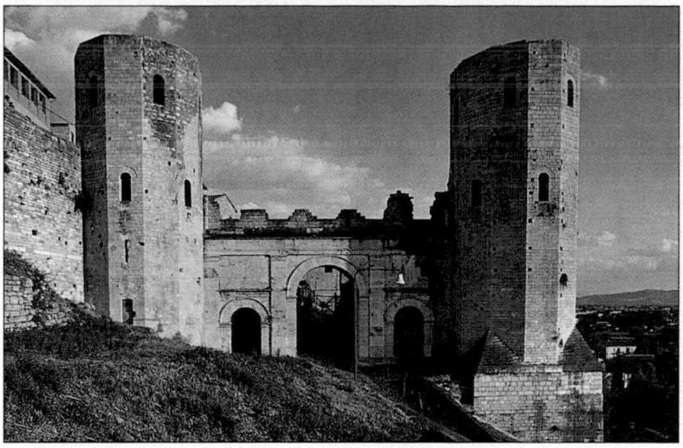
Roman Porta Venere, with its two characteristic 12-sided towers

the Augustan era: the structure that you see today originally had a double curtain giving way to an internal courtyard. The gate offers good views over the surrounding countryside.

Porta dell'Arce
Via Arco Romano.
One of the oldest entrances to the town, this gate is an example of how Roman buildings were integrated into the medieval fortifications. Nearby is the terrace of the Belvedere, from which the Topino valley, as well as the outline of Assisi's Santa Maria degli Angeli, can be admired.

San Claudio
Via Fontevecchia.
From the Belvedere, you can descend to the plain via the narrow Via dei Cappuccini and then the long Via Fontevecchia. Here, you'll find the delightful church of San Claudio, dating from the 12th century. Perhaps Spello's most interesting church architecturally, it has retained intact its Romanesque decoration and layout. The simple façade is topped by the original belfry.

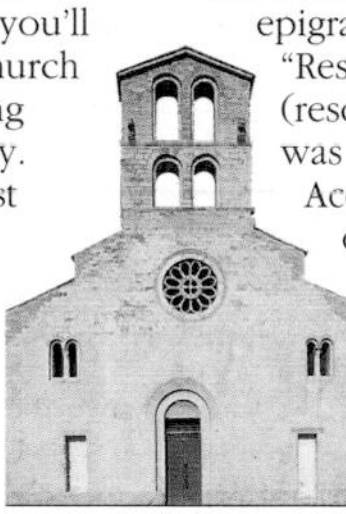
The Romanesque façade of San Claudio

VISITORS' CHECKLIST

Perugia. **Road Map** D4. *8,000. FS Rome–Ancona line. Pro Loco, Piazza Matteotti 3, 0742 301 009. Corpus Domini Infiorata, late May, early Jun.*

Roman Ruins
Via Centrale Umbra.
The Roman city was built at a lower level than the medieval town, which was constructed more defensively on the hill. The amphitheatre, near the church of San Claudio on the main road to Foligno, dates from the 1st century AD, but little survives.

A kilometre from Spello towards Perugia is **Villa Fidelia**, once at the centre of the Roman city, and where an epigraph, known as the "Rescritto di Costantino" (rescript of Constantine), was found in 1733. According to this ordinance, the great emperor, in the years between 324 and 337 AD, authorized the Umbrians to hold their celebrations at Spello and not in Orvieto.

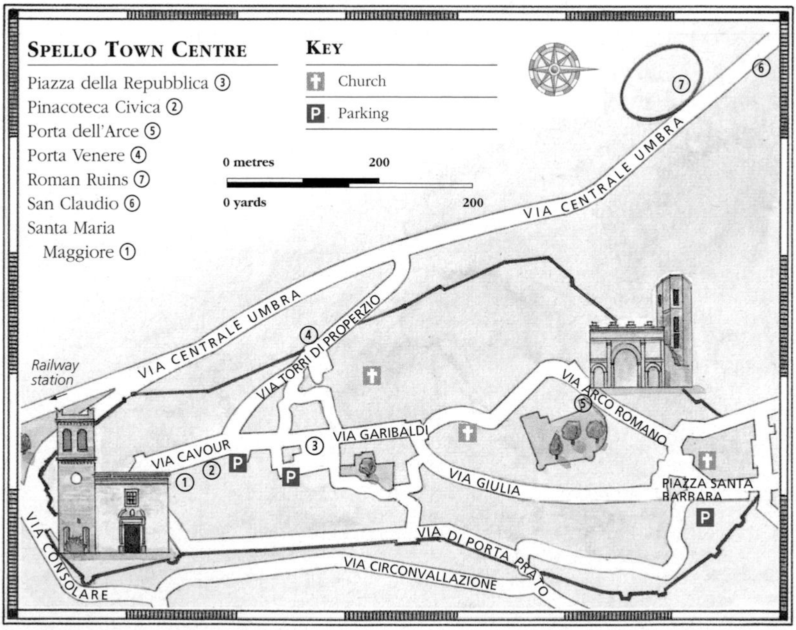
SPELLO TOWN CENTRE
Piazza della Repubblica ③
Pinacoteca Civica ②
Porta dell'Arce ⑤
Porta Venere ④
Roman Ruins ⑦
San Claudio ⑥
Santa Maria Maggiore ①
KEY
Church
Parking
0 metres 200
0 yards 200
VIA CENTRALE UMBRA
VIA CENTRALE UMBRA
Railway station
VIA TORRI DI PROPERZIO
VIA CAVOUR
VIA GARIBALDI
VIA ARCO ROMANO
VIA GIULIA
PIAZZA SANTA BARBARA
VIA DI PORTA PRATO
VIA CIRCONVALLAZIONE
VIA CONSOLARE

Foligno's Piazza della Repubblica with the cathedral's south façade

Foligno ❷

Perugia. **Road Map** D4.
🏛 *56,000.* 🚉 *Rome–Ancona line.*
🚌 🛈 *Porta Romana 137, 0742 350
493.* 🎭 *Giostra della Quintana,
2nd Sun in Sep.*

THE TOWN OF Foligno, of
Roman origin, lies in
the plain of the river
Topino, which skirts
its northern edge.
One of the few
Umbrian towns to
be built on flat land,
Foligno was sited
at the crossroads
of two commercial
roads of great
importance: the Via
Flaminia and the
road from Perugia
to Assisi.

*Madonna di Foligno,
now in the Vatican*

The principal
manufacturing and commercial
centre in the region, with the
exception perhaps of Perugia,
Foligno is a lively, dynamic
city. Because of its location,
the city has been able to
sprawl out onto the plain,
helped by the destruction of
the 14th-century walls after
the unification of Italy. While
the original oval layout can
still be discerned, the historic
centre features a mix of old
and modern architecture.

The railway station, east of
the centre, is both a good
point of reference and a good
place from which to start a
tour. From here, passing by
streets where walls once
stood, you rapidly reach the
historic centre along Via
Ottaviani and Via Umberto I.
Halfway along Via Umberto I
is Via Piermarini, named after

the famous Foligno architect
who designed La Scala opera
house in Milan. Opposite
is the entrance to Via dei
Monasteri, where you'll find
the **monastery of Sant'Anna**.
While still in possession of
several precious works of art,
the monastery is most famous
as the former home (until
1798) of Raphael's
celebrated *Madonna
di Foligno*, removed
by Napoleon's men
and now on display
in the Vatican
museum in Rome.

Back on Via
Umberto I, at the
corner with Via
Garibaldi you come
to the little brick
church of the
Nunziatella (late
15th century), of
interest because of two works
by Perugino. Above the right-
hand altar is a *Baptism of
Jesus* and, in the lunette, a
God the Father. Both works
date from 1507.

From here it is just a short
distance to the central **Piazza
della Repubblica**, the heart
of the city and home to the
main centres of religious and
civic power, as was traditional
in the Middle Ages. These
include the **duomo**, built and
modified between 1133 and
1512 and restored to its
original Romanesque form in
the early 20th century. The
cathedral is unusual for
having two façades. The main
façade faces the small Piazza
del Duomo. The building's
better side, however, is the
south front, with its richly
decorated lateral façade

adorned with a splendid
doorway (1201), which looks
onto Piazza della Repubblica.

Opposite is the **Palazzo
Comunale**, with a Neo-
Classical façade. Originally
built in the 13th century, the
palace was rebuilt several
times and altered completely
following the earthquake
of 1832. The only historic
element to be kept was the
battlemented tower, which,
however, succumbed to the
earthquake of 1997.

The palace is linked to
Palazzo Orfini, which is
famous because it was
probably the home of the
printing house of Orfini. This
was among the earliest of all
Italian printing houses (1470),
and the first to publish a
work in Italian, Dante's
Divine Comedy (1472).

On the northwestern side of
Piazza della Repubblica is
another important building,
Palazzo Trinci, home of the
Pinacoteca Comunale and the
Museo Archeologico. Among
many works of art in the
gallery are pictures by three
notable painters born
in Foligno: Ottaviano Nelli,
Niccolò Alunno and Pier
Antonio Mezzastris.

Via Gramsci, which leads
west off the piazza, contains
several palaces dating from
the 16th to 18th centuries,
some constructed over older
medieval buildings. Of these,
the Renaissance **Palazzo Deli**
(Via Gramsci 6) is the most
beautiful. It features a

Nativity, **Niccolò Alunno, church
of San Niccolò**

Well from 1340 in the Romanesque cloister of the abbey of Sassovivo

Altopiano di Colfiorito ❸

Perugia. **Road Map** E4.
🚆 *Foligno, 24 km (15 miles),*
Rome–Ancona line. 🚌 ℹ️ *Porta*
Romana 137, Foligno, 0742 350 493.

HEADING EAST FROM Foligno along main road no. 77, shortly before the border of Le Marche you reach the Altopiano of Colfiorito. This upland plain, which reaches over 700 m (2,300 ft) above sea level, consists of seven broad basins, once part of a lake which was drained in the 15th century. Of the original natural formation, a marsh called the Palude di Colfiorito remains. The 100-ha (250-acre) wetland is of great interest for its aquatic vegetation and associated wildlife.

Various calcareous plains alternate with steep slopes, in a fascinating undulating landscape. Silhouetted around the fringes are the Apennine peaks of Monte Pennino, Monte Acuto, Monte Le Scalette, Monte Profoglio and Col Falcone.

This upland plain and the surrounding area now form part of the Parco Regionale di Colfiorito, a protected area that was set up to preserve this unique region. Now that the park is well established, visitors can explore the Altopiano using a series of signposted routes. There are also traces of ancient human habitation, the most obvious of which are the so-called "castellieri", pre-Roman villages. The most visited is that of Monte Orve.

medieval tower that was once part of **Palazzo Trinci**.

In Piazza San Domenico, at the end of Via Gramsci, is the Romanesque church of **Santa Maria Infraportas**, whose exterior portico dates from the 11th or 12th century. Inside is the Cappella dell'Assunta (12th century), which has Byzantine-like frescoes that are of interest even though they are in a rather bad state. Another fine work in the church is a *St Jerome and Two Angels* by Mezzastris.

The façade of Santa Maria Infraportas

The church of **San Niccolò**, nearby on Via della Scuola di Arti e Mestieri, was rebuilt in the 14th century by Olivetan monks, remodelled in the following century and then completely rebuilt again in the 18th century. Inside are several works by Niccolò Alunno, among them the *Polyptych of the Nativity*, one of his best-known works. The School of Arts and Crafts, after which the street is named, was based in the monastery alongside.

In Piazza XX Settembre, reached from San Niccolò along Via Mezzalancia, is one of the most beautiful private palazzi built in the 17th century, **Palazzo Monaldi-Bernabò**, now a school.

🏛 **Museo di Palazzo Trinci**
Piazza della Repubblica.
📞 *0742 357 697.*
🕙 *10am–7pm Tue–Sun.*

ENVIRONS: Heading east out of Foligno along the main road no. 77, then taking a fork to the right after about 2 km (1 mile), you come to the scenic road that leads up to the **Abbazia di Sassovivo**, surrounded by a dense forest of holm oaks. Founded in around 1000, the Benedictine abbey was an important political and cultural centre at least until the 15th century. The abbey church is of much less interest than the Romanesque cloister (13th century), which is the finest of its kind in the region. This features 128 variegated double or spiral columns which support 58 round arches, decorated with coloured marbles and two bands of mosaics. There is a 13th-century fresco, too. Also of note is the Loggia del Paradiso in the monastery.

The slopes of Monte Pennino and the marsh of Colfiorito

**Piazza Silvestri, in the heart of
Bevagna**

Bevagna ❹

Perugia. **Road Map** D4. 🚶 4,600.
🚆 Foligno, 9 km (6 miles), Rome–
Ancona line. 🚌 ℹ️ Pro Loco, Piazza
Silvestri, 0742 361 667. 🎪 Mercato
delle Gaite, Jun.

Sᴵᴛᴜᴀᴛᴇᴅ ᴀᴛ ᴛʜᴇ western
margins of the Valle
Umbra, Bevagna has
long been at the centre
of a busy road network,
Inhabited probably
since the 7th century
BC, ancient *Mevania*
experienced its most
afflluent period under
the Romans, thanks
largely to its position
on the Via Flaminia.
Many illustrious citizens
of ancient Rome built
their country houses
here. Following a
period of decline
during the Lombard era,
when this branch of the Via
Flaminia lost importance, the
town experienced a revival in
the 12th century, and this was
when Bevagna acquired its
current appearance. Town
walls, incorporating part of

**Artemis,
Museo Comunale**

the Roman walls, were built,
with a main square at the
centre. Not only are the walls
still a feature, but remarkably
little has been built outside
them since the Middle Ages.
Porta Foligno is the main
entrance into the town, from
where Corso Matteotti leads
to the heart of the city, Piazza
Silvestri. Around this clearly
medieval piazza stand the
Gothic **Palazzo dei Consoli**
and three churches: **San
Silvestro**, **San Michele
Arcangelo** and **Santi
Domenico e Giacomo**.
Corso Matteotti follows the
route of the "cardo" – one
of the main streets through
the Roman settlement. In
the northern part, where the
Forum stood, various traces
of the Roman era still survive,
among them the ruins of a
temple (incorporated into the
church of the Madonna
della Neve), a theatre
and baths. In the same
district, off Piazza
Garibaldi, is the 13th-
century church of **San
Francesco**. Inside are
frescoes by an artist
known as Fantino.
This painter was born
in Bevagna at the end
of the 16th century and
left works of art in many
local towns. The church
also contains a stone
which is said to have
been mounted by
St Francis when he
preached to the birds *(see
pp22–3)*, an event which
happened nearby.
Also worth a visit is the
Museo Comunale, which has
many Roman and pre-Roman
finds, as well as the fine
Ciccoli Altarpiece (1565–70)

by Dono Doni. There is also
a fascinating section devoted
to the local artists who
worked here in the 16th and
17th centuries.

🏛 **Museo Comunale**
Corso Matteotti 70.
📞 0742 360 031. ⬭ Apr, May, Sep:
10:30am–1pm, 2:30–6pm daily; Jun
& Jul: 10:30am–1pm, 3:30–7pm daily;
Aug: 10.30am–1pm, 3–7:30pm daily;
Oct–Mar: 2:30–7pm Tue–Sun.

**Ciccoli Altarpiece, 1565–70, by
Dono Doni, Museo Comunale**

Montefalco ❺

Perugia. **Road Map** D4. 🚶 5,592.
🚆 Foligno, 12 km (7 miles),
Rome–Ancona line. 🚌 ℹ️ Porta
Romana 137, Foligno, 0742 350 493.
🎪 Agosto Montefalchese, Aug.

Pᴇʀᴄʜᴇᴅ ʜɪɢʜ on a hill
dominating the valleys of
the rivers Topino and Clitunno,
Montefalco offers superb
views over central Umbria,
and has been nicknamed "the
balcony of Umbria". It is also
famous for its Sagrantino wine.
The small medieval comune,
known as Coccorone, was
badly damaged in 1249 in the
course of bitter battles fought
between the pope and
emperor Frederick II. When
the latter rebuilt the town, he
decided to call it Montefalco,
in honour of his imperial
eagle insignia. The town's
artistic high point came in the
14th century, followed by
decline once Montefalco
came under papal jurisdiction.
Montefalco retains some
elements of Roman origin, but

Historic Bevagna, at the fringes of the Valle Umbra

the atmosphere is, above all, medieval, focused on the circular Piazza del Comune. This feudal nucleus is enclosed within a circle of medieval walls with five gates, from which five main streets lead, in the shape of a star, to the central piazza.

The main access to the town is via the 14th-century Porta Sant'Agostino, which has a tower on top. From here, Via Umberto I and then Corso Mameli lead up to the main square. Along the way is the church of **Sant'Agostino**, (late 13th century), whose façade is adorned with slender columns and a rose window. Inside the church are a number of interesting frescoes, among them one attributed to Ambrogio Lorenzetti. You also pass palazzos Tempestini, Langeli and Moriconi.

Laid out during the 14th century, the central Piazza del Comune is home to the **Palazzo Comunale**, heavily reworked in the 19th century, the former church of San Filippo Neri (now a theatre) and the **Oratorio di Santa Maria**, which was used as a public meeting place during the Renaissance.

Just north of Piazza del Comune, along Via Ringhiera Umbra, is the most important monument in the town, and indeed one of the most famous in the entire region – the former church of **San Francesco**. The attached monastery houses the **Museo Comunale**. The highlight of a

Scenes from the Life of St Clare, detail, church of Santa Chiara

visit to the deconsecrated 14th-century church are the frescoes painted by Benozzo Gozzoli (1420–97), a pupil of Fra Angelico and famous above all for his exquisite frescoes in the Palazzo Medici in Florence. Gozzoli's frescoes in San Francesco are found in the Cappella di San Girolamo and, more importantly, in the central apse, where the magnificent and colourful *Life of St Francis* (1452) is the most important pictorial cycle dedicated to the saint after the one in the Basilica di San Francesco in Assisi.

The church-cum-museum also contains works of art salvaged from other local churches, as well as other objects: note, in particular, a *Crucifix* by the Maestro Espressionista di Santa Chiara (late 13th–early 14th centuries), a *Madonna and Child* from the workshop of Melozzo da Forlì (late 15th century), a *Nativity* painted by Perugino (1503) and, among the sculptures, a *Coronation of the Virgin* from the workshop of Andrea della Robbia (16th century).

From Piazza del Comune, a flight of steps leads southwards down to the medieval church of **San Bartolomeo**, and to the town gate of the same name. Beyond is Viale Federico II (named in honour of the emperor who stayed in the town in 1240 during his battles against the pope), which leads on to the quarter

Crucifix, **Museo Comunale**

called Borgo di San Leonardo. Walking westwards, outside the old walls, you reach the convent and church of **Santa Chiara**. These are dedicated not to the famous Clare of Assisi, but to Chiara di Damiano of Montefalco (1268–1308), who had the complex built here in the 13th and 14th centuries, on the site of the older Cappella di Santa Croce. The chapel (opened on request by the nuns who still live in the convent) is now the apse of the church. It is completely covered in 14th-century frescoes by Umbrian artists, narrating the lives of the saints Chiara, Caterina (Catherine) and Biagio (Blaise), and of the Virgin. On the wall of the altar a *Calvary* includes more than 45 figures.

A short distance south, along Via Giuseppe Verdi, is the Renaissance church of **Santa Illuminata**, which was built from 1491 on the site where Santa Chiara and her sister were locked up by their father.

The Franciscan convent of **San Fortunato**, in a lovely wooded spot about 1 km south the town, is worth visiting for the frescoes by Benozzo Gozzoli (1449) in the church.

🔒 San Francesco and Museo Comunale

Via Ringhiera Umbra.
📞 0742 379 598. ⏲ Nov–Aug: 10:30am–1pm, 2–6pm; Sep–Oct: 10:30am–7pm. 🔒 Mon. 🖼 ♿

Porta Sant'Agostino (or dello Stradone), gateway to Montefalco

Trevi ❻

Perugia. **Road Map** D4.
🏛 *7,000.* FS *Perugia–Terni line.*
ℹ *Piazza Mazzini 16, 0742 781 150.*

THE HISTORIC CENTRE of Trevi "unwinds" in a stunning spiral fashion around a steep conical hill, Monte Serano, which dominates the plain of Spoleto. Flooding from the nearby river Clitunno used to be a constant threat and forced the inhabitants of Roman Trevi to move to higher ground. Once this threat was averted, however, the modern city – the so-called Borgo Trevi – was free to develop down on the plain, among the fields and olive groves.

Trevi converted early to Christianity; according to legend, this was because of the presence of the martyr Emiliano. In the 4th century, after a brief period of liberty, the town became part of the papal states and remained so until the unification of Italy.

The central Piazza Mazzini is home to the **Palazzo Comunale**, built in the 14th century but with important later additions, such as the 15th-century portico. From here, Via San Francesco passes the monumental **Palazzo Valenti** en route to the enormous church of **San Francesco**.

This church, together with the adjacent **Raccolta d'Arte di San Francesco**, is the principal artistic attraction in the town. The church itself, which dates from the 13th

Coronation of the Virgin, detail

century, contains interesting works, including a fine organ from 1209. However, Trevi's most important works of art are on display in the Raccolta, which has been housed in the church monastery since 1997. The finest work is the *Coronation of the Virgin* (1522), by Giovanni di Pietro, known as Spagna, which was commissioned by the friars of the church of San Martino *(see below)*; the predella includes two scenes from the lives of the saints: *St Martin gives away his Cloak* and *The Stigmata of St Francis*. The art collection also includes paintings from the Umbrian school from the 14th century, among the most complete anywhere; in particular, do not miss the *Life of Christ* by Giovanni di Corraduccio (first half of the 14th century).

Painted cross (15th century), Raccolta di San Francesco

The cathedral of **Sant'Emiliano** stands at the summit of the hill. It was extensively restored in the 20th century, but still has the three original apses (12th century), which are among the best examples of Romanesque in the region. Next door is the Palazzo Lucarini, which houses the **Flash Art Museum**, with a small permanent collection of contemporary art by Italian and foreign artists, as well as changing exhibitions.

A ten-minute walk along pedestrian Viale Ciuffelli takes you to the 14th-century parish church of **San Martino**, built in a panoramic position on the northeastern edge of town. Inside the church are works by Tiberio d'Assisi and Fantino *(see p104)*, among the most famous artists of the Umbrian school. It is also worth visiting the **Santuario della Madonna delle Lacrime**, just south of the centre (not far from the train station), where there is a lovely *Epiphany* by Perugino (1512), as well as an important cycle of frescoes by Lo Spagna, in the chapel of San Francesco.

🏛 **Flash Art Museum**
Via del Duomo.
🕐 *3:30–6:30pm Wed–Fri, 10:30am–12:30pm, 3:30–6:30pm Sat & Sun.*

ENVIRONS: Around 5 km (3 miles) north of Trevi rises the 14th-century church of **Santa Maria a Pietrarossa**. Its name derives from the red stone *(pietra rossa)* in the presbytery, to which miraculous powers were attributed. The church has an extensive portico, beneath which is a vast cycle of votive frescoes dating from the 15th century. A few metres from the church is the San Giovanni spring, whose water is said to be therapeutic.

Interior of the church of San Martino

The pool formed by the Fonti del Clitunno springs, framed by weeping willows and poplars

Fonti del Clitunno **7**

Perugia. **Road Map** D4. **FS** *Trevi, 10 km (6 miles), Perugia–Terni line.*

THESE FAMOUS springs emerge alongside the Via Flaminia, at Vene, and have been known since antiquity. The cool, limpid waters of this series of karst springs create a large pool dotted with small islands as well as a river of the same name.

On a literary level, the historic reputation of the springs derives from the oracular skills attributed to the god of the river Clitunno (Clitumnus, the messenger god). The oracle was often cited by poets through the ages, from Virgil to Byron. This does not mean that drinking the water makes you a good orator. The waters'

The Roman Tempietto

main effect, some people say, is to remove the urge to imbibe alcohol.

The site really owes its fortune to the fertility of the soil and the sheer abundance of water, which rises in such quantity that at one time the river was navigable. The Romans exploited the site and created a holiday area here, using the springs to create public baths. Numerous buildings were constructed, including several villas dotted along the river banks, although today they have almost totally disappeared. Votive buildings include the **Tempietto**, which many experts now believe was built in the 8th century, using the materials from an earlier Christian building. Standing about one kilometre north of the Fonti, the temple consists of a crypt and a room for

worship. The latter is decorated with 7th-century frescoes, thought to be the oldest paintings with sacred subjects in Umbria.

🏛 Fonti del Clitunno
📞 *0743 275 085.*
⏰ *Mar: 9am–6pm; Apr: 9am– 7:30pm; May–Aug: 8:30am–8pm; Sep: 9am–7pm; Oct: 9am–6pm; Nov–Feb: 10am–4:30pm.*
🏛 Tempietto
⏰ *Apr–Oct: 9am–8pm; Nov–Mar: 9am–2pm.*

ENVIRONS: Just south of the springs is **Campello sul Clitunno**, whose church of the Madonna della Bianca has fine 16th-century frescoes. For a fantastic view, follow the steep road up from the village to **Castello di Pissignano**, where Barbarossa once stayed.

A trapezoid tower, part of the Castello di Pissignano

UMBRIAN OLIVE OIL

Olive oil made in Umbria can bear the label "denominazione di origine controllata" (denomination of controlled origin) if it conforms to the high quality standards set for the product. Umbria has been divided into five producing districts, each with differing quality criteria. The strictest rules are applied in the district centred around Trevi, one of the most important olive-growing areas.

Parco Nazionale dei Monti Sibillini ❽

The park logo

Oᴺᴇ ᴏꜰ ᴛʜᴇ ᴍᴏꜱᴛ recently established of Italian national parks, the mountainous Sibillini park is exceptional. Extending over 70,000 ha (173,000 acres), the park is divided between Umbria and Le Marche and offers a bewitching combination of nature and history. There are numerous abbeys and medieval hill towns as well as rich natural diversity. Trails cover the entire park and are suitable for both walkers and mountain bikes. The windy upland plains are popular for hang-gliding, and in winter the mountains attract skiers. Among the refuges higher up are Rifugio Città di Ascoli (Passo di Forca Canapine), Capanna Ghezzi (above the plains of Castelluccio) and Rifugio San Severino Marche.

Abbazia di Sant'Eutizio
The buildings of this abbey date from the late 12th century, but the area drew hermits from the 6th century onwards, and was important politically and culturally during the early Middle Ages.

Visso, now the park headquarters, was said to have been founded 907 years before Rome. From the Middle Ages to the 18th century its territory was divided into five districts called "guaite" (guards). Castles and look-out towers are visible.

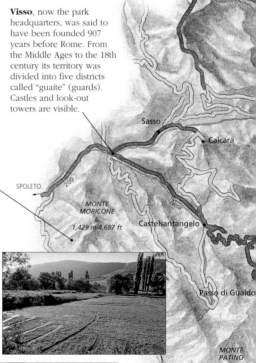

Marcite di Norcia
These irrigated meadows benefit from the water that flows from karstic springs.

Wɪʟᴅʟɪꜰᴇ ɪɴ ᴛʜᴇ Mᴏɴᴛɪ Sɪʙɪʟʟɪɴɪ

The park is an ideal habitat for many species. In terms of mammals, the wolf and wildcat are present in small numbers, but there are healthy populations of roe deer, marten and especially wild boar (to the degree that they are becoming a problem). Lynx have been seen, but doubt has been cast on sightings of the Marsican bear. The birdlife in the mountains is very varied. Foremost is the golden eagle, an elegant predator which is easily spotted in the area. Some rarer species such as the peregrine falcon and the goshawk are also present. Alpine choughs and wall creepers are common.

Golden eagle

Park Flora
Rare species of plant can be observed in flower on the northern slopes, including alpine orchids and daisies like these.

VISITORS' CHECKLIST

Road Map F5. 🚗 🛈 *Ento Parco, Visso, 0737 972 711.*
Ⓦ www.sibillini.net

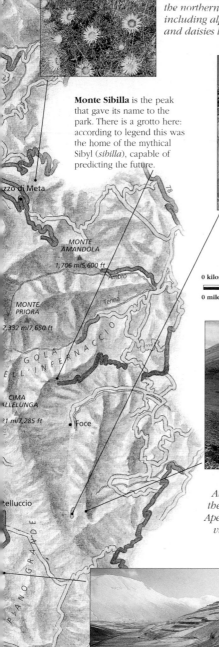

Monte Sibilla is the peak that gave its name to the park. There is a grotto here: according to legend this was the home of the mythical Sibyl (*sibilla*), capable of predicting the future.

zzo di Meta

78

MONTE
AMANDOLA

1,706 m/5,600 ft

Ambro

MONTE
PRIORA

2,332 m/7,650 ft

Tenna

G O L A

E L L ' I N F E R N A C C I O

CIMA
ALLELUNGA

21 m/7,285 ft • Foce

elluccio

P I A N O   G R A N D E

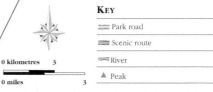

Lago di Pilato
According to legend, Pontius Pilate was buried in this lake after the buffaloes pulling his hearse refused to go any further; though another story says that a remorseful Pilate drowned himself here.

KEY

▬▬	Park road
▬▬	Scenic route
⌁	River
▲	Peak

0 kilometres   3

0 miles   3

Monte Vettore
At 2,476m (8,121 ft), this is the highest peak in the park and one of the major mountains in the Apennine chain. From the summit there are fine views over the entire massif: the dark waters of Lago di Pilato dominate the scene below.

Plains of Castelluccio
There are three high plains at over 1,300m (4,264 ft) on the western slopes of the park above the isolated village of Castelluccio (famous for its lentils). In spring, the ground here is carpeted in a breath-taking abundance of flowers, known as the fioritura.

Spoleto ⑨

**Detail of a lunette,
San Nicolò**

SPOLETO IS ONE OF THE most important towns in Umbria. It occupies a striking hillside position, at the foot of Monteluco, is home to a host of fine monuments, and enjoys an international reputation. The last started with the travellers on the Grand Tour and continues today with the cosmopolitan crowd that has flocked to the famous Festival di Spoleto since 1958.

The first settlement here was founded, probably by the Umbri, high up where the fortress was later built: traces of the massive 4th-century-BC walls are still visible. Spoletium, founded in 241 BC, became a major Roman colony, thanks partly to its proximity to the Via Flaminia, used by people travelling to Rome from the north. Spoleto later became the seat of a Lombard dukedom and then an important commune. Numerous monastic orders were established here and the town maintained its prosperity over the centuries.

View of the city of Spoleto dominating the Spoletine valley

Exploring Spoleto

The main approach into the city is from the northern side, over the Ponte Sanguinario, a Roman bridge. From here, the route of the tour climbs leads upwards, via several sites of importance, to the highest and oldest part of the city, where both the duomo and the Rocca d'Albornoz, essential sights on a visit to Spoleto, are found.

🏛 San Gregorio Maggiore
Piazza Garibaldi.
Just over Ponte Sanguinario, the gateway to the town, is Piazza Garibaldi, home to the church of San Gregorio Maggiore. It was founded in the 4th century, in the early Christian era, outside the walls, as were all the oldest churches in the city. It was renovated in the 12th century, incorporating materials from various Roman remains. The façade is adorned with statues and a huge campanile

(notice the Roman blocks used in the lower half) and has a portico modelled on that of the duomo (see p113). Despite frequent restoration and embellishment, the Romanesque interior still bears traces of interesting medieval frescoes.

The façade of San Gregorio with portico and bell tower

The entrance to San Nicolò, framed by Gothic arches

🏛 San Nicolò
Via Cecili.
From Piazza Garibaldi, Via dell'Anfiteatro heads towards the centre, past the meagre ruins of a 2nd-century-AD Roman amphitheatre. Continuing up Via Cecili you reach the deconsecrated church of San Nicolò.

What looks like a single church is, in fact, a complex of religious buildings placed one on top of the other over the course of the centuries. The imposing Gothic church, which played host to Martin Luther in 1512, is now used for plays and concerts.

🏛 San Domenico
Via Pierleoni.
Via Cecili leads to Piazza della Torre dell'Olio, with the 14th-century tower of the same name. Taking Via Pierleoni, which runs south, you reach the large monastic church of San Domenico (13th century), with its distinctive pink and white striped design.

Restored to its original Gothic form in the 1930s, the church has a single, unusually long nave. Here, you can admire interesting frescoes dating from the 14th and 15th centuries, some of which have come to light only in recent decades. In particular, linger over the Cappella di San Pietro Martire (the first on the left), the Cappella di Santa Maria Maddalena, on the right-hand side of the apse, and the Cappella Benedetti di Montevecchio, on the left of the presbytery.

The Roman Theatre in Spoleto, dating from the 1st century AD

VISITORS' CHECKLIST

Perugia. **Road Map** D5.
⌖ 38,000.
🚆 Rome–Ancona line, 892021.
🚌 800 512 141 🛈 Piazza della
Libertà 7, 0743 238 920.
🎭 Festival di Spoleto, Jun–Jul.

🛈 Santi Giovanni e Paolo

Via Filitteria.
Heading up Via Sant'Andrea
from San Domenico, you pass
the **Teatro Nuovo**, a grand
theatre built over the ruins of
a monastery and inaugurated
in 1864. A little further on
is the deconsecrated church
dedicated to saints John and
Paul in 1174. It is worth a visit
for the frescoes inside: the
oldest is the one depicting the
Martyrdom of Thomas Becket,
painted after his canonization
in 1173.

🏛 Galleria Comunale d'Arte Moderna

Corso Mazzini. 📞 0743 464 34.
◯ mid-Mar–mid-Oct: 10:30am–1pm,
3–6:30pm Tue–Sun; mid-Oct–mid-
Mar: 10:30am–1pm, 2:30–5:30pm. 🎫
Housed in Palazzo Spada,
the collection in this modern
art gallery is divided into
three sections. The most
interesting is the first, which
has works by contemporary
Italian artists, participants in
the "Premio Spoleto" (Spoleto
Prize), among them Arnaldo
Pomodoro and Giulio Turcato.

🏛 Teatro Romano

Piazza della Libertà.
Corso Mazzini eventually
widens out into Piazza della
Libertà. This is the site of a
much-restored Roman theatre,
built in the 1st century AD
and with a capacity of 3,000.
It was excavated only in the
late 19th century. It is used
for festival performances.
In the nearby monastery of
Sant'Agata, one of the oldest
religious buildings in the city,
is the **Museo Archeologico
Nazionale**, with important
pre-Roman finds.

🏛 Museo Archeologico Nazionale

Via Sant'Agata 18. 📞 0743 223
277. ◯ 8:30am–7:30pm (9am–1pm
Sun, public hols). 🎫

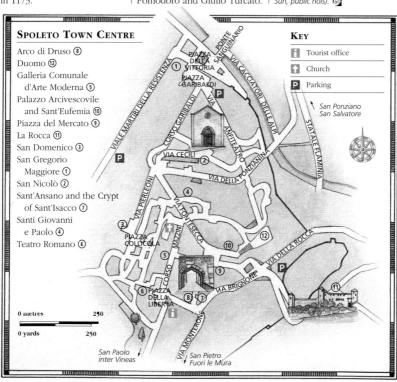

SPOLETO TOWN CENTRE

Arco di Druso ⑧
Duomo ⑫
Galleria Comunale
   d'Arte Moderna ⑤
Palazzo Arcivescovile
   and Sant'Eufemia ⑩
Piazza del Mercato ⑨
La Rocca ⑪
San Domenico ③
San Gregorio
   Maggiore ①
San Nicolò ②
Sant'Ansano and the Crypt
   of Sant'Isacco ⑦
Santi Giovanni
   e Paolo ④
Teatro Romano ⑥

KEY

🛈 Tourist office
🛉 Church
🅿 Parking

↖ San Ponziano
   San Salvatore

0 metres   250
0 yards   250

San Paolo
inter Vineas

San Pietro
Fuori le Mura

🔒 Sant'Ansano and the Crypt of Sant'Isacco

Via Brignone.

Climbing up towards the oldest part of Spoleto, you follow the route of the "cardo maximus", one of the main roads through the Roman settlement. The church of Sant'Ansano is, in fact, built on the ruins of a 1st-century temple. What you see today dates from the 18th century, but the church has a complex architectural history. The crypt of Sant'Isacco (St Isaac) provides evidence of a 12th-century church dedicated to both saints. It contains Roman columns and striking Byzantine-style frescoes. The church above contains a *Madonna* by Spagna (first half of the 16th century).

The Crypt of Sant'Isacco, beneath Sant'Ansano

🔒 Arco di Druso

Piazza del Mercato.

The Arch of Drusus, one of many arches scattered around the town, marked the point where the *cardo maximus* entered the forum (now Piazza del Mercato). It was erected in AD 23 in memory of the son of emperor Tiberius.

🏛 Piazza del Mercato

This square lies at the heart of the oldest part of Spoleto. With an open market, shops and bars, it is always buzzing with activity.

In terms of monuments, of particular note is a fountain built in the mid-18th century with material taken from other buildings, among them four coats of arms and a slab commemorating Pope Urban VIII. In the north-western corner is one side of the **Palazzo Comunale**, originally medieval but rebuilt in the late 1700s, after earthquake damage. The **Pinacoteca Comunale** inside

The fountain in Piazza del Mercato, built in 1746–48

has a decent collection of paintings by Umbrian artists: of note are the 13th- and 14th-century crucifixes and a *Mary Magdalene* by Guercino.

Nearby is a **Casa Romana** (Roman house), dating from the 1st century BC and with some lovely mosaic floors.

🔒 Casa Romana

Via di Visiale.
📞 0743 437 222. ⏰ *mid-Mar–mid-Oct: 10am–1pm, 3–6:30pm daily; mid-Oct–mid-Mar: 10am–6pm.* ⦿ Tue (Oct–Mar). 🖼

🏛 Pinacoteca Comunale

Via Saffi. 📞 0473 459 40. ⏰ *mid-Mar–mid-Oct: 10:30am–1pm, 3–6:30pm daily; mid-Oct–mid-Mar: 10:30am–1pm, 2:30–5pm.* ⦿ Tue (Oct–Mar). 🖼

🏛 Palazzo Arcivescovile

Via Fontesecca.
⏰ *10am–1pm, 3–6pm Tue–Sun.* 🖼
The architectural history of this palace, in front of Palazzo Comunale, constitutes a

virtual narrative in stone of the history of Spoleto. It began with the construction of a Roman building (still partially visible), above which it is thought that the large Palazzo dei Longobardi was built when Spoleto was a duchy. In the 12th century the building was incorporated into a monastery, and then finally, in the 16th–17th centuries, it became the bishop's palace.

Inside is a good collection of works of art and, in the courtyard, the 12th-century church of **Sant'Eufemia**. Recently restored, the church is Romanesque but more Lombard than Umbrian in style, with three aisles and women's galleries inserted above the side aisles.

🔒 La Rocca

Via della Rocca.

In 1359, when the city was an outpost of a Church intent on reconquering Umbria, Cardinal Albornoz, papal legate for Innocent VI, ordered the construction of a military fortress (*rocca*) at the highest point of the city. It was linked to the hill behind, Monteluco, by the impressive Ponte delle Torri, which still straddles the Valle del Tessino *(see p113)*. La Rocca can be reached on foot or by shuttle bus (buses run hourly from Piazza Campello).

The fortress is built on a rectangular plan around two courtyards, the Corte d'Armi and the Cortile d'Onore, both surrounded by towers. Over the centuries, La Rocca has

The Rocca, seen from the far side of the Ponte delle Torri

been home to various notable figures, among them Lucrezia Borgia, whose caprices were perhaps responsible for the naming of the tower called "della Spiritata" (the spirited one). Converted into a prison for over a century, in 1984 the Rocca underwent lengthy restoration.

The highlights inside are the frescoes in the **Camera Pinta** (in one of the main towers). These chivalric scenes were painted by artists from the school of Terni in the 14th–15th centuries. There are more frescoes in other parts of the fortress.

Behind La Rocca is the masterly, ten-arch **Ponte delle Torri**, crossing the river Tessino. It is 230 m (755 ft) long and over 70 m (230 ft) high: the date of construction is uncertain and it is probable that today's bridge evolved from a Roman bridge cum-aqueduct. In the middle of the bridge is an opening offering good views. The bridge leads to the Fortezza dei Mulini.

Mosaic by Solsternus on the façade of the duomo

🔒 Duomo

Piazza del Duomo.

🕐 8:30am–12:30pm, 3:30–7pm (Nov–Feb: 6pm) daily.

A short climb from Piazza del Mercato leads to the sloping Piazza del Duomo, home of Spoleto's cathedral. As a backdrop to the Festival di Spoleto, this church's image is now world-famous.

The cathedral, built and consecrated at the end of the 12th century, is dedicated to Santa Maria Assunta, and rises on a site where there were at least two earlier religious buildings. The façade, one of

The duomo's façade, backdrop to the annual Festival di Spoleto

the most superb examples of Umbrian Romanesque, is divided into three orders and is the result of at least three successive phases of construction.

The original project resulted in the basilica layout, and the bell tower probably dates from the same era (12th century). A second phase of construction (early 13th century) saw the building of the façade, with the mosaic of Solsternus (1207) and the three upper rose windows, which frame the original Cosmatesque one underneath, one of the most beautiful in central Italy. The portico, with its magnificent central door, was added at the end of the 15th century. The bronze bust of Urban VIII above the central door was sculpted by Gian Lorenzo Bernini in 1640.

The interior of the church, rebuilt in Baroque style in 1648, is built on a Latin cross plan, divided into three aisles separated by a colonnade. There are various important works of art here. Just past the entrance, on the right, is the Cappella del Vescovo Costantino Eroli, built in 1497 and entirely decorated with frescoes by Pinturicchio. Don't miss those in the chapel altar niche, depicting *God the Father and Angels, The Madonna and Child* and

John the Baptist and St Stephen. There is also a fine series of figures from the Old Testament on the vault. The other important cycle of frescoes (1467–69), by the artist Filippo Lippi, is found on the walls of the apse. The subject is the life of Mary. Among the scenes are an *Annunciation*, a *Transition of the Virgin*, a *Nativity* and a *Coronation of the Virgin*. The sarcophagus of the Tuscan artist is also kept in the church, although his remains are no longer here.

On the two sides of the apse, extending outwards from the main body of the church, are two chapels, the Cappella della Santissima Icona and the Cappella del Sacramento. In the first is an image of the Virgin in the form of a icon, much venerated because it is attributed to St Luke. On the left, to the side of the transept is the lovely Cappella delle Reliquie. Besides some fine frescoes and painted panels, this chapel contains a 14th-century wooden statue of a *Madonna and Child* and a letter written by

Transition of the Virgin, Filippo Lippi, detail

St Francis to his disciple Fra Leone. On the first altar on the left, in the nave, hangs a *Crucifix* by Alberto Sotii, painted on parchment applied to board, dated 1187. Other similar treasures are kept in the Archivio Capitolare.

Detail of a Pinturicchio fresco in the duomo's Cappella Eroli

Detail of a bas-relief on the façade of the church of San Pietro Fuori le Mura

🔒 San Paolo inter Vineas
Via San Paolo.

The first of four important churches, which form a curve around the eastern side of the historic centre of Spoleto, lies south of the city, beyond the Giardino Pubblico (public gardens) and the stadium.

San Paolo inter Vineas was built on the site of an early Christian religious building, mentioned by St Gregory the Great in the 6th century. The present Romanesque church, flanked by a cloister, dates from the 12th and 13th centuries, and was skilfully restored in the latter half of the 20th century. The most important feature inside is the fresco cycle, which was painted in the early 13th century and is considered to be among the oldest in the region. It depicts the *Prophets* and *Scenes from the Creation of the World*.

The Romanesque church of San Paolo inter Vineas

🔒 San Pietro Fuori le Mura
Via Matteotti, then via Roma, beyond main road SS Flaminia.

Whereas at San Paolo inter Vineas it is the interior frescoes which are the most important feature, here it is the decorations on the façade.

San Pietro Fuori le Mura ("outside the walls"), which lies south of the town centre, stands at the top of a flight of steps on a plateau from where there are fine views.

The building has ancient origins, probably dating back to the 5th century, when the relics of the chain of St Peter were moved here. The current church dates mainly from the 12th century. The carved stone reliefs on the façade are regarded as one of the most prized examples of Umbrian Romanesque. The reliefs on the lower, older part

Façade of San Pietro Fuori le Mura

of the structure, produced in the 12th and 13th centuries, tell complex stories rich in symbolism. They relate lay episodes, taken from medieval encyclopedias, and other religious stories linked to the life of Christ.

🔒 San Ponziano
SS Flaminia, road to the cemetery.

This church lies northeast of the centre, alongside Via Flaminia, and at the foot of the Cinciano hill. It occupies the site of the tomb of the martyr Ponziano, patron saint of Spoleto, who is commemorated on 14 January. This is a convent church, first the home of Poor Clares and later Augustinian nuns, with a Romanesque exterior and an interior which was completely restructured in 1788 by Giuseppe Valadier. (He also designed the doors and altars of the cathedral.)

The main feature of interest is the crypt, which is original. Divided into three aisles, like the church above, and with

---

THE FESTIVAL DI SPOLETO

The most important event in Spoleto's recent history occurred when it was chosen by the Italian-American composer Gian Carlo Menotti as the venue for the Festival dei Due Mondi, which was to become a major international arts event. The choice fell on Spoleto because of its central location within Italy, its historic appeal and its plentiful theatres and cinemas. In 1958 a performance of Verdi's *Macbeth*, directed by Luchino Visconti, inaugurated the first festival. Since then, despite the controversy with which the festival has always been associated and the change of name (today it is called the "Festival di Spoleto"), every summer the event attracts an enthusiastic audience, as well as artists from all over the world, to this splendid city.

A closing concert at the Festival

five apses, this contains
Roman fragments and some
pretty votive frescoes, which
include one showing the
Archangel Michael with a
globe and staff, in the right-
hand apse. On the left is an
Enthroned Madonna.

**The formal interior of the church
of San Salvatore**

🔒 San Salvatore

Via del Cimitero, off SS Flaminia.

From San Ponziano, the road
goes up the Cinciano hill and
brings you to the last, and the
most historically interesting,
of all the religious buildings
close to Spoleto.

The church of San Salvatore
is an exceptional example,
perhaps unique in Umbria, of
a building constructed using
mainly salvaged material,
almost all dating from the
Roman era. The columns,
decorative elements, capitals,
architraves – most of the
architectural features in the
three-aisled basilica church, in
fact – date from the Roman
period. For this reason, it has
been difficult for art historians
to date San Salvatore with any
great precision, although it is
undoubtedly one of the oldest
churches in the country. Two
theories circulate currently.
According to the first, the
church dates from the early
Christian period, and bears
witness to the heights of
splendour achieved in late
Roman art in this area (the
Tempietto del Clitunno
would be of the same era).
According to the second
theory, however, the building
dates from the 8th and 9th
centuries.

San Pietro
in Valle ⑩

Perugia. **Road Map** D5 🚇 *Terni,
20 km (12 miles), Perugia–Terni line.*
🚌 🛈 *0742 380 011.* ⊡ *Mar–Oct:
10:30am–12.30pm, 2:30–6pm daily;
Nov–Feb: 2:30–4:30pm.*

IT IS DIFFICULT to try to rank
Umbrian abbeys in order of
importance, but clearly no
classification could omit the
Benedictine abbey of San
Pietro in Valle, situated in the
lower part of the Valnerina,
just north of the village of
Ferentillo (*see p123*).

Set against a backdrop of
wooded hills, San Pietro in
Valle is of significant artistic
and religious interest. The
abbey's roots lie
deep in legend. Its
foundation, as one
of the frescoes in
the left-hand
transept of the
church testifies,
traditionally dates
from the 5th century
AD, when the
Lombard duke of
Spoleto, Faroaldo II,
met the Syrian
hermit Lazarus. St
Peter had suggested
to the duke in a
dream that he should
transform the hermit's small
chapel into a rich and
powerful abbey, and so San
Pietro in Valle was built.
Faroaldo subsequently
decided to remain here,
becoming a monk, and he
rests here still: his splendid
sarcophagus can be seen in
the right-hand transept.

**Capital,
San Pietro in Valle**

The abbey was severely
damaged by the Saracens in
the 9th century, but was
restored in around 1000 by
Ottone III and then by his
successor Enrico II. In the
1930s, extensive renovation
revealed the medieval linear
forms which the building had
managed to retain, despite all
the alterations. Today, the
abbey is privately owned, and
has been converted into an
appealing, sought-after hotel,
part of the Relais & Chateaux
chain, though parts are open
to the general public.

The abbey church is owned
by the state and is well worth
a visit. Long and formal, with
a single nave ending in a
short transept and three
apses, the church contains
some superb works of
art. On the walls is
a cycle of frescoes,
which ranks among
the finest examples
of Romanesque
painting in Italy in its
complexity and in
the precision of its
execution. On the left-
hand wall and on the
upper right-hand
side are *Stories
from the Old
Testament*, while in
the remaining space on the
right-hand side are *Scenes
from the Life of Christ*. The
inner façade and the transept
are decorated with works
from later eras.

Look out for the beautifully
preserved Lombard altar (8th
century), which bears the self-
portrait and signature of the
sculptor: "Ursus".

The medieval Benedictine abbey of San Pietro in Valle

The broad Piazza San Benedetto, in the centre of Norcia

Norcia ⓫

Perugia. **Road Map** 5F. 🏛 *5,000*.
🚌 ℹ️ *Via Solferino 22, 0743 828
173*. 🌐 *www.norcia.net* 🎪 *Mostra
Mercato del Tartufo Nero, Feb.*

AT THE FOOT OF the Monti
Sibillini, on the edge of
the plain of Santa Scolastica,
and on the borders of the
ancient duchies of Spoleto
and Benevento, Norcia was a
trading city and a staging post
for centuries. Today, the town
is known above all for its
local produce, in particular
for its black truffles and
for the production of
high-quality meat,
sausages and
salami. (The word
"norcino" – from
Norcia – is now
synonymous with
superior meat
products.) Browsing around
the wonderful *salumerie* and
other food shops is a highlight of any visit to the town.

**Lunette from the door of
San Benedetto, detail**

The walls built by the
Romans (who conquered the
city in 290 BC) were replaced
by another, heart-shaped set
in the 13th century. These
walls, and the city itself, have
been damaged by disastrous
earthquakes over the years.
Along the perimeter, however,
the ancient gates (eight in all)
can still be seen.

One of these gates, Porta
Romana, marks the start of
Corso Sertorio, which leads
to Piazza San Benedetto, the
heart of the town since the
Middle Ages. At its centre is a
statue of St Benedict (1880).
Facing onto the square is

Palazzo Comunale, of 14th-
century origin but partly
rebuilt after the earthquake in
1859. The portico is original
while the soaring bell tower
dates from the 18th century.

Alongside the palazzo is the
church of **San Benedetto**,
which was founded in the
Middle Ages and extensively
rebuilt in 1389 and at various
later dates. The 14th-century
façade is dominated by a
monumental doorway (1578),
with two statues
representing St
Benedict and Sta
Scolastica on either
side. On the right
side of the church is
a 16th-century
portico, the Portale
delle Misure, which
has a stone step
bearing the
commercial
measures used for the sale of
grain. The interior, which was
reconstructed in the 18th
century, contains a crypt built
on the site where, according
to tradition, St Benedict and
Sta Scolastica were both born.
Traces of the oldest church
and fragments of frescoes are
visible in the crypt.

The cathedral of **Santa
Maria Argentea**, built in the
16th century and remodelled
in the 18th, also stands on the
piazza but is of little interest.
Much more impressive is the
Castellina, a fortress built for
Pope Julius III in 1554. Its
square layout, centred on a
courtyard with a loggia, was
the work of the prestigious
architect Jacopo Barozzi, also
known as Vignola. The fort

houses the **Museo
Civico Diocesano**,
where the highlights
include two crucifixes
and a five-figured
sculptural group of
the *Deposition* (13th
century). The latter is
perfectly preserved and
provides important
evidence of the popular
art being done at that
time (such groups were
carried in processions).

For a taste of Norcia
of old, follow Via Roma
as far as Porta Ascolana,
past several churches,
or take Via Anicia from
the main square to the
highest part of the city. The
palazzi here date from the
17th and 18th centuries, when
Norcia was a major trading
centre on the borders with
the Adriatic regions. Here,
too, is **Sant'Agostino**, with
some fine 16th-century
frescoes by local artists.
Also of note are the Gothic
church of **San Francesco**, on
Piazza Garibaldi, and the 14th-
century **Tempietto** (on Via
Umberto), which has some
pretty bas-reliefs.

Museo Civico Diocesano
Piazza San Benedetto. 📞 *0743 751
010.* ♿ ⭕ *Oct–Mar: 10:30am–1pm
3–5pm Sat, Sun & public hols; April:
10:30am–1pm, 4–6:30pm daily; May
& Jun: 10:30am–1pm, 4–6:30pm Fri–
Sun; Jul & Sep: 10:30am–1, 4–6:30pm
Tue–Sun; Aug: 10:30am–1pm, 4–7pm.*

**The courtyard of the Castellina
with its loggia and gallery**

A LAND RENOWNED FOR SAINTS

Two of the most important saints in Umbrian history (St Francis apart) were born in this area, just a few kilometres from each other but separated by nearly one thousand years.

St Benedict, founder of the oldest monastic order in the West, was born (with his twin sister Santa Scolastica) in Norcia, in 480. After studying in Rome he settled at Montecassino, where he wrote his famous *Rule*. This became a major influence on medieval monastic life. The patron saint of Norcia (as well as of Europe), St Benedict's saint's day is celebrated on 21 March.

Santa Rita (born Rita Lotti, commemorated on 21 May) was born at Roccaporena, near Cascia, in around 1380, and died in the mid-15th century. The factional struggles between the Guelfs (pro the papacy) and the

Monument to St Benedict by Giuseppe Prinzi, 1880

Ghibellines (pro the German emperors) caused her much suffering. Her parents were part of the so called "peacemakers of Christ", or mediators between the two factions, and Rita carried on their work, even after the assassination of her husband and the subsequent murder of her two sons, killed while trying to avenge their father.

Rita entered the Augustine convent of Santa Maria Maddalena at Cascia, where she remained for 40 years, until her death in 1457. She developed a sore on her forehead, which was said to have been caused by a thorn falling from a crown of thorns as she knelt in prayer beneath a statue of Christ; it was viewed by fellow nuns as a stigmata. The miraculous story of Rita gave rise to a popular cult that has lasted for centuries. Indeed, it was thanks only to a popular campaign that Rita was eventually made a saint, on 24 May 1900.

View of Roccaporena, with the cliff of Santa Rita behind

Cascia ⑫

Perugia. **Road Map** 5E. 🏛 *3,300.* 🚌 🚶 *Via G. da Chiavano, 0743 714 01.* 🎭 *Celebrazioni per Santa Rita, 21–22 May.*

INHABITED SINCE late antiquity, because of its strategic position, Cascia has had a turbulent past: Umbrian, then Roman and Byzantine, then part of the Duchy of Spoleto, but independent from the 10th century. In the early Middle Ages, it was a Ghibelline city, locked in bitter struggle with Norcia

and Spoleto, cities owing allegiance to the pope. Taken by Rome in 1517, Cascia immediately acquired great importance because of its position on the border with the Kingdom of Naples. This brought great prosperity.

With the unification of Italy, Cascia lost its political relevance and fell into a long period of decline, halted in the 20th century only thanks to religious tourism, which brought large numbers of pilgrims dedicated to the memory of Santa Rita.

The cult is still a significant feature of life in Cascia today, so the focus is no longer the now-destroyed hilltop fortress, but a modern **Sanctuary** dedicated to the saint. It was built in 1947, replacing a church dating from

1577. To the left of the sanctuary is the convent of Santa Rita, where the saint lived for much of her life.

Other sites to visit in the town include the **Museo Civico** (divided between Palazzo Santi and the church of Sant'Antonio Abate), in particular for the fine wooden sculptures, and the churches of **San Francesco** and Santa Maria. In the outskirts of the town is **Roccaporena**, Rita's birthplace, dominated by a hill known as the "scoglio" (cliff) of Santa Rita. The area's many castles and towers, which formed an effective system of fortification, are evidence of the historical importance of the region.

Not far from Cascia is the Parco Nazionale dei Monti Sibillini (see pp108–9).

Fresco in the lunette above the door to the church of San Francesco

Terni ⑬

THE ONLY UMBRIAN PROVINCIAL CAPITAL apart from Perugia, Terni has always been the most developed centre for industry in the region – the result of its position: at the centre of a plain and at the confluence of the River Nera and the Serra and Tescino streams. The availability of water was crucial for the development of heavy industry during the 19th century (the famous Italian steelworks Acciaierie Breda is based here). Terni is also crossed by the Via Flaminia, an extremely important route since Roman times, linking Rome with the north and the Adriatic coast. Terni's industrial importance made it a target for heavy bombardment during World War II and today, despite its Bronze Age origins, it looks decidedly modern compared with most other Umbrian towns. Terni is the unlikely birthplace of St Valentine, the patron of lovers and one of the world's most popular saints.

Madonna and Saints, Benozzo Gozzoli

Exploring Terni

Although it is a fairly large city, Terni – or at least the most important sights – can be visited in a relatively short time and on foot: the historic centre, located on the western side of the River Nera, is reasonably compact.

If you leave your car near the railway station (to the north of the centre), it is easy to follow Viale della Stazione to Piazza Tacito, from where Corso Cornelio Tacito leads directly to the heart of Terni. This is focused around the squares of Piazza della Repubblica, where the main public buildings are located, and Piazza Europa. The latter is home to Palazzo Spada, which was designed, according to local tradition, by Antonio da Sangallo the Younger.

⌂ San Francesco
Piazza San Francesco.
○ *8am–12:30pm, 3:30–7:30pm daily.*
Halfway along Corso Tacito, it is worth making a detour to the right to look at this 13th-century church, which was originally designed in typical Franciscan style with a single nave and transept. In the course of the 15th century,

the lateral aisles and the bell tower were added. Inside, the Cappella Paradisi contains a cycle of frescoes (*The Last Judgment*), painted by Bartolomeo di Tommaso, of the Giotto school. The cycle dates from the middle of the 15th century.

▦ Pinacoteca Comunale
Palazzo Gazzoli, Via del Teatro Romano 13.
℡ *0744 434 209.*
○ *10am–1pm, 4–7pm Tue–Sun.* ▨
Palazzo Gazzoli is the new seat of the Pinacoteca Comunale, one of the richest and most varied art galleries in Umbria. It houses contemporary works (highlights are by Mirò, Kandinsky and Chagall) and works representative of the medieval Umbrian school, by Benozzo Gozzoli (*The Marriage of St Catherine*), Spagna and Nicolò Alunno.

⌂ Sant'Alò
Via Sant'Alò.
℡ *0744 407 148.* ○ *by appt.*
This Romanesque church, just off Via XI Febbraio, dates from the 11th century and is notable for the abundant re-use of Roman statuary on the exterior. It is thought that the church was built on the ruins of an earlier pagan temple.

⌂ Duomo (Santa Maria Assunta)
Piazza Duomo.
○ *9am–noon, 3:30–7pm daily.*
The duomo, located south of the city centre, near the public gardens, was built on

A huge ladle in action in a steelworks

INDUSTRIAL TERNI

The industrial importance of Terni goes back to the dawn of the industrial revolution in Italy (beginning of the 19th century), when the Vatican ironworks were based here. During the 19th century the industries multiplied: foundries, saw-mills, wool mills, as well as the hugely successful Acciaierie Breda steelworks. All found an ideal environment on this plain, which is well supplied with water and in a strategic position for trade. Industry has altered both the countryside and the town itself. Today the factories are, for the most part, dismantled or converted for other use, but the industrial archaeology of Terni is still a reason to visit the area. There are other reasons, of course: this "outdoor museum" extends to cover Terni itself, the waterfalls of Marmore and the town of Narni.

Detail of the decoration on the main door of the duomo

the site of earlier religious buildings, the first of which existed at least by the 6th century; numerous churches were later built on the same site. The current basilica is the result of reconstruction in 1653, although there are still some traces of a Romanesque church. Look out for the bird and animal reliefs on the main door as you enter.

⋔ Roman Amphitheatre

Piazza Duomo, Giardini Pubblici.
This amphitheatre (1st century AD), not far from the duomo, is very much a ruin but is still one of the best preserved Roman sites in Terni. Used as a quarry and later covered by buildings, it was discovered in the mid-19th century and was finally excavated in the 1930s.

On the left is Palazzo Vescovile, whose curvilinear rear façade follows the line of the old bastions. There are lovely views from the adjacent public gardens.

⋔ San Salvatore

Via San Salvatore.
◯ 9am–noon, 4–6pm daily.
The town's most interesting church, just off Piazza Europa,

The round church of San Salvatore

was erected on the ruins of Roman buildings, but it has been impossible to establish exactly when. The main body of the church, built on a circular plan, was thought to have been a Roman temple to the sun but is now believed to date from the 11th century; the rectangular avant-corps is more recent, built perhaps in the 12th century.

Inside the church are traces of frescoes; the ones in the Cappella Manassei date from the 14th century.

VISITORS' CHECKLIST

Road Map D6.
🏠 110,000. **FS** Rome–Ancona line, 892021. 🚌 800 512 141.
ℹ️ Via Cesare Battisti, 0744 423 047. @ info@umbriatour.it
🎭 Feste di San Valentino, 14 Feb; Cantamaggio, May.

⋔ San Pietro

Piazza San Pietro.
◯ 8am–noon, 3:30–7:30pm daily.
This 14th-century church, not far from Palazzo Comunale, was enlarged and restored several times. It contains many 14th- and 15th-century frescoes representative of the local school.

⋔ Mostra Permanente di Paleontologia

Ex-chiesa di San Tommaso, Largo Liberotti. 📞 0744 434 202. ◯ 10am–1pm, 4–7pm Wed, Thu, Sat 🖼️
An indispensable tool for anyone studying the early history of Umbria, this permanent exhibition has a rich collection of fossils, the remains of several ancient mammals, and a diorama of Umbria when it was covered by the waters of the ancient Tiberine Lake.

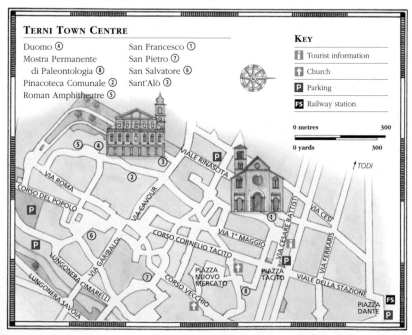

TERNI TOWN CENTRE

Duomo ④
Mostra Permanente di Paleontologia ⑧
Pinacoteca Comunale ②
Roman Amphitheatre ⑤
San Francesco ①
San Pietro ⑦
San Salvatore ⑥
Sant'Alò ③

KEY

ℹ️ Tourist information
⋔ Church
P Parking
FS Railway station

0 metres 300
0 yards 300

Narni ⑭

Terni. **Road Map** C6. 🚶 20,000.
🚉 Rome–Ancona line. 🚌
🛈 Piazza dei Priori 3, 0744 715 362.
🖥 www.comune.narni.tr.it 🎭 Corsa
dell'Anello, mid-May for two weeks.

THIS FINE AND unspoilt hill
town, located dramatically
above a bend in the River
Nera, is the geographical
centre of Italy. Its origins date
back to the Umbri people,
who founded *Nequinum*. This
settlement was conquered
by Rome in 299 BC and was
renamed *Narnia*, after the
nearby river. Its importance
under the Romans derived
from the fact that it was the
birthplace of Emperor Nerva,
in AD 32, and also a major
stopping point on the Via
Flaminia. Narni grew until
occupied the entire rocky
spur above the Nera.

Medieval Narni knew
tough years during the wars
between the papacy and the
empire, but it continued to
grow, even after the establishment of papal rule in the mid-
14th century. The building
of a great fortress, on the
orders of Cardinal Albornoz,
emphasized papal authority.
In the 16th century, Narni
was devastated by the
Lanzichenecchi on their
return north after the Sack of
Rome. During the following
centuries, the slow rate of
growth kept the town centre
in the form in which it can
still be seen today.

Detail of the bas-reliefs to the right of the door of Palazzo del Podestà

Porta Ternana, on the Via
Flaminia, is the main point of
entry to Narni. From here, Via
Roma leads straight to Piazza
Garibaldi, at one time known
as Piazza del Lago because of
a great subterranean cistern,
fed by the Roman aqueduct
of Formina; this now supplies
the water for a 14th-century
fountain with a bronze basin.

Most of the sights
are close to the
main axis of the
town, formed by Via
Garibaldi and Via
Mazzini. At one end
is Piazza Garibaldi,
home of Narni's
duomo, an
imposing and
beautiful building
dedicated to San
Giovenale, the
town's patron saint.
It was founded in
1047, but reconstructed in
the 12th century. The façade
has a portico and a portal
decorated with carvings.
Inside, two low arcades
separate the three aisles. On
the right is the mausoleum of
the bishops of Narni, which
is dominated by a tombstone
dating from 558.

From the duomo, it is a
short walk up Via Garibaldi to
the central Piazza dei Priori,
the attractive seat of civic
power in Narni. Facing the
square are the **Palazzo dei
Priori**, with a portico and an
impressive loggia designed by
Gattapone – responsible also
for the Palazzo dei Consoli
in Gubbio *(see p60)* – and
the **Palazzo del Podestà** (or
Palazzo Comunale); both date
from the 14th century. In the
atrium of the Palazzo del
Podestà is a series of Roman

Detail of the fountain in Piazza Garibaldi

and medieval archaeological
stones and finds, while inside
is a superb *Coronation of the
Virgin* by Ghirlandaio, and
frescoes by Benozzo Gozzoli
and others. **Casa Sacripanti,**
also in the square, features
three medieval bas-reliefs of
gryphons and knights.

Beyond Piazza dei Priori,
the main street (now Via
Mazzini) continues
north. Immediately
on the right is the
façade of the little
Romanesque church
of **Santa Maria in
Pensole**, built in
around 1175. Of
particular interest is
the exterior, with its
attractive portico
and three doorways
carved with classical
motifs. A little
further on, where the
road widens out into Piazza
XIII Giugno, is the church
of **San Domenico** (12th
century). Now deconsecrated,
it houses the Public Library,
Historical Archive and the
town art gallery. The main
reason to go inside is to see
some of the most interesting
medieval frescoes in Narni:
among the often faint
fragments, of particular note
are those by the Zuccari
family, found in the large
chapel off the left-hand aisle.
San Domenico also has many
other works from other
churches in the town, among
them an *Annunciation* by
Benozzo Gozzoli, at the end
of the right-hand aisle. In the
underground areas of the
church, you can visit the
Inquisition cells, with graffiti
made by the prisoners of the
ecclesiastical court.

The duomo, facing onto Piazza
Garibaldi

To return to Piazza dei Priori from San Domenico, make your way along the narrow streets which run parallel to Via Mazzini. This area is home to the church of **San Francesco**, built in the 14th century on the site where it is said that St Francis stayed during his sojourn in Narni in 1213, and where he founded an oratory. The church is Romanesque, but with some Gothic elements. Among these, the most important feature of the exterior is the doorway, with a niche above. Inside, frescoes adorn every inch of wall: of special interest are the frescoes by Mezzastris, in the first chapel, depicting *Scenes from the Life of St Francis* and *Scenes from the Life of St Benedict*, as are those by Alessandro Torresani (16th century), in the sacristy.

On top of the hill that dominates Narni is a vast fortress known as the **Rocca**. It was built in the 1370s by Gattapone, at the behest of Cardinal Albornoz, one of the most important figures in the history of the early Middle Ages in Umbria (*see p41*), and responsible for numerous fortresses which still bear his name. Narni's fortress was abandoned for years, but it has now been restored. There are fine views from the site.

ENVIRONS: Heading out of Narni, towards Terni, you reach, after a short detour to the left, a bridge over the River Nera. Though easy to

The Romanesque abbey of San Cassiano, dating from the 12th century

miss among the modern development of industrial Narni Scalo, this is the best possible observation point from which to admire a majestic Roman arch in the middle of the river, the only one surviving from the **Ponte d'Augusto**. At 160 m (525 ft) long and 30 m (98 ft) high, this must have been one of the most impressive bridges in the whole of Umbria when it was built. It is known as the Augustan bridge because it dates from the era of the first emperor (27 BC). This bridge was one of the most popular sights on the Grand Tour.

Continuing along the same road, over the Nera, a climb leads to the **Abbazia di San Cassiano**, perhaps the most important of the many religious buildings that dot the Narni countryside. Set in a panoramic position, the Romanesque, 12th-century complex is enclosed by battlemented walls and

includes a pretty church with a bell tower.

To the southeast, 13 km (8 miles) from Narni, is the **Convento del Sacro Speco**, founded in 1213 by St Francis, who often prayed in a cave nearby. The place is imbued with a mystical atmosphere.

Visciano **⑮**

Terni. **Road Map** C7.
FS *Narni, 8 km (5 miles), Rome–Ancona line.* 🚌 🛈 *Piazza dei Priori 3, Narni, 0744 715 362.*

HEADING SOUTH from Narni, a tortuous but scenic road leads up to the hilltop hamlet of Visciano. The reason for coming here is to visit the small and simple church of **Santa Pudenziana** (if it is closed, ring the bell of the family next door and they will let you in). This is a typical example of Umbrian Romanesque, built in the 12th and 13th centuries, and making abundant use of Roman materials. It has a tall stone campanile and a sober façade with a small portico. The interior is divided into three aisles, with an inlaid floor of precious marble and fragments of Roman mosaics.

The church is famous for its frescoes. Behind the façade are *Christ, San Vittore* and *San Medico*, and other saints, as well as the *Madonna and Child*, all contemporary with the construction. The other figures, such as *Santa Pudenziana*, date from the 14th and 15th centuries.

The Rocca, one of many fortresses built by Cardinal Albornoz

Parco Fluviale del Nera ⑯

KNOWN AS THE "WATER PARK", this natural park extends along the course of the River Nera from Terni to Ferentillo, leading to the heart of the National Park of the Monti Sibillini *(see pp108–9)*, and thereby forming what is virtually a single protected reserve of huge interest. Within the park is one of the most famous and much-loved sights in Italy, the Cascata delle Marmore, the highest waterfalls in the country, where the waters from the River Velino spill over from the upland of the Marmore down into the River Nera. Visitors should note that the water for the waterfall is switched on only for brief periods, which vary from month to month, so you should call ahead if you don't want to miss the spectacle. The park has much else of interest, however, and offers excellent opportunities for water sports.

Sweet violets, found in the pasture areas in the park

Cascata delle Marmore

The tremendous spectacle of the falls, a popular destination with travellers throughout the ages, is created by the River Velino, which reaches this point via an artificial channel. Water then cascades down in three stages, over a total height of 165 m (541 ft), to reach the River Nera below. The falls can be seen from both the lower road (SS209) and the upper road (S79).

The Observatory along the upper road, in the village of Marmore, is one of many points from which to admire the falls in all their glory. It dates from 1781.

TERNI

209

Nera

Nera

Marmore

Velino

CONSTRUCTING A WATERFALL

In antiquity, the River Velino did not spill into the River Nera as it does today, but stagnated in the marshes of the Rieti plain. In 271 BC the Romans decided to link the two by digging a channel, the Cavo Curiano, which feeds today's main waterfall. Since then, the Cascata delle Marmore has been at the centre of the entire river system of central Italy, provoking bitter debate between those who wanted to close it down and others who wanted to extend it. The latter option was chosen in the 15th and 16th centuries, with the work entrusted by the popes to the great architects of the day (Antonio da Sangallo, Giovanni Fontana and Carlo Maderno), who were to transform the falls. The latest alterations, to adapt the falls for hydroelectric power, took place in the 1920s.

The hydroelectric plant at the Marmore falls, one of Italy's main sources of energy

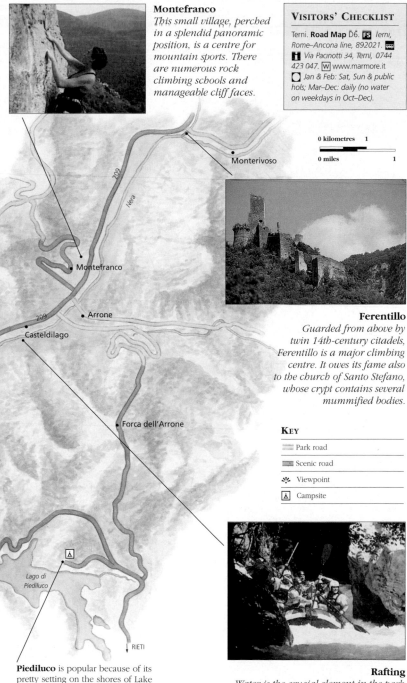

Montefranco
This small village, perched in a splendid panoramic position, is a centre for mountain sports. There are numerous rock climbing schools and manageable cliff faces.

VISITORS' CHECKLIST

Terni. **Road Map** D6. **FS** *Terni, Rome–Ancona line, 892021.* ▦ ♠ *Via Pacinotti 34, Terni, 0744 423 047.* W www.marmore.it ○ *Jan & Feb: Sat, Sun & public hols; Mar–Dec: daily (no water on weekdays in Oct–Dec).*

Monterivoso

0 kilometres 1

0 miles 1

209

Nera

Montefranco

209

Arrone

Casteldilago

Forca dell'Arrone

Lago di Piediluco

Ⓐ

↓ RIETI

Ferentillo
Guarded from above by twin 14th-century citadels, Ferentillo is a major climbing centre. It owes its fame also to the church of Santo Stefano, whose crypt contains several mummified bodies.

KEY

⚏	Park road
▬	Scenic road
☼	Viewpoint
Ⓐ	Campsite

Piediluco is popular because of its pretty setting on the shores of Lake Piediluco, the second largest lake in Umbria after Trasimeno, and just outside the park. The church of San Francesco is worth a visit, and boat rides on the lake are recommended.

Rafting
Water is the crucial element in the park and various water sports can be practised here, including rafting, canoeing and kayaking.

The 17th-century Porta Romana, inserted into the ancient walls

Amelia ⑰

Terni. **Road Map** C6.
👥 *11,000.* 🚆 *Narni, 11 km (7 miles), Rome–Ancona line.* 🚌
ℹ️ *Via Orvieto 1, 0744 981 453.*

PERCHED ON A HILL between the Tiber and Nera valleys, Amelia is a city of ancient origin. In fact, it was in antiquity that the town knew its greatest importance, when it was located on the Via Amerina, one of several Roman roads linking southern Etruria with Umbria.

Still standing today are parts of the impressive **Mura Poligonali** (Polygonal Walls), built by the Umbri and among the oldest walls in Italy. Their age is not certain, but they date from no later than the 5th century BC. Some 8 m (26 ft) high, and 3 m (10 ft) wide, the bastions are, for the most part, made up of vast polygonal stone blocks, fitted together without mortar. The size of the walls can best be seen at **Porta Romana**, framed by a Classical-style 17th-century arch.

This same gate is also the main entrance to the historic centre. Close by, in Palazzo Boccarini, is the **Museo Archeologico**, home to all manner of Roman finds from tablets to sarcophagi. Of huge interest is a magnificent statue of the Roman general Germanicus; discovered locally, it was for years kept in Perugia; Amelia has won it back, for the time being at least.

A short way up Via della Repubblica is the 13th-century church of **Santi Filippo e Giacomo**. It contains seven tombs of the Geraldini family, one of the most important dynasties in Amelia. Cardinal Alessandro Geraldini is famous for helping to persuade the Spanish monarchy to authorize the first voyage of Christopher Columbus to the Indies. The church's funerary monuments include the 15th-century tombs of Elisabetta and Matteo Geraldini, the work of Agostino di Duccio.

Palazzo Farattini, just off Via della Repubblica, is Amelia's most impressive private building. It was designed by Antonio da Sangallo the Younger in the 16th century for the Farattini, the other family to feature large in the history of Amelia. Via della Repubblica climbs further to Piazza Marconi, the town's lovely main square, and then continues up Via Duomo to the highest point of the city and the **duomo**.

The cathedral's appearance today is the result of almost total reconstruction in the 17th century, which replaced the original Romanesque church, though the fine 11th-century bell tower remains. Inside are several works of importance: these include a panel with a *Madonna and Child* attributed to Antoniazzo Romano, and two paintings by Nicolò Pomarancio in the Oratorio del Sacramento.

Returning to the lowest part of the town along Via Geraldini, you reach Piazza Matteotti, whose architectural highlight is the charming **Palazzo Comunale**.

Beyond Porta Romana, you can visit the country church of **Santa Maria delle Cinque Fonti**, built on the site where St Francis is said to have given a sermon in 1213. The church is named after a fountain with five spouts that stands nearby.

Detail from the tomb of Matteo and Elisabetta Geraldini

🏛 **Museo Archeologico**
Piazza Augusto Vera.
📞 *0744 978 120.* ⏰ *Apr–Sep: 10:30am–1pm, 4–7pm Tue–Sun (Jul & Aug: daily); Oct–Mar: 10:30am–1pm, 3–5:30pm Fri–Sun.* ♿

View of Amelia, showing how the village expanded down the hillside

◁ **The impressive Cascata delle Marmore, with the second level in the foreground**

ENVIRONS: The area around Amelia is dotted with abbeys and sanctuaries which are easy to reach and a delight to visit. About 4 km (2 miles) southwest of Amelia, on the road to Attigliano, is the 13th-century **Monastery of the Santissima Annunziata**, which belongs to the Friars Minor. There is a *Last Supper* on the wall of the refectory.

Heading eastwards, past the village of Capitone – which was the castle of nearby Narni in the Middle Ages – you reach the village of La Cerqua and the **Sanctuary of the Madonna della Quercia**. This was built in the 16th century to hold an image of the Virgin Mary, now on the apse altar.

The Roman **Via Amerina** is a historical object in itself, and has maintained its role as a communication route.

Lago di Alviano, along the border with neighbouring Lazio

Interior of Santa Maria Assunta, in Lugnano

Lugnano in Teverina ⑱

Terni. **Road Map** C6.
🏠 *1,600.* 🚉 *Attigliano, 11 km (7 miles), Milan–Rome line.* 🚌 🛈 *Via Orvieto 1, Amelia, 0744 981 453.*
🎭 *Christmas concerts and Living Nativity, 24 Dec–6 Jan.*

FOLLOWING THE MAIN road 205 from Amelia towards Lago di Alviano, after around 10 km (6 miles) you come to the small town of Lugnano in Teverina. Set in a panoramic position along a ridge and enclosed by medieval walls,

Lugnano began life as the feudal village of a Provençal count, in around 1000.

Although some way from the usual tourist trails, Lugnano is well worth visiting simply to see one of the most interesting Romanesque churches in Umbria, the church of **Santa Maria Assunta**. The building dates from the 12th century, although it has undergone much restoration, especially in the 15th century. In common with various other Umbrian churches of the same era, such as the cathedral of Spoleto, the façade features a beautifully decorated portico, some of which is the work of the famous Roman marble workers, the Cosmati. There is more Cosmati work inside, both in the nave (which has a Cosmatesque pavement) and in the crypt, which also has a finely sculpted screen. Other works of art include a triptych of the *Annunciation* by Niccolò Alunno, in the apse, and a *Crucifixion* of the Giotto school.

Capital in Santa Maria Assunta

ENVIRONS: A short distance southwest of the town centre are traces of the Assisi saint in the church of **San Francesco**. It was erected in 1229 on the spot where a miracle is said to have taken place, as shown in the fresco above the right-hand altar.

After passing the ruins of an ancient Roman villa, the road descends towards the Tiber and the hamlet of **Attigliano**. Proceeding north on the Via Amerina, along the banks of the Tiber, after about 8 km (5 miles) you come to the **Lago di Alviano**. This is part of an artificial basin created to generate hydroelectricity and today is an oasis run by the World Wide Fund for Nature and part of the Parco Fluviale del Tevere *(see p133)*. From the nearby medieval town of Alviano, birthplace of condottiere Bartolomeo di Alviano, steps lead to **Santa Illuminata**, a pilgrimage site linked to an order of hermits called the Camaldolese.

A lovely 10-km (6-mile) stretch of the Via Amerina runs to **Montecchio**, with an interesting necropolis (6th–4th centuries BC) nearby.

One of the chambers in the necropolis near Montecchio

**Gate at the entrance to the
medieval town of San Gemini**

San Gemini ⑲

Terni. **Road Map** D6.
🏛 4,300. 🚉 Terni, 11 km (7 miles),
Rome–Ancona line. 🚌 ℹ Via
Garibaldi, 0744 630 130.

THE MEDIEVAL TOWN OF San
Gemini was built over the
ruins of an ancient Roman
settlement, alongside the Via
Flaminia. The only traces of
the Roman town are a tomb,
the so-called Grotta degli
Zingari and a ruined villa.

The heart of San Gemini
is Piazza di Palazzo Vecchio,
home to the medieval
Palazzo Pubblico, whose
tower was much altered in
the 1700s. Under an exterior
arcade is an image of St
George, patron saint of the
town. The 13th-century
Oratorio di San Carlo,
nearby, has striking frescoes.

On the edge of town
are the churches of **San
Francesco**, with a fine
Gothic doorway, and **San
Giovanni Battista**, with a
13th-century façade and a
lovely Romanesque door
decorated with mosaics. One
of the façade inscriptions
bears the date of its founding,
1199, with the names of the
architects and sculptors
Nicola, Simone and Bernardo.

Just outside San Gemini's
old gateway is the privately-
owned church of San Nicolò.
The beautifully sculpted
Romanesque portal is a copy,
since the original is in the
Metropolitan Museum in New
York. There is more fine (and
original) sculpture inside.

ENVIRONS: Just to the north, on
flatter ground, is the modern
spa town of San Gemini
Fonte, with facilities for spa
water treatments. The famous
mineral waters of Sangemini
and Fabia are bottled here.
Sangemini water, known in
antiquity and exploited since
the late 19th century, is rich
in calcium but with low levels
of chlorine and sodium, so is
particularly recommended for
children. Fabia water has
average levels of minerals and
is today promoted as a light
table water. It is said to be
good for the digestion.

**The ancient spring at the Terme
di San Gemini**

Carsulae ⑳

Terni. **Road Map** D6. 🚉 Terni,
14 km (9 miles), Rome–Ancona line.
🚌 ℹ Soprintendenza archeologica
dell'Umbria, 0744 630 420.
🕐 dawn–dusk daily.

FROM SAN GEMINI FONTE a
detour of 3 km (2 miles)
along part of the old Via
Flaminia brings you to the
ruined Roman town of
Carsulae, founded in the 3rd
century BC on the slopes of
the mound bearing the pretty
name of Chiccirichì.

At first merely a staging and
garrison post, then a village
Carsulae eventually became a
town in Augustus' Region VI.
It experienced its greatest
period of splendour between
30 and 10 BC, when work
was being done on the Via
Flaminia. The town was
abandoned following the
decline in importance of the
road. Carsulae was attacked
and raided by barbarians and
marauders on a number of
occasions, and was also badly
damaged by earthquakes.

From the 16th century
onwards, the aristocratic
families of the region, in
particular the Cesi family of
Acquasparta, began to carry
out excavations in search of
objects of interest for their
own private collections.
The modern archaeological
excavations date back to the
1950s, when a number of
sites used in public life were
uncovered, including a
basilica, the old forum, and
temples. The great value of
Carsulae as an archaeological
site lies in the fact that the
original layout has remained
complete for the most part,
despite the encroachment of
the modern Via Flaminia,
which crosses the site.

The small church of **San
Damiano** was built in the
11th century, using the
remains of a Roman temple.
From here, you can follow a
stretch of the original Via

The little church of San Damiano, inside Carsulae's archaeological area

The ruins of the Roman theatre at Carsulae, showing clearly the supports for the stalls

Flaminia to the **Forum**, with an adjacent basilica with three aisles and an apse. In front of the forum is a public square where numerous low walls – the ruins of religious and secular buildings – can be seen: among them are the bases of the **Tempietti Gemelli** (twin temples) and the remains of baths.

Continuing up the old Via Flaminia, you arrive at the **Arco di San Damiano**, a monumental gate which once had three arches: only the central one survives. A burial site is nearby. Behind the basilica, beyond the modern Via Flaminia, are the **Amphitheatre**, built in a natural depression and used for circus games, and the **Theatre**, of which only the foundations of the stage and the supports for the stalls remain.

Acquasparta ㉑

Terni. **Road Map** D6.
👥 4,500. 🚆 Terni, 20 km (12 miles), Rome–Ancona line. 🚌
ℹ Corso Lincei, 0744 930 045.
🎭 Arte estate, Jul–Aug.

T HE FIRST RECORDS of Acquasparta date from the 10th century. The name derives from the local spa waters, which were known to the Romans and, it is said, taken by St Francis. Acquasparta's appearance today recalls the influence of the Cesi family, who changed the face of the town during the 15th and 16th centuries. Among the features dating from this era are a palace named after the noble family, walls and towers.

Palazzo Cesi, commissioned by the Cesi family from the architect Giovanni Domenico Bianchi, was completed in 1565. The interior of this aristocratic residence is richly decorated: Giovan Battista Lombardelli produced the first paintings, while an artist from the north was responsible for the remainder. The rooms have splendid coffered wooden ceilings; the one in the Sala di Ercole (Room of Hercules) is particularly fine. Palazzo Cesi belongs to the University of Perugia and is used for seminars and

Palazzo Cesi, now part of the University of Perugia

conferences as well as a summer art exhibition.

Along Corso Umberto I, the main street, are the church of **Santa Cecilia** and the **Oratorio del Sacramento**, where a mosaic floor from the ruins of Roman Carsulae has been put into new use.

The 200,000-year-old fossil forest at Dunarobba

ENVIRONS: A detour 15 km (9 miles) west of Acquasparta, skirts Casteltodino and leads to the fossil forest of **Dunarobba**, close to the village of Avigliano Umbro. This ancient forest, which dates from the Pliocene age, is made up of around 40 petrified trunks of large trees similar to today's sequoia. Preserved for centuries under a blanket of clay on the shores of Lago Tiberino (which once filled the Tiber Valley), the upright trunks seem almost alive.

A few kilometres north is the medieval castle and village of **Casigliano**. Within is Palazzo Atti, a project of Antonio da Sangallo the Younger which was based on Roman designs. It was the inspiration for Palazzo Cesi.

Todi ⓒ

THE CITY OF TODI occupies a stunning spot, on a hilltop halfway between Perugia and Terni. First built on land occupied by the Umbri, Todi was later appropriated by the Etruscans (its name derives from the Etruscan word *tutere*, meaning "border") and then, in 89 BC, by the Romans. Under the Romans, Todi's two hilltops were levelled out to make Piazza del Popolo and new walls were built around the Etruscan ones. Todi today would not have looked very different during the Middle Ages, a time of great splendour, when the town expanded southwards and was divided into four districts, surrounded by a third circle of walls. The city became a papal possession, along with all the other towns of Umbria, and there was only minor subsequent modification during the Renaissance.

St Peter, in the duomo

Exploring Todi

The centre of the city is, as it was in Roman times, Piazza del Popolo. This truly magnificent square contains the duomo, as well as three fine monuments to temporal power: Palazzo del Popolo, Palazzo del Capitano and Palazzo dei Priori. Following years of research, this largely medieval square was chosen as the starting point for excavations which have provided the information necessary to reconstruct the layout of the ancient city.

The eagle of Todi, Palazzo dei Priori

built between 1293 and 1385. At the top left of the façade is an eagle in bronze, the symbol of the city and the work of Giovanni di Gigliaccio in 1339. (According to tradition, the original Umbrian town was built where an eagle had dropped a tablecloth taken from a local family.) Over the centuries the palazzo has housed the city's various and varied rulers, including the leaders of the medieval commune and the papal governors.

🏛 Palazzo dei Priori

Piazza del Popolo. 📞 075 894 4148. 🚫 to the public.
This palace, situated on the southern side of Piazza del Popolo, is the least attractive of the three palazzi. It was

🏛 Palazzo del Popolo

Piazza del Popolo. 📞 075 894 41 48. 🚫 see Palazzo del Capitano.
This is one of the oldest buildings of its type in Italy: construction began in 1213, though the palace has been

considerably restored. Built in Lombard-Gothic form, the palace's left-hand side faces Piazza del Popolo, while the front can be admired from nearby Piazza Garibaldi. In particular, look out for the swallowtail crenellations (a Guelf motif) and the external staircase, which gave access to the hall on the first floor, above the porticoed space of the ground floor. Public assemblies were held here.

The palace shares an entrance with Palazzo del Capitano and houses part of the Museo Pinacoteca.

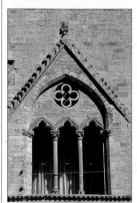

Three-mullioned window, Palazzo del Capitano

🏛 Palazzo del Capitano

Piazza del Popolo.
Museo Pinacoteca 📞 075 894 4148. 🕐 Apr–Aug: 10:30am–1pm, 2:30–6pm daily (Apr: Tue–Sun); Mar & Sep: 10:30am–1pm, 2–5pm daily; Oct–Feb: 10:30am–1pm, 2–4:30pm daily.
This palace dates from the late 13th century and faces the eastern side of the square. The façade has mullioned Gothic windows and a monumental arched staircase

Piazza del Popolo, an excellent example of a well-preserved medieval square which serves both the Palazzo del Capitano and the adjacent Palazzo del Popolo. In particular, it gives access to the Sala del Capitano, with remains of frescoes, medieval coats of arms and a 14th-century *Crucifixion*.

Sculptural detail from the door of the duomo

The **Museo** Pinacoteca, which spans the adjacent palazzi, includes a decent archeological collection, the **Museo Etrusco-Romano**, as well as paintings, of which the most significant is a *Coronation of the Virgin* (1507–11) by Giovanni di Pietro, known as Spagna.

🏛 Duomo

Piazza del Popolo.

☎ 075 894 30 41. ◻ summer: 8:30am–12:30pm, 2:30–6:30pm; winter: 8:30am–4:30pm Mon–Sat, 8:30am–12:30pm, 2:30–6:30pm Sun. Dedicated to Maria Santissima Annunziata, the duomo was founded in the 12th century, probably on the site of a Roman temple, but wasn't

completed for another 200 years, with further additions being made after that. The simple façade, which is divided horizontally by cornices, is lovely. An 18th-century flight of steps leads up to a carved 16th-century door set into a decorative framework, above which, as befits the façade's Romanesque simplicity, is a beautiful rose window (1515). Pilaster strips, small loggias and mullioned windows decorate the right-hand side and the tall apse.

Inside, the church has a decorative beamed roof and splendid Gothic capitals, as well as a superb 16th-century choir. The entire central space as well as the chapels contain various works of art, the most interesting of which are near the altar: two paintings by Spagna, to the sides, and, above, a painted wooden Crucifix dating from the 13th

VISITORS' CHECKLIST

Perugia. **Road Map** C5.
🚉 *17,000.* **FS** *Perugia–Terni line, 892021* 🚌 *800 512 141*
ℹ️ *Piazza Umberto I, 075 894 3395.* 🎭 *Todifestival, Sep.*

and 14th centuries. There is also a crypt, which contains three figures originally on the façade, as well as a handful of Roman remains.

The magnificent rose window on the façade of the cathedral

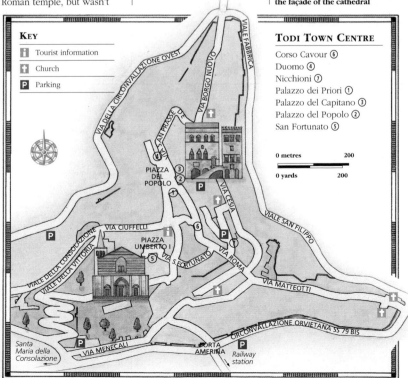

KEY

ℹ️	Tourist information
🏛	Church
P	Parking

TODI TOWN CENTRE

Corso Cavour ⑥
Duomo ④
Nicchioni ⑦
Palazzo dei Priori ①
Palazzo del Capitano ③
Palazzo del Popolo ②
San Fortunato ⑤

0 metres   200
0 yards   200

VIALE FABBRICA
CIRCONVALLAZIONE OVEST
VIA BORGO NUOVO
VIA DELLA
VIA SAN PRASSE DE
PIAZZA DEL POPOLO
VIA CESIA
VIALE SAN FILIPPO
VIA CIUFFELLI
PIAZZA UMBERTO I
VIA S. FORTUNATO
VIA ROMA
VIA MATTEOTTI
VIALE DELLA CONSOLAZIONE
VIALE DELLA VITTORIA
Santa Maria della Consolazione
VIA MENECALI
PORTA AMERINA
Railway station
CIRCONVALLAZIONE ORVIETANA SS 79 BIS

Detail from the main door of the church of San Fortunato

⛪ San Fortunato

Piazza Umberto I.
🕐 *summer: 9:30am–noon, 3–5pm; winter: 9am–12.30pm, 3–7pm.* ⬤ *Mon.*

Heading south along Via Mazzini, skirting the medieval heart of Todi, you reach the enormous hilltop church of San Fortunato, a sight not to be missed.

This is a Franciscan church, but with many anomalies: the dedication, for example, is not to the Assisi saint but to Fortunato, patron of Todi. (The reason for this was that the church replaced a building used by Benedictine monks.) The construction took place in two phases: the first from 1292–1328, the second in the 1400s. It was commissioned by the bishop of Todi, Matteo d'Acquasparta.

The unfinished façade, a mixture of Romanesque and Gothic styles, stands out at the top of an imposing flight of steps. Through the fine Gothic central doorway lies a wonderfully airy Gothic interior, which does not follow the traditional Franciscan model. It is a rare example in Italy of a Gothic hall church; that is, in which the two side aisles are as high as (though much narrower than) the nave. Note the lovely and unusual ribbed cross vaults, the fine late 16th-century choir stalls, the raised chapels along the sides, and the Gothic baptismal font.

Frescoes decorate many of the chapels and include, in the fifth chapel on the left, some scenes from the *Life of St John the Baptist* by the Giotto school, and, in the fourth chapel on the right, a *Madonna and Child* (1432) by Masolino di Panicale.

The church is also famous for the tomb of Jacopone da Todi, in the crypt beneath the altar. Jacopone was a rich merchant who, following the death of his devout wife, Vanna, became a mystic and a poet. His devotion was reputedly so extreme that he was rejected even by the Franciscans. He was accused of heresy on a number of occasions and is mainly remembered for his *Laudi*, one of the fundamental texts in the birth of Italian literature (*see p30*). The great man, a native of Todi, died in 1306 and gradually became the symbol of the medieval city. He is still the best-known figure in the cultural history of Todi.

Extending westwards from San Fortunato is a large public park, where a fortress commissioned by Cardinal Albornoz stood until 1503.

🏛 Corso Cavour

Descending the steps of Via San Fortunato brings you to the steep Corso Cavour, the "Rua degli Speziali" (spice sellers' street) of medieval Todi. Halfway along is a fountain known as the **Fonte Rua** (1606), or Fonte Cesia (after the bishop who had it built), and, at the end, **Porta Marzia**, a medieval arch made out of material salvaged from other buildings.

The 17th-century Fonte Rua, in Corso Cavour

🏛 Nicchioni

Piazza del Mercato Vecchio.
Walk through Porta Marzia, and turn left into Via Mercato Vecchio, which leads to Piazza Garibaldi (a car park). The level part of this street, the old medieval market square, is dominated by four Roman arches, the so-called Nicchioni (niches). These most probably date from the Augustan era, and either supported a raised street, or formed part of the wall of a Roman basilica.

⛪ Santa Maria della Consolazione

Viale della Consolazione.
🕐 9:30am–12:30pm, 2:30am–6:30pm (winter: 2–5pm). ⬤ Mon.
This church, located outside the city walls, is one of the masterpieces of the Umbrian Renaissance. Begun in 1508

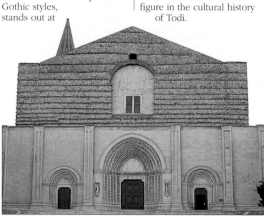

The unfinished façade of the church of San Fortunato

The church of Santa Maria della Consolazione, outside Todi

and finished in 1607, it has been attributed by some to Bramante, the architect of St Peter's in Rome. In fact, there is no documentary evidence of any such project by the great architect, though it is just possible that Cola di Caprarola, who started the project, may have used drawings by Bramante.

The distinctive silhouette of the church – familiar from the covers of dozens of publications devoted to Todi – is built on a square plan and rises to a great dome. Encircling the main structure are four apses, of which one, to the north, is semicircular and three are polygonal; they have two orders of pilasters, with a mixture of capitals, and are pierced by elegant windows. The drum which supports the great dome is narrower than the main body of the church, leaving space for a raised terrace, guarded by four eagles sculpted by Antonio Rosignoli in the 17th century. There are great views from here. The Baroque doorways date from the 18th and 19th centuries.

The airy and light interior, in the form of a Greek cross, is also Baroque and contains statues of the apostles. In the apse is the venerated fresco of the *Madonna della Consolazione* (15th century). The church was built to protect the fresco.

Eagle on the terrace, Santa Maria della Consolazione

Parco Fluviale del Tevere ㉓

Terni. **Road Map** C5. **FS** *Orvieto, Milan–Rome line; Todi, Perugia–Terni line.* **Ⓘ** *Ente parco, Civitella del Lago, Baschi, 0744 950 732.* **W** *www.parcotevere.It*

THIS RIVER PARK extends for some 295 ha (18,025 acres) from the bridge of Montemolino, at the gates of Todi, south as far as Lago di Alviano, and has great wildlife and lovely scenery. It includes around 50 km (31 miles) of land along the banks of the Tiber, the largest river in central Italy, and two artificial lakes (Alviano and Corbara). The main access to the park is at the medieval hill town of Baschi, about 24 km (15 miles) from Todi, close to the junction of road S448 and the motorway.

The Tiber river, one moment placid and the next turbulent, is home to a variety of birds, among them blue heron and kingfishers, as well as freshwater fish. Poplars, alders and willows, typical riverside vegetation, cloak the sides.

Steep valleys sweep away from the river and extend as far as the Apennines: the wildest is the **Gole del Forello**, considered one of the most interesting biotopes in the region. On the northern banks of Lago di Corbara, not far from the fortified village of Prodo, winds the **Gole di Prodo**, a deep gorge best suited to hikers or experienced and well-equipped mountain climbers. Diverse birds of prey, including buzzards, sparrowhawks and kites, can be seen in these inaccessible areas, where the vegetation consists mainly of trees such as holm oaks and hornbeams and shrubs such as broom and heather. The marshes in the Lago di Alviano basin *(see p127)*, with its own particular birdlife and plants, are also of great interest.

Besides the natural beauty and the opportunities for outdoor sports, the park also incorporates sites of historical and archaeological interest. Digs are under way in various spots, including in the Vallone di San Lorenzo (site of several necropolises) and in the area of the ancient river port of **Pagliano**, at the confluence of the Paglia and Tiber rivers; the port's existence confirms the importance of the Tiber as a communication route of the central Italic peoples.

The wild Gole del Forello, a fascinating wildlife habitat

Orvieto ㉔

A SHEER TUFA OUTCROP, the remains of ancient volcanoes fractured by millennia of ice, sun and rain, rises abruptly from the plain and supports the spectacular medieval city of Orvieto. All around, the fertile soil feeds the vines that produce the area's famous white wines. In the Etruscan era a city called Velzna stood here and became rich through commerce with traders from the Tyrrhenian Sea (part of the Mediterranean) and the north. The Romans took over in 264 BC and virtually destroyed the town. Revival came only in the Middle Ages, when Orvieto developed into a free and powerful commune, albeit one troubled by civic strife. The Black Death of 1348 was devastating, however, and Orvieto eventually came under papal control. The old city, with its superb duomo, has changed little in the last 500 years, and attracts millions of tourists every year.

The imposing tufa platform supporting Orvieto

⛪ Duomo
See pp136–7.

⛫ Museo Archeologico Nazionale
Piazza del Duomo.
☎ 0763 341 039. ◯ 8:30am–7pm daily (1pm Sun, public hols). ⬚ ♿
On the scenic Piazza del Duomo, next to the imposing mass of the cathedral, stand the **Palazzi Papali**, which include three 14th-century buildings, commissioned by Popes Urban IV, Gregory X and Martin IV and later combined into one complex.

The **Museo Archeologico Nazionale,** housed in the Palazzo del Martino IV, has a particularly fine Etruscan collection, including bronzes and mirrors. Several tombs and funerary objects are among the exhibits of special interest, including frescoes from 2nd-century-BC tombs and two painted 4th-century tombs from Settecamini.

⛫ Museo dell'Opera del Duomo
Piazza del Duomo. ☎ 0763 342 477. ◯ for long-term restoration.
The Palazzi Papali also house a museum dedicated to the cathedral. Exhibits include

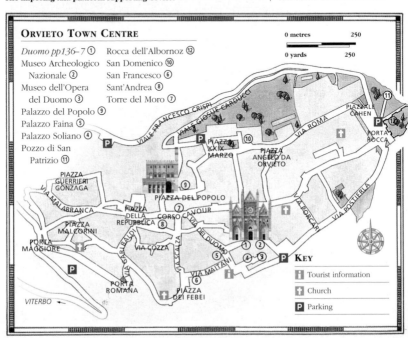

ORVIETO TOWN CENTRE

0 metres   250
0 yards   250

VIALE FRANCESCO CRISPI
VIALE GIOSUE CARDUCCI
VIA ROMA
PIAZZALE CAHEN
PORTA ROCCA
PIAZZA XXIX MARZO
PIAZZA ANGELO DA ORVIETO
PIAZZA GUERRIERI GONZAGA
VIA MALABRANCA
PIAZZA DEL POPOLO
PIAZZA DELLA REPUBBLICA
CORSO CAVOUR
VIA DEL DUOMO
VIA PORCARI
VIA POSTIERLA
PIAZZA MALCORNI
PORTA MAGGIORE
VIA GARIBALDI
VIA COZZA
VIA SCALZA
VIA MAITANI
PORTA ROMANA
PIAZZA DEI FEBEI
VITERBO ◄

KEY

🛈	Tourist information
✝	Church
P	Parking

UNDERGROUND ORVIETO

Sotterranei
Società Speleotecnica. *0763 344 891 (phone ahead to book English tours).* tours at intervals from 11am–5.15pm.

Pozzo di Via della Cava
Trattoria Sciarra, Via della Cava 28. *0763 342 373.* 8am–8pm daily.

Passages below the town

The people of Orvieto are used to living with cellars: every house or shop has its own cave, and every family has its own story to tell of the underground. Marco Marino, for example, an antiques dealer in Via della Cava, found the remains of the oldest ceramics kiln known in the world by digging in his cellar. He uses it to display his collection of 15th-century ceramics.

A group of enthusiasts developed a project to open up some of Orvieto's caves to visitors, and the Società Speleotecnica is one of the groups to run tours. The caves underneath the embankment that separates the hospital from the walls of the cliff are examples of underground Orvieto: caves which were re-used over the centuries, as workshops, and storerooms for cereals, oil and wine. In addition to the intriguing Pozzo di San Patrizio *(see p138),* it is well worth visiting the Pozzo di Via della Cava, an Etruscan well. Used in the 16th century and then covered up, the well now forms part of the basement of a restaurant called Trattoria Sciarra.

VISITORS' CHECKLIST

Perugia. **Road Map** B5.
22,000. FS Milan–Rome line, 892021. Piazza del Duomo 24, 0763 341 772.
Corpus Domini procession; Palombella Pentecoste, 30 May.

Palazzo Faina (Museo Civico and Museo Claudio Faina)

Piazza del Duomo. *0763 341511.* Apr–Sep: 9:30am–6pm daily; Oct–Mar: 10am–6pm. Mon in Jan, Feb, Nov, Dec.

This 19th-century palazzo opposite the duomo houses two museums. The Museo Civico, on the ground floor, is of much less interest than the Museo Claudio Faina, an extraordinarily rich private collection gathered by the Faina counts in the 19th century. Among the exhibits are beautiful Etruscan vases, superb jewellery from the 5th century BC onwards, and a series of exquisite Attic vases. There is a wonderful view of the duomo from the top floor.

paintings, statues and other works of art that once filled the cathedral, dating from the Middle Ages up to the 18th century. Among them are paintings by Simone Martini, a series of large statues formerly in the cathedral and also a collection of church ornaments.

Detail from an Etruscan fresco, Museo dell'Opera del Duomo

Palazzo Soliano and Museo Emilio Greco

Piazza del Duomo. *0763 344 605.* 10:30am–1pm, 2:30–6pm (Oct–Mar: 6:30pm) Tue–Sun.

The austere, tufa Palazzo Soliano was commissioned by Pope Boniface VIII in 1297, but was not completed until 1359. In the early days, the palace was used as a storehouse by the Fabbrica del Duomo (cathedral works). Later, from the mid-16th century onwards, the hall on the ground floor was used by Orvieto's stonemasons. The structure is very simple, consisting of two large rooms one on top of the other. The lower room has a line of pilasters and arches and opens out into a grand, monumental staircase.

Palazzo Soliano houses a substantial collection of 20th-century sculptures, drawings and lithographs given to the city by Emilio Greco, a contemporary Sicilian artist well known in Italy.

Cinerary urn kept in the Museo Civico, Palazzo Faina

San Francesco

Piazza dei Febei.
The Romanesque church of San Francesco was founded in 1240, but it has been much altered over the centuries.

The large church has a tufa façade with three arched doorways and mullioned windows. Inside, the vault is supported by wooden trusses of enormous dimensions given the era in which they were made.

Look out for the 14th-century wooden *Crucifixion,* attributed to Maitani (involved in the construction of the duomo) or his school.

Orvieto: Duomo

Lunette on the door with the *Madonna and Child*

Orvieto's magnificent duomo, which dominates the skyline, was founded by Pope Nicholas IV in 1290. Things got off to a bad start and, in 1308, the Sienese architect and sculptor, Lorenzo Maitani, was brought in to save the building. It wasn't finished for another 300 years. Maitani himself was largely responsible for the 52-m (170-ft) façade, with his own magnificently detailed bas-reliefs of scenes from the Old and New Testaments, a superb rose window, 16th-century statues and multi-coloured mosaics (not original). The striped design outside is carried through into the Romanesque nave, divided by columns with elaborate capitals. Inside, the masterpiece is the chapel of the Madonna di San Brizio, with frescoes by Fra Angelico and Luca Signorelli and portraits of famous poets and writers, including Ovid and Dante.

Stained Glass
Among the stained glass in the apse is this Nativity by Giovanni Bonino di Assisi.

Sanctuary
The sanctuary walls feature 14th-century frescoes by Ugolino di Prete Ilario, a local artist. Above is a detail from the Adoration of the Magi.

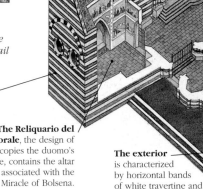

The Reliquario del Corporale, the design of which copies the duomo's façade, contains the altar cloth associated with the Miracle of Bolsena.

The exterior is characterized by horizontal bands of white travertine and blue-grey basalt.

Cappella del Corporale
This chapel contains the superb 14th-century Madonna dei Raccomandati *(left) by the Sienese artist Lippo Memmi, and frescoes (1357–64) of the* Miracle of Bolsena *and* Miracles of the Sacrament *by Ugolino di Prete Ilario.*

STAR FEATURES

★ **Façade**

★ **Cappella della Madonna di San Brizio**

FRESCOES BY LUCA SIGNORELLI

A fascinating cycle of frescoes narrating events related to the Apocalypse unfolds on the walls of the Cappella della Madonna di San Brizio. Signorelli tackles the themes of the Last Judgment – *The Day of Judgment, The Preaching of the Antichrist, The Resurrection of the Dead, The Damned Consigned to Hell, The Blessed Entering Heaven,* and *Angels Guide the Elect to Paradise* – blending spatial harmony and dynamism in a synthesis of the art of central Italy of the time. The three-dimensionality and energy emanating from the figures heighten the drama and anticipate the painting of Michelangelo in the Sistine Chapel.

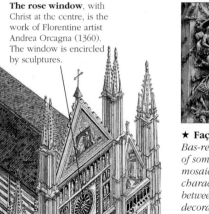

Detail from the fresco of *Day of Judgment* by Signorelli

VISITORS' CHECKLIST

Piazza del Duomo.
0763 341 167.
summer: 7:30am–12:45pm, 2:30–7:15pm daily; winter: 7:30am–12:45pm, 2:30–6:15pm.

★ Cappella della Madonna di San Brizio
The fresco cycle in this Gothic chapel, begun by Fra Angelico (1447) with the assistance of Benozzo Gozzoli, and later completed by Luca Signorelli (1499–1504), is one of the finest of the Renaissance.

The rose window, with Christ at the centre, is the work of Florentine artist Andrea Orcagna (1360). The window is encircled by sculptures.

★ Façade
Bas-reliefs and statues (the originals of some are in the Museo dell'Opera), mosaics, pilasters and arches characterize this perfect synthesis between architecture and the decorative arts. It is a stunning example of Italian Gothic.

Main Door
The decorated bronze panels of the main door were the work of Emilio Greco in the 1960s.

♛ Torre del Moro

Corso Cavour.
○ Mar, Apr, Sep, Oct: 10am–7pm;
May–Jul: 10am–8pm; Jan, Feb, Nov,
Dec: 10am–1pm, 2:30–5pm daily.

The 12th-century "Tower of
the Moor" towers 42 m
(137 ft) above Corso Cavour,
Orvieto's main street, where it
meets Via del Duomo. It owes
its name to the figure on the
coat of arms of the Pucci, a
local family. Its 14th-century
bell is still in working order.

Alongside the tower is the
Palazzo dei Sette (1300),
built as the seat of the seven
(*sette*) magistrates in charge of
the commune, and later the
seat of the papal governor.

**The Torre del Moro rising above
the roofs of old Orvieto**

♙ Sant'Andrea

Piazza della Repubblica.

This church is one of the
oldest buildings in Orvieto.
Founded in the 7th century,
Sant'Andrea was built upon
walls of probable Etruscan
origin, over which a Roman
temple was later built. It was
then rebuilt in stages during
the 12th–14th centuries.

Sant'Andrea was once the
most important church

in Orvieto. It was here that
Pope Innocent III proclaimed
the Fourth Crusade in 1201
and that Martin IV was
crowned pope in 1281, in the
presence of Charles of Anjou.

Important elements include
the Gothic door, by Marco da
Siena, designed by Maestro
Vetrino (1487), and the
imposing 12-sided bell tower,
with three orders of two-
mullioned windows and a
series of coats of arms, placed
here when restoration was
undertaken in 1920–30. The
interior is supported by great
granite columns, probably
Roman, and is decorated with
fragments of frescoes and a
10th-century pulpit.

♛ Palazzo del Popolo

Piazza del Popolo. ☎ 0763 343 768.
● to the public.

The heart of the city in
ancient times, Piazza
del Popolo is home
to the Palazzo del
Popolo, first
described in the
town records at the
end of the 13th
century. Built from
the local tufa stone
and topped by a
bell tower, it is an
important example
of Orvieto civic
architecture from the
late 13th century.
Ornamentations include an
external staircase, an open
loggia, crenellations, and
mullioned windows linked
by a cornice. It is now a
conference centre.

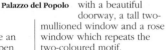

**Detail from the
Palazzo del Popolo**

**The façade of San Domenico with
the original striped pilasters**

♙ San Domenico

Piazza XXIX Marzo.

It was here that the unusual
striped stonework, in dark-
coloured basalt and pale
travertine, appeared for the
first time in Orvieto, in the
late 13th century.
The style was then
extensively used in
the duomo and
became a signature
motif for the city.
Despite substantial
restoration in the
Baroque era, the
façade maintains its
simple Romanesque-
Gothic austerity,
with a beautiful
doorway, a tall two-
mullioned window and a rose
window which repeats the
two-coloured motif.

Half the church was taken
down in the 20th century to
make room for the nearby
barracks; the interior space
today consists merely of the
original transept and the
tribune. The most important
work of art is the splendid
tomb of Cardinal Guglielmo
de Braye by Arnolfo di
Cambio (1282), but there are
also frescoes and other
examples of sculpture.

♫ Pozzo di San Patrizio

Viale Sangallo. ☎ 0763 343 768.
○ Apr–Sep: 10am–6:45pm;
Oct–Mar: 10am–5:45pm daily. ♿
Located at the eastern end
of Corso Cavour is one
of Orvieto's best-known
monuments. Commissioned
in 1527 by Pope Clement VII
and designed by Antonio da
Sangallo the Younger, the

The church of Sant'Andrea with its unusual 12-sided tower

The impressive depths forming the Pozzo di San Patrizio

62-m (203-ft) well is a superb piece of engineering. Crucial to the design are two 248-step spiral staircases: one was used for the descent and one for the ascent, so that donkeys carrying pitchers of water would not meet on the way. The stairways are lit by 72 windows.

Looking over the plain from the bastions of the Rocca

⋔ Rocca dell'Albornoz
Viale Sangallo. 【 0763 343 768. ◯ always open. 🎫

Dominating the eastern end of Orvieto, near the terminus of the funicular that connects the old city with the railway station down on the plain, is the **Rocca**, built by Cardinal Albornoz in 1364 to bolster the power of the papacy. The locals destroyed it soon afterwards, and not much remains today.

The Rocca is an excellent vantage point from which to enjoy views over the city and the plain, as well as being a tranquil spot, surrounded as it is by pretty gardens.

ENVIRONS: Around 1.5 km (1 mile) north of Orvieto, at the foot of the tufa cliff, is the **Necropoli del Crocifisso del Tufo**. This Etruscan cemetery complex dates from the 6th–3rd centuries BC and consists of small chambered tombs built of tufa blocks and containing a stone bench for laying out the corpse. On the lintel over the entrance to each tomb is the name of the person or family buried there. The site seems to have an essentially "urban" layout, following what would be defined today as a town plan.

The site was discovered only in the 19th century, by foreign archaeologists who passed on some of the finds to the Louvre and the British Museum. It wasn't until 1880 that the site was first explored in a scientific, non-intrusive way and finally began to arouse the interest of the Italian authorities. Over 100 tombs have now been found. The majority of the important funerary

objects discovered in the tombs are now distributed among Orvieto's museums.

On the south side of the cliff is the **Necropoli della Cannicella**, another burial site used by the Etruscans from the 7th–3rd centuries BC. It follows a similar layout to the necropolis at Crocifisso del Tufo.

Around 3 km (2 miles) south of Orvieto, just off SS71, is the **Abbazia di Santi Severo e Martino**, a great medieval monastery complex. Now partly converted into a hotel, the monastery belonged to the Benedictine Order until 1221, and then passed to the Premonstratensians (a French Order founded in 1120 by St Norbert).

Apart from the rooms used by the hotel, several areas of the monastery can still be visited. There is much that dates from the original construction (12th–13th-centuries). The splendid 12-sided Romanesque tower dates from the 12th century. The church, reached through a great 13th-century arch, features a single nave with a ribbed vault, an inlaid marble floor in the Cosmatesque style and several fragments of medieval frescoes. The barrel-vaulted Oratorio del Crocifisso, once the monks' refectory, is adorned with a 13th-century fresco depicting the *Crucifixion with Saints*. Also of interest is the 13th-century Abbot's House.

⋔ Necropoli del Crocifisso del Tufo
【 0763 343 611. ◯ 8:30am–7pm (winter: 5pm) daily. 🎫 ♿

Etruscan necropolis of the Crocifisso del Tufo, 6th century BC

TRAVELLERS'
NEEDS

WHERE TO STAY 142–151
WHERE TO EAT 152–167
SHOPPING IN UMBRIA 168–171

WHERE TO STAY

IN RECENT YEARS the range of accommodation in Umbria has developed noticeably. As well as hotels in the old historic centres, some famous for their charm, the region now has an extensive network of inns and country hotels that can offer a range of services. *Agriturismo*, or lodging in farmhouses, is now widespread and represents an excellent option not just

Logo of the consortium of Umbria hoteliers

for a brief stay, but for longer holidays, too. In addition to offering accommodation, these places offer facilities for adults and children alike. Hotels suitable for groups – usually built to cater for pilgrimage tour groups – can be found in Umbria's more famous towns. There are also campsites throughout the region, and many towns can accommodate camper vans.

GRADING AND PRICES

HOTELS IN UMBRIA are classified according to the standards followed in the rest of Italy. The categories run from one to five stars, plus a top luxury hotel category (L). Services offered are generally good. Prices vary according to the season and are higher during festivals and major cultural events. In general, the three-star category offers the best value for money.

Most hotels accept credit cards, except perhaps some in the lower-starred categories. If in doubt, it is best to check beforehand.

BOOKING

UMBRIA DOES not have much of a low season, although visitor numbers drop between November and February. Booking ahead is strongly advised; a fax or an e-mail to confirm the booking is often requested.

HOTELS

WHICHEVER UMBRIAN city or hill town you choose to stay in, various types of accommodation, from luxury hotels to family-run pensions are available. Accommodation lists are published annually, with prices, by the Perugia tourist office (APT), and are available on request.

HISTORIC HOTELS

EVERY TOWN AND VILLAGE in Umbria preserves some trace of the past: a castle, an abbey, or houses once occupied by the nobility. Umbria can offer numerous examples of historic buildings adapted for the purpose of accommodation. They are usually refurbished to the highest standards, with prices to match.

Anyone looking for the tranquillity of a monastery could choose to stay in the 13th-century cloisters of La

A luxury hotel complex created out of 17th-century farm buildings

Badia just outside Orvieto (*see p149*), for example, or in the Eremo delle Grazie near Spoleto (*see p151*). Those aspiring to the role of lord of the manor, on the other hand, could opt for the Villa di Monte Solare in Fontignano (*see p145*). Hotels housed in aristocratic palazzi within town walls include the Hotel Fonte Cesia in Todi (*see p151*) and the Palazzo Dragoni in Spoleto (*see p151*).

AGRITURISMO AND COUNTRY HOUSES

THE FORMULA for *agriturismo* is simple: working farms in the countryside offer rooms and facilities to visitors. Such places can offer guests a unique insight into everyday life in rural Umbria.

The scale ranges from the small family farm able to offer only a handful of rooms to much larger properties, which may be less traditional but can provide a wider range of facilities, such as tennis courts. Many have a children's play area and a swimming pool as well as horses and bikes. The

The welcoming reception area at Le Silve hotel in Assisi

◁ **Market traders in the Piazza del Mercato in Spoleto**

food is authentic and uses local produce (including some from the farm). Across the region, around 5,000 beds in more than 400 farms are available.

Many require a stay of anything from two to seven nights in high season; the price charged for an overnight stay usually includes breakfast.

For a more up-market alternative, choose a country house hotel. Such hotels are also in rural locations but offer more luxurious rooms and restaurants, and provide more sports facilities and perhaps beauty treatments.

The tourist office issues an annual listing of *agriturismo* properties. Two guides, pubished annually but most easily available in Umbria, are: *Agriturist*, published by **Agriturist Umbria**, and *Vacanze e Natura*, published by **Terranostra Umbria**.

CAMPSITES

THERE ARE campsites all over Umbria: all the historic towns have at least one, and the area around Lake Trasimeno has a range of sites suited to tents, camper vans or caravans.

All Umbrian campsites are registered with the authorities and listed in regional tourist guides issued by the Perugia and Terni tourist offices.

Sites are usually clean and well run, and often located in attractive settings. Overnight stops by camper vans are strictly regulated; overnight stays are prohibited in historic centres, while in the modern or less touristy centres there are often designated parking places.

Falconry, available on some farm holidays

Hilltop hamlet converted into agriturismo accommodation

SELF-CATERING APARTMENTS

ONE OPTION DURING the summer months is to rent an apartment, whether it's in a town, a village, by a lake or in the mountains. The demand for apartments in Perugia, largely by students, continues all year round.

There are many agencies that deal with short-term lets; these are listed in the relevant booklets produced by the tourist offices.

LODGINGS FOR PILGRIMS

NUMEROUS religious communities offer simple accommodation to visitors. This may be in the form of a no-frills hotel, but some convents or monasteries provide special lodgings for pilgrims. There is a wide choice in Assisi, a major pilgrimage destination, but it is also worth looking in much smaller places, such as Bevagna or Spello. Meals are not normally provided, with the exception of the busy hostels in Assisi. The accommodation lists supplied by the tourist office are the best source of information.

YOUTH HOSTELS AND STUDENT ACCOMMODATION

PERUGIA, a university town, has youth hostels and student accommodation of various types: for sources of information, *see p175*.

BED & BREAKFAST

ESTABLISHMENTS OFFERING bed-and-breakfast accommodation are found mainly in Umbria's historic towns. This can often turn out to be both a comfortable and economical choice.

Some bed-and-breakfasts exist in the countryside, but, unlike farms involved in *agriturismo*, they cannot provide an evening meal.

Swimming pool at Le Casette agriturismo near Montecchio

Choosing a Hotel

THESE HOTELS HAVE BEEN selected across a wide price range for their good value, facilities and location. They are listed by area, corresponding to the sightseeing regions in this guide. Use the colour-coded thumb tabs, which indicate the areas covered on each page, to guide you to the relevant sections of the chart. Towns or villages are listed in alphabetical order.

	CREDIT CARDS	GARDEN OR TERRACE	SWIMMING POOL	PARKING	RESTAURANT OR BAR
NORTHERN UMBRIA					
ASSISI: *La Castellana di Milena Salari (Agriturismo)* € Costa di Trex 4. **(** *075 801 9046 or 360 71 4672.* **FAX** *075 801 9046.* W *www.agriturismolacastellana.it* Relaxing 14th-century farmhouse just outside Assisi, on the Sentiero della Pace. Archery, art and meditation courses on offer. ⚏ 🛏 **Rooms:** *6.*	AE DC MC V	●		●	
ASSISI: *Country House 3 Esse* € Via Di Valecchie 41. **(** *075 81 6363.* **FAX** *075 81 6155.* W *www.countryhousetreesse.com* Less than a kilometre from the centre of Assisi, this 1920s villa is set among peaceful countryside. Rooms are furnished with antiques. 🗐 🛏 **Rooms:** *15.*	AE DC MC V	●	■	●	■
ASSISI: *Castel San Gregorio* €€ San Gregorio 16/a. **(** *075 803 8009.* **FAX** *075 803 8904.* ● *mid-Jan–early Feb.* This small medieval castle is surrounded by a large park, some 8 km (5 miles) northwest of Assisi. The rooms have an age-old fascination, with antique furniture and bathrooms set into the circular towers. 🛏 **Rooms:** *12.*	AE DC MC V	●		●	■
ASSISI: *Hotel Umbra* €€ Via degli Archi 6. **(** *075 81 2240.* **FAX** *075 81 3653.* W *www.hotelumbra.it* ● *Jan–Feb.* A delightful hotel in the historic centre with spacious rooms and small balconies. The garden and the terrace are very pleasant and the kitchen offers good regional cooking. 🗐 **Rooms:** *25.*	AE DC MC V	●			■
ASSISI: *Locanda dell'Angelo (Agriturismo)* €€ Via Mora 24. **(** **FAX** *075 803 9780.* @ *locandangelo@libero.it* Growing vines, olives and fruit, and raising horses, sheep and pigs are among the agricultural activities going on at this farm The main house is an 18th-century villa, located within the park of Monte Subasio. Sales of oil, wine, jam and honey. ⚅ ⚏ 🕱 🅄 🛏 **Rooms:** *11.* **Apartments:** *1.*	AE DC MC V	●	■	●	■
ASSISI: *Il Noceto Umbro (Agriturismo)* €€ Petrignano, Via Campagna 43. **(** **FAX** *075 800 0838.* W *www.ilnocetoumbro.com* An estate of 6 ha (15 acres), about 5 km (3 miles) west of Assisi, devoted to the cultivation of fruit, cereal crops and vegetables. Guests are accommodated in restored farm buildings, each room with a private bathroom. Sales of jam, fruit and honey. ⚅ ⚏ 🕱 🅄 **Rooms:** *7.*	AE DC MC V	●	■	●	
ASSISI: *Le Silve di Armenzano* €€€ Caparrochie, Frazione Armenzano. **(** *075 801 9000.* **FAX** *075 801 9005.* W *www.lesilve.it* ● *mid-Nov–mid-Mar.* A lovely farmhouse converted for 21st-century needs. In a gorgeous spot 10 km (6 miles) east of Assisi. Good service. **Rooms:** *13.*	AE DC MC V	●	■	●	■
ASSISI: *Subasio* €€€€ Via Frate Elia 2. **(** *075 812 206.* **FAX** *075 816 691.* A historic hotel located near the St Francis basilica. Cared-for rooms have elegant furniture and furnishings. There is a lovely view from the terrace, where dinner is served in summer. 🗐 🛏 **Rooms:** *61.*	AE DC MC V	●		●	■
BETTONA: *Natura Amica (Agriturismo)* € Fratta, Via dei Cacciatori 7. **(** **FAX** *075 982 922.* ● *Nov–Feb.* Set on a hillside just outside Bettona, the old stone farm buildings have been restored and simply furnished. 🅄 🛏 **Rooms:** *7.* **Apartments:** *3.*		●	■	●	
CASTIGLIONE DEL LAGO: *I Romiti (Agriturismo)* € Vaiano, Via Poggio del Sole 10. **(** *075 952 7216.* **FAX** *075 952 7163.* W *www.romiti.com* This old farmhouse, on a hill near Castiglione del Lago, offers comfortable lodgings, lawn bowling and archery. ⚅ ⚏ 🕱 🛏 **Rooms:** *5.* **Apartments:** *4.*	AE DC MC V	●	■	●	

Price categories for a standard double room per night, with tax, breakfast and service included:

€ under 80 euros
€€ 80–130 euros
€€€ 130–180 euros
€€€€ 180–230 euros
€€€€€ over 230 euros

CREDIT CARDS
Cards accepted: American Express, Diners Club, MasterCard, Visa.
GARDEN OR TERRACE
Hotel with a garden or with a terrace offering good views.
SWIMMING POOL
Unless specified otherwise, this means a pool outdoors.
PARKING
Parking places available inside or outside the hotel.
RESTAURANT OR BAR
Restaurant or bar, open to non-residents as well.

	CREDIT CARDS	GARDEN OR TERRACE	SWIMMING POOL	PARKING	RESTAURANT OR BAR
CASTIGLIONE DEL LAGO: *Agricola Il Melograno (Agriturismo)* €		●	▣		
CASTIGLIONE DEL LAGO: *Miralago* €€	AE DC MC V	●			▣
CITTÀ DELLA PIEVE: *Antica Frateria (Agriturismo)* €€	AE DC MC V	●	▣	●	▣
CITTÀ DI CASTELLO: *La Valle dei Falchi (Agriturismo)* €€	AE DC MC V	●	▣	●	▣
COSTACCIARO: *Oasi Madre del Buon Consiglio (Agriturismo)* €€		●			
DERUTA: *Il Pino (Agriturismo)* €		●	▣	●	▣
FONTIGNANO: *Villa di Monte Solare* €€€	AE DC MC V	●	▣	●	▣
GUBBIO: *La Ginestra (Agriturismo)* €	AE DC MC V	●	▣	●	
GUBBIO: *Oderisi-Balestrieri* €		●			
GUBBIO: *Semidimela (Agriturismo)* €	AE DC MC V	●	▣	●	▣

CASTIGLIONE DEL LAGO: *Agricola Il Melograno (Agriturismo)* €
Ferretto, Via dei Pieracci. **FAX** *057 821 459 or 057 821 459.*
W www.kou.net/melograno
An 18th-century farmhouse on a hill within the Parco del Trasimeno, where fallow deer and moufflon are raised. Fitness courses, music, fishing and archery are some of the activities on offer. Honey, jam, cheese, oil and wine are on sale. **Rooms: 5. Apartments: 5.**

CASTIGLIONE DEL LAGO: *Miralago* €€
Piazza Mazzini 6. *075 951 157.* W www.miralago.com Jan–Feb.
In a lovely spot on the shores of Lake Trasimeno, the Miralago is a small and friendly family-run hotel. There is also a very good restaurant serving fish-based dishes. **Rooms: 19.**

CITTÀ DELLA PIEVE: *Antica Frateria (Agriturismo)* €€
Poggio al Piano 44. *057 829 8805.* **FAX** *057 829 7055.* W www.anticafrateria.it
An old friary set in 24 ha (59 acres) of grounds devoted to growing olives, fruit, vegetable and forage crops. All sorts of activities available, including cookery courses. **Rooms: 5. Apartments: 1.**

CITTÀ DI CASTELLO: *La Valle dei Falchi (Agriturismo)* €€
Felcino Candeggio. **FAX** *075 852 6184.* W www.lavalledeifalchi.com
Housed in an old princely residence in the state forest of Candeleto-Pietralunga, where birds of prey are raised. Activities include archery and falconry courses. **Apartments: 6.**

COSTACCIARO: *Oasi Madre del Buon Consiglio (Agriturismo)* €€
Chiascio Grande. **FAX** *075 917 0780.* @ kjsdpe@tin.it
This estate, close to the park of Monte Cucco, is devoted to raising animals and growing cereal crops. There's bowling and table tennis as well as courses in cookery and the study of medicinal herbs. **Apartments: 4.**

DERUTA: *Il Pino (Agriturismo)* €
Via Castelleone. *075 870 7338 or 971 06 03.* **FAX** *075 870 7338.*
W www.agriturismoilpino.com
Renovated cottages within an area used for hunting. There is a small lake for fishing and a bowling alley. Riding holidays, art and pottery classes. Sales of honey, oil, wine and jam. **Rooms: 2. Apartments: 1.**

FONTIGNANO: *Villa di Monte Solare* €€€
Colle San Paolo, Via Montali 7. *075 832 376.* **FAX** *075 835 5462.*
W www.villamontesolare.it Dec–Jan.
This charming 18th-century villa south of Lake Trasimeno has many original features: terracotta floors, furniture and frescoes. **Rooms: 24.**

GUBBIO: *La Ginestra (Agriturismo)* €
Santa Cristina, Colonnata 18, Valmarcola. **FAX** *075 920 088.*
W www.agriturismolaginestra.it
These stone cottages, just south of Gubbio, are equipped with every kind of comfort. Courses wrought-iron work and weaving can be taken as an alternative to outdoor activities. **Rooms: 6. Apartments: 3.**

GUBBIO: *Oderisi-Balestrieri* €
Via Mazzatinti 2/12. *075 922 0662.* **FAX** *075 922 0663.* W www.rosatihotels.com
Located in the medieval town, this hotel offers comfortable rooms with wood prevalent, in the beds, tables and beams. Polite staff. **Rooms: 35.**

GUBBIO: *Semidimela (Agriturismo)* €
Scritto, Petroia 36. **FAX** *075 920 039.* W www.semidimela.com
Jan–mid-Mar.
This 18th-century cottage just south of Gubbio has rustically furnished rooms (each with bathroom), in keeping with the rest of the building and the delightful setting. Home cooking with vegetarian specials. **Rooms: 8.**

Price categories for a standard double room per night, with tax, breakfast and service included:
€ under 70 euros
€€ 80–130 euros
€€€ 130–180 euros
€€€€ 180–230 euros
€€€€€ over 230 euros

CREDIT CARDS
Cards accepted: American Express, Diners Club, MasterCard, Visa.
GARDEN OR TERRACE
Hotel with a garden or with a terrace offering good views.
SWIMMING POOL
Unless specified otherwise, this means a pool outdoors.
PARKING
Parking places available inside or outside the hotel.
RESTAURANT OR BAR
Restaurant or bar, open to non-residents as well.

GUBBIO: *Bosone Palace* €€
Via XX Settembre 22. ☎ 075 922 0688. FAX 075 922 0552.
W www.mencarelligroup.com
Housed in Palazzo Raffaelli, one of the oldest palazzi in the historic centre, the Bosone has comfortable rooms, decorated in different styles. The atmosphere is relaxing and cordial. Rooms: 30.

Credit Cards: — | Garden or Terrace: ● | Swimming Pool: — | Parking: ● | Restaurant or Bar: ■

GUBBIO: *Villa Montegranelli* €€
Monteluiano. ☎ 075 922 0185. FAX 075 927 3372. W www.villamontegranelli.it
A noble country residence dating from the late 18th century, 4 km (2 miles) from Gubbio. Both the suites and the rooms are well cared for and have a lovely view over the surrounding countryside. Rooms: 21.

Credit Cards: AE DC MC V | Garden or Terrace: ● | Swimming Pool: — | Parking: ● | Restaurant or Bar: ■

MAGIONE: *Casale Il Picchio (Agriturismo)* €€
Via Case Sparse 58, Montecolognola. ☎ 075 84 1595. FAX 075 847 8630.
W www.casaleilpicchio.it
A typical Umbrian farmhouse situated on a hillside near Lake Trasimeno and with 10 ha (25 acres) of land given over to olive trees. The olive oil produced on the farm is on sale to guests. Apartments: 4.

Credit Cards: — | Garden or Terrace: ● | Swimming Pool: ■ | Parking: ● | Restaurant or Bar: —

MARSCIANO: *Torre Colombaia (Agriturismo)* €
San Biagio della Valle. ☎ FAX 075 878 7381. W www.torrecolombaia.it
An organic farm in the hills, equidistant from Marsciano, Perugia and Lake Trasimeno, with lodgings in an 18th-century farmhouse. There are courses in organic agriculture for those who are interested. Good food using organic produce. Apartments: 8.

Credit Cards: — | Garden or Terrace: ● | Swimming Pool: — | Parking: — | Restaurant or Bar: ■

MONTE SANTA MARIA TIBERINA: *I Muri (Agriturismo)* €
Gioiello, I Muri. ☎ 075 857 1001 or 349 883 0867. FAX 075 857 1077.
W www.imuriagriturismo.com
Rural but comfortable cottages in the hills west of Città di Castello, all with a private bathroom. Guests can take part in theatre sessions and courses in cooking, embroidery and sewing. Sales of oil, wine, dessert wines, spirits and jam. Rooms: 6. Apartments: 3.

Credit Cards: — | Garden or Terrace: ● | Swimming Pool: ■ | Parking: ● | Restaurant or Bar: ■

NOCERA UMBRA: *Villa della Cupa (Agriturismo)* €
Via Colle 141. ☎ 074 281 0666 or 074 281 0329. FAX 074 281 0666.
W www.villadellacupa.it
Built from rose-coloured stone, this villa has welcoming rooms, all with bathrooms. Natural remedies based on clay are made and sold here, and courses of lectures on the countryside as well as nature trails are also on offer. Rooms: 19.

Credit Cards: — | Garden or Terrace: ● | Swimming Pool: — | Parking: ● | Restaurant or Bar: ■

PACIANO: *Locanda della Rocca* €€
Via Roma 4. ☎ 075 830 236. FAX 075 830 155. W www.locandadellaroccabuitoni.it
⬤ Jan–Feb.
Just south of Lake Trasimeno, this is a charming inn, created from an old stone house and watermill. The suite, built in a 17th-century tower with panoramic windows, is lovely; the dining room is in the old cellars. Rooms: 10. Apartments: 1.

Credit Cards: AE DC MC V | Garden or Terrace: ● | Swimming Pool: — | Parking: ● | Restaurant or Bar: ■

PERUGIA: *La Pernice (Agriturismo)* €
Monte Petriolo, Via dei Muri 1. ☎ FAX 075 600 132. W www.umbriamaison.it
Agriturismo in the hills, with apartments created from a typical Umbrian stone house. Rooms are rustic and simply furnished. Apartments: 4.

Credit Cards: AE DC MC V | Garden or Terrace: ● | Swimming Pool: ■ | Parking: ● | Restaurant or Bar: —

PERUGIA: *Il Rosciolo (Agriturismo)* €
Piccione, Strada per Fratticiola Selvatica, 1. ☎ 075 603 530.
FAX 075 603 9140. @ ilrosciolo@libero.it
Some 16 km (10 miles) northeast of Perugia, this farmhouse offers all kinds of facilities, including guided walks and archery. There is an adult and children's pool. Sales of produce from the estate. Rooms: 9.

Credit Cards: AE DC MC V | Garden or Terrace: ● | Swimming Pool: ■ | Parking: ● | Restaurant or Bar: ■

PERUGIA: *Lo Spedalicchio* €€
Ospedalicchio, Piazza Bruno Buozzi 3. 📞 FAX 075 801 0323. W www.lospedalicchio.it
Midway between Perugia and Assisi The rooms in Lo Spedalicchio,
built within the walls of a 14th-century fortress, are simple, comfortable
and tastefully furnished. Good value for money. Rooms: 25.

PERUGIA: *Locanda della Posta* €€€
Corso Vannucci 97. 📞 075 572 8925. FAX 075 573 2562.
An old staging post, housed in an important palazzo in Perugia's historic
centre. Much of the original furnishing has been maintained intact and
some rooms even have valuable frescoes. 🗐 🔟 Rooms: 39.

PERUGIA: *Relais San Clemente* €€€ AE DC MC V
Bosco. 📞 075 501 5100. FAX 075 591 5001. W www.relais.it
This hotel, east of Perugia on the Gubbio road, is housed in a lovely villa
named after the church that forms part of the complex. A swimming pool,
tennis courts and mountain bike trails are provided within the large and
delightful gardens. 🏊 🔟 🗐 🔟 Rooms: 64.

PERUGIA: *Castello dell'Oscano* €€€€ AE DC MC V
Cenerente, Strada Forcella 37. 📞 075 584 371. FAX 075 690 066.
W www.oscano.com
Surrounded by a forest of ancient oaks and sequoias, just north of Perugia,
Oscano is an old manor house, converted into a delightful hotel. The
rooms and suites are sumptuously decorated. 🗐 Rooms: 22.

PERUGIA: *Brufani* €€€€€ AE DC MC V
Piazza Italia 12. 📞 075 573 2541. FAX 075 572 0210. W www.sinahotels.com
The rooms in this luxury hotel, which opened in 1884, were painted by
Lillis, the German designer. The panorama is stupendous, and it is just a
short stroll to the principal sights. Rooms: 94.

PIEGARO: *Bulletta (Agriturismo)* € AE DC MC V
Castiglion Fosco, Via Fontana. 📞 075 839 259 or 075 839 496.
FAX 075 839 7035.
Lying in the hills east of Piegaro, south of Lake Trasimeno the farm grows
vines, olives, fruit and grain, and raises animals. Accommodation is
available in a series of 17th-century stone farm buildings. One of the
apartments is equipped for the disabled. 🏊 🔟 🔟 Apartments: 5.

PIETRALUNGA: *Sant'Andrea (Agriturismo)* € AE DC MC V
Sant'Andrea Alessandro 7. 📞 FAX 075 933 058. W casadellapace.org
Rooms with shared facilities in an old stone village, and courses in
meditation, yoga and self-awareness. Organic and vegetarian food, using
tofu and vegetables from the garden. 🏊 🔟 Rooms: 8.

UMBERTIDE: *Caigherardi (Agriturismo)* €
Via Bacciana 2/A. 📞 FAX 075 930 6257.
In the hills near Montone, just north of Umbertide, stands this old house in
brick and stone, with welcoming and stylishly furnished apartments. The
farm produces wine and tobacco and raises livestock. Guests are invited
to take part in farm life. 🏊 Apartments: 7.

UMBERTIDE: *La Chiusa (Agriturismo)* €€
Niccone 353. 📞 075 941 0848. FAX 075 941 0774. W www.lachiusa.com
Agriturismo in the Valle del Niccone on the borders with Tuscany, in an old
farmhouse surrounded by green countryside. Spacious, well-maintained
rooms. Cookery courses available. 🏊 Rooms: 4. Apartments: 1.

UMBERTIDE: *Fattoria del Cerretino (Agriturismo)* €€
Calzolaro, Via Colonnata 3. 📞 075 930 2166. W www.cerretino.it
Restored apartments and rooms in a farm complex in a hilltop village
overlooking the Alta Val Tiberina. Wine, sweet vin santo, honey and olive
oil for sale, as well as truffles in season. Traditional local cooking. Fishing.
🏊 🏊 🔟 🔟 🔟 🔟 Rooms: 3. Apartments: 7.

SOUTHERN UMBRIA

AMELIA: *Azienda Agrituristica Oliveto (Agriturismo)* €
Strada di Cecanibbio 38. 📞 0744 981 101. W agriturismooliveto.it
In a tranquil and sunny setting, six cosy apartments in old stone farm
buildings clustered around a pool. Cookery lessons are on offer as well as
the opportunity to join in the grape or olive harvests, or corn-reaping.
🏊 🔟 Apartments: 6.

Price categories for a standard double room per night, with tax, breakfast and service included:

€ under 80 euros
€€ 80–130 euros
€€€ 130–180 euros
€€€€ 180–230 euros
€€€€€ over 230 euros

CREDIT CARDS
Cards accepted: American Express, Diners Club, MasterCard, Visa.
GARDEN OR TERRACE
Hotel with a garden or with a terrace offering good views.
SWIMMING POOL
Unless specified otherwise, this means a pool outdoors.
PARKING
Parking places available inside or outside the hotel.
RESTAURANT OR BAR
Restaurant or bar, open to non-residents as well.

	CREDIT CARDS	GARDEN OR TERRACE	SWIMMING POOL	PARKING	RESTAURANT OR BAR
BASCHI: *Pomurlo Vecchio (Agriturismo)* € Lago di Corbara, Pomurlo Vecchio. 074 495 0190. FAX 074 495 0500. W www.pomurlovecchio-lecasette.it A restored 13th-century farmhouse in a hillside setting, within the Parco Fluviale del Tevere, 5 km (3 miles) east of Baschi. Services include a reading room, tennis lessons and the sale of farm produce. Fishing. Rooms: 17. Apartments: 2.	AE DC MC V	●	■	●	■
BEVAGNA: *Il Corbezzolo (Agriturismo)* € Castelbuono, Voc. San Sisto 59. 074 236 19 33 or 347 379 72 59. FAX 074 236 90 42. W www.ilcorbezzolo.it This hillside farm offers lodgings in a carefully restored stone farmhouse, furnished in Umbrian style. Rooms: 6.	AE DC MC V	●	■		■
CALVI DELL'UMBRIA: *San Martino (Agriturismo)* € Colle San Martino 10. 074 471 0644 or 368 435 100. FAX 074 471 0644. W www.guesthousetravel.com This farm, run on organic principles, lies in the far southern tip of Umbria, some 20 km (12 miles) south of Narni. The rooms for guests are housed in a restored farmhouse. Apartments: 4.		●	■		■
CAMPELLO SUL CLITUNNO: *Il Vecchio Mulino* €€ Via del Tempio 34. 074 352 1122. FAX 074 327 5097. W www.perugiaonline.com/vecchiomolino ● Nov–Feb. A small inn housed in a 15th-century water mill. Rooms are elegantly and individually furnished. Inside, some of the original mill workings can still be seen. Rooms: 13.	AE DC MC V	●		●	■
CASCIA: *Casale Sant'Antonio (Agriturismo)* € Casali Sant'Antonio 59. 074 376 819 or 074 376 232. A small mountain farmstead, in a natural green oasis, southwest of Cascia; a lovely place for relaxing. Honey and vegetables produced on the farm are on sale. Rooms: 3.	AE DC MC V	●			
CASTEL RITALDI: *Gli Olmi (Agriturismo)* € Torregrosso 43. FAX 074 325 2031 or 074 351 109. W www.aaagriturismo.it This farm lies in the lovely Umbrian hills north of Spoleto. A good base for exploring the local countryside, either on foot or horseback. Rooms: 2. Apartments: 4.		●		●	
DERUTA: *Relais Il Canalicchio* €€€ Collazzone, Canalicchio, Via della Piazza. 075 870 7325. FAX 075 870 7296. W www.relaisilcanalicchio.it Canalicchio is a genuine 11th-century fortified village in a wonderful position south of Deruta. Each room bears the name of a noble personage from the history of the village. Rooms are embellished with antique furniture and fabrics. Rooms: 43. Apartments: 16.		●	■	●	■
FICULLE: *La Casella (Agriturismo)* €€ Strada La Casella, 4. 076 386 684. FAX 076 386 588. W www.lacasella.com About 20 km (12 miles) north of Orvieto, in the Valle del Chiani, stand these four old farmhouses, which have been converted into a welcoming place to stay. La Casella is a large complex offering various sports activities and a health centre for mind and body treatments, including massage. Cookery courses are available. Rooms: 32.		●	■	●	■
MONTECASTRILLI: *Le Macchie (Agriturismo)* € Le Macchie 147. FAX 074 494 0657. W www.paginegialle.it/lemacchie This organic farm, which is devoted to livestock and cheese production, lies in the hills between Acquasparta and Amelia. The guest rooms are in typically Umbrian farm buildings, which have been restored. Cheese and oil are among the products on sale. Rooms: 15.	AE DC MC V	●	■	●	■

MONTECCHIO: *Le Casette (Agriturismo)* € AE DC MC V
Le Casette. **C** *074 495 7645.* **FAX** *074 495 0500.*
W *www.pomurlovecchio-lecasette.it*
This farm is situated south of Lago di Corbara, within the Parco Fluviale del
Tevere. Guests stay in converted stone farm buildings. Good food, with
traditional Umbrian dishes. **Rooms: 16.**

MONTEFALCO: *Ringhiera Umbra* € AE DC MC V
Via Goffredo Mameli 20. **C** *074 237 9166.* **W** *www.ringhieraumbra.com*
This modest hotel in the town centre is part of an old palazzo. Panoramic
views, and well-priced food in the small vaulted restaurant. **Rooms: 11.**

MONTEFALCO: *Villa Pambuffetti* €€€€€
Via della Vittoria 20. **C** *074 237 9417.* **FAX** *074 237 9245.*
W *www.villapambuffetti.com*
This elegant villa has been run by the same family for many years. Visitors
are welcomed as though they are personal guests. The lovely tower suite
has a wonderful panoramic view. **Rooms: 15.**

MONTEFRANCO: *La Vaccheria (Agriturismo)* €
Vaccheria 13, S.S. Valnerina. **C** **FAX** *074 438 7070.*
W *www.digilander.iol.it/lavaccheria*
A farm by the River Nera, 10 km (6 miles) from the Cascata delle
Marmore. Guests are accommodated in a simple but comfortable
building. **Rooms: 16. Apartments: 1.**

MONTEGABBIONE: *Il Colombaio (Agriturismo)* €
Via di Parrano. **C** **FAX** *076 383 8495.* **W** *www.agriturismo.com/colombaio*
Lodgings at Il Colombaio are organized in several early 19th-century stone
houses, in the hills southeast of Città della Pieve. The restaurant is housed
in the old stables, with solid wood furniture and a fireplace.
Rooms: 8.

NARNI: *Colle Abramo delle Vigne (Agriturismo)* €
Vigne, strada di Colle Abramo. **C** *074 479 6428 or 335 529 1135.*
FAX *074 479 6428.* **W** *www.colleabramo.com*
This farm is a few kilometres south of Narni, in open country in the lower
Nera valley. The rooms are well equipped and there is lots to do: table
tennis, table football, volleyball, archery, courses in furniture restoring
and, on request, rally driving in jeeps on dirt roads. Wine and oil are on
sale. **Rooms: 5.**

NORCIA: *Il Casale nel Parco (Agriturismo)* € AE DC MC V
Fontevena. **C** **FAX** *0743 816 481.* **W** *www.casalenelparco.com*
About a kilometre north of Norcia and framed by the Monti Sibillini, this
ancient stone farmhouse has been carefully restored. Facilities include trips
to the Monti Sibillini National Park, lawn bowling, table tennis and archery.
Salami, olive oil, lentils and honey for sale. **Rooms: 5.**

NORCIA: *Garden* € AE DC MC V
Viale XX Settembre 2b. **C** **FAX** *0743 816 687.* **W** *www.nursia.com*
This hotel is close to the historic centre of Norcia, in an excellent position
for visiting the city. Simple but welcoming rooms. **Rooms: 43.**

ORVIETO: *Corbara (Agriturismo)* €
Corbara. **C** *0763 304 003.* **FAX** *0763 304 152.* **W** *www.tenutadicorbara.it*
A stone's throw from the Lago di Corbara and the Tiber, both easily
reached on horseback: one of the many activities on offer. Accommodation
is in converted farm buildings. **Rooms: 5. Apartments: 6.**

ORVIETO: *L'Elmo (Agriturismo)* € AE DC MC V
Via San Faustino 18. **C** *0763 215 219 or 0347 228 4907.* **FAX** *076 321 5790.*
W *www.lelmo.it*
A peaceful atmosphere is guaranteed at L'Elmo. The food is
authentically Umbrian, from the home-made bread and pasta to the
wine. Cookery courses and art classes are available.
Rooms: 3. Apartments: 4.

ORVIETO: *Fattoria di Titignano (Agriturismo)* €€ AE DC MC V
Titignano, Prodo. **C** **FAX** *076 330 8 22.* **W** *www.titignano.it*
A large farm set against the lovely backdrop of Titignano, a medieval
village surrounded by green hills just north of Lago di Corbara. Rooms are
furnished in elegant rustic style, with locally made furniture and fireplaces.
Rooms: 6.

Price categories for a standard double room per night, with tax, breakfast and service included:

€ under 80 euros
€€ 80–130 euros
€€€ 130–180 euros
€€€€ 180–230 euros
€€€€€ over 230 euros

CREDIT CARDS
Cards accepted: American Express, Diners Club, MasterCard, Visa.
GARDEN OR TERRACE
Hotel with a garden or with a terrace offering good views.
SWIMMING POOL
Unless specified otherwise, this means a pool outdoors.
PARKING
Parking places available inside or outside the hotel.
RESTAURANT OR BAR
Restaurant or bar, open to non-residents as well.

	CREDIT CARDS	GARDEN OR TERRACE	SWIMMING POOL	PARKING	RESTAURANT OR BAR

ORVIETO: *Virgilio* €
Piazza Duomo 5/6. [0763 341 882. FAX 0763 343 797. W www.hotelvirgilio.com
● Jan–Feb.
This modest but comfortable hotel is in a central location. Some rooms have a good view of the cathedral. ▸ Rooms: 13.
Credit cards: AE DC MC V

ORVIETO: *Villa Ciconia* €€
Orvieto Scalo, Ciconia. [0763 305 582. FAX 0763 302 077.
W www.hotelvillaciconia.com
This lovely riverside villa is an oasis in an unpromising location just north Orvieto. Rooms have terracotta floors and four-poster beds in wrought iron, and several retain their 16th-century frescoes. ▤ Rooms: 12.
Credit cards: AE DC MC V · Garden or terrace · Parking · Restaurant or bar

ORVIETO: *La Badia* €€€
La Badia. [0763 301 959. FAX 0763 305 396. W www.labadiahotel.it ● Jan–Feb.
This elegant inn is housed in a 13th-century abbey 5 km (3 miles) south of town, with tennis courts, swimming pool and a lovely view of Orvieto and the surrounding hills. Service is very good, as is the food. ▤ Rooms: 28.
Credit cards: AE DC MC V · Garden or terrace · Swimming pool · Parking · Restaurant or bar

OTRICOLI: *Brincadeira (Agriturismo)* €
Vallefigliola 152. [FAX 074 471 9550. W www.brincadeira.it
Just 30 minutes from Rome. Visitors are surrounded by the old Wild West, with rooms completely done out in perfect country style. There are horses and a saloon where good tex-mex food is served. Rooms: 3.
Garden or terrace · Parking · Restaurant or bar

PARRANO: *Il Poggiolo di Parrano (Agriturismo)* €
Bagni, S.P. Parranese km 8.5. [0763 838 471 or 0368 305 7435.
FAX 0763 838 776. W www.ilpoggiolo.com
This 19th-century farm north of Orvieto has tasteful rooms. There is an astronomical telescope for star-watching, and guests can use the nearby thermal pools of San Casciano. Rooms: 1. Apartments: 4.
Credit cards: AE DC MC V · Garden or terrace · Swimming pool · Parking · Restaurant or bar

SPELLO: *Le Due Torri (Agriturismo)* €
Via Torre Quadrato 1. [0742 651 249 or 0330 646 124. FAX 0743 270 273.
W www.seeumbria.com
These farm buildings on the edge of Spello are built of the pink stone of Monte Subasio and are perfect for people who love peaceful surroundings. Wine, vinegar, olive oil and honey are produced and sold here. Rooms: 5. Apartments: 5.
Credit cards: AE DC MC V · Garden or terrace · Parking · Restaurant or bar

SPELLO: *La Bastiglia* €€
Via dei Molini 17. [074 265 1277. FAX 074 230 1159. W www.labastiglia.com
● Jan–Feb, Jul.
Formerly a stone mill, La Bastiglia is now a small, charming hotel in Spello's old centre. Lovely views over the countryside from the spacious rooms on the top floor and from the large garden terrace. ▤ Rooms: 33.
Garden or terrace · Swimming pool · Parking · Restaurant or bar

SPELLO: *Palazzo Bocci* €€€
Via Cavour 17. [0742 301 021. FAX 0742 301 464. W www.palazzobocci.com
Modern fittings have been tastefully used in this elegant period residence, with stuccoes of landscapes on the lounge walls, some antique furniture in the rooms and a terrace overlooking Spello's rooftops. ▤ Rooms: 23.
Credit cards: AE DC MC V · Garden or terrace · Parking · Restaurant or bar

SPOLETO: *Il Casale Grande (Agriturismo)* €
Beroide, Via San Paolo di Beroide 16. [0743 275 780. FAX 0743 270 273.
W www.seeumbria.com
This farm west of the Fonti del Clitunno offers accommodation in 19th-century farm buildings. Olive oil for sale. Apartments: 4.
Credit cards: AE DC MC V · Garden or terrace · Swimming pool · Parking · Restaurant or bar

SPOLETO: *Aurora* €
Via Apollinare 3. [0743 220 315. FAX 0743 221 885. W www.hotelauroraspoleto.it
A hotel in the historic centre. Functional rooms equipped with a minibar. Linked to the excellent Apollinare restaurant. Rooms: 23.
Restaurant or bar

Spoleto: *Charleston* €€
Piazza Collicola 10. **(** 0743 220 052. **FAX** 0743 221 244. **W** www.hotelcharleston.it
The Charleston is located in a 17th-century palazzo in the centre of
Spoleto. Both modern and traditional furnishing. Relaxing family
atmosphere. **▤ ✛ Rooms:** 21.

Spoleto: *Gattapone* €€€
Via del Ponte 6. **(** 0743 223 447. **FAX** 0743 223 448. **W** www.hotelgattapone.it
This historic Spoleto hotel is high up enough to offer lovely views over
the city. Rooms combine functionality with aesthetics, featuring a blend
of modern fittings and some antique pieces. **✛ Rooms:** 15.

Spoleto: *Palazzo Dragoni* €€€
Via del Duomo 13. **(** 0743 222 220. **FAX** 0743 222 225.
This 16th-century period residence is in the medieval heart of Spoleto.
Public areas consist of delightful rooms with arched windows. The suites
and rooms are beautifully decorated. **▤ ✛ Rooms:** 15.

Spoleto: *Eremo delle Grazie* €€€€
Monteluco. **(** 0743 49 624. **FAX** 0743 49 650. **W** www.eremodellegrazie.it
Up a winding road east of Spoleto is an ancient hermitage that has been
converted into a luxury hotel. The rooms are converted monks' cells, and
the public areas are embellished with antiques, making this as much a
museum as a hotel. **✛ Rooms:** 9 suites.

Todi: *San Lorenzo Tre* €€€
Via San Lorenzo 3. **(FAX** 075 894 4555. **W** www.todi.net/lorenzo ● mid-Jan–Feb.
This delightful pensione occupies a 17th-century palazzo in a small street
in the centre of Todi and is ideal for anyone who doesn't want to spend a
great deal but wants to be in the heart of the old town. Immaculate rooms
with 19th-century furnishings. **Rooms:** 6.

Todi: *Tenuta di Canonica (Agriturismo)* €€
Canonica 75/76. **(** 075 894 7545. **FAX** 075 894 7581.
W www.tenutadicanonica.com
This hotel has been charmingly converted from a medieval lookout tower,
from which there are wonderful views over Todi and the lake of Caldara.
This building and the adjacent main house have bedrooms, a small library,
a TV room with video and a pretty dining room. **⚡ ✈ ᴓ ✛ Rooms:** 11.

Todi: *Hotel Bramante* €€€
Via Orvietana 48. **(** 075 894 8381. **FAX** 075 894 8074. **W** www.hotelbramante.it
Set in rolling parkland on Todi's hillside, in a converted 12th-century
convent, with beautifully furnished rooms with every comfort. Within easy
walking distance of Todi's historic centre. **▮ ☢ Rooms:** 57.

Todi: *Fonte Cesia* €€€
Via Leonj 3. **(** 075 894 3737. **FAX** 075 894 4677. **W** www.fontecesia.it
This smart hotel is situated in a palazzo in the historic centre of Todi,
with elegantly tasteful and comfortable rooms and lounges with armchairs,
divans and antique furniture. The restaurant is located in the palace's old
cellars. **▤ Rooms:** 34.

Todi: *Relais Todini* €€€
Collevalenza, Cervara. **(** 075 887 521. **FAX** 075 887 182.
W www.relaistodini.com
Just south of Todi, this splendid hotel is housed in a superbly furnished
14th-century palace. It is part of a large estate, with a wildlife reserve,
exotic animals, rare plants and lakes where guests can go boating. Lovely
views of Todi and the surrounding hills. **☢ ᴓ ▤ Rooms:** 12.

Torgiano: *Le Tre Vaselle* €€€€
Via Giuseppe Garibaldi 48. **(** 075 988 0447. **FAX** 075 988 0214.
W www.3vaselle.it
One of the most enchanting hotels in Umbria, housed in an old noble
residence in the famous wine-producing area of Torgiano. It is elegantly
furnished, with fireplaces and beamed ceilings in the lounges and
bedrooms. Minibus service to Perugia and Assisi. **☢ Rooms:** 60.

Trevi: *I Mandorli* €
Bovara, Fondaccio 6. **(FAX** 0742 786 69. **W** www.seeumbria.com/mandorli
Guests are accommodated in rooms and apartments in medieval stone
buildings located next to the main house. Guests may also use the library.
⚡ ᴓ ✛ Rooms: 6. **Apartments:** 3.

For key to symbols see back flap

WHERE TO EAT

ONE OF THE main reasons to visit Umbria is in order to experience the excellent food. A land of robust flavours and old culinary traditions, Umbria is brimming with trattorias and restaurants where you can taste the local produce. Trattorias are usually family-run and less smart than restaurants, but also decidedly cheaper. As far as high-class restaurants are concerned, Umbria has made great strides forward in recent years: there

Ciaramicola, a Carnival cake

are now some very elegant and prestigious restaurants. The region's numerous local festivals and fairs also offer the opportunity to try all sorts of regional produce; some may be devoted to a particular crop such as chestnuts, truffles or olives. *Agriturismo* (farm lodgings) also offers visitors an excellent opportunity to taste good and authentic Umbrian food, cooked in a farmhouse kitchen using produce from the farm.

OPENING HOURS AND PRICES

RESTAURANT AND trattoria opening hours in Umbria are similar to those found all over central Italy. Generally, lunch is served from noon to 2:30pm, and evening meals from 7pm onwards – this is to cater for tourists used to eating earlier than Umbrians, who tend not to go out to eat before 8:30pm. Closing times depend on the season and on the type of place: earlier for trattorias and in winter, later in summer and in smarter restaurants in historic centres.

Prices obviously vary enormously. In some famous restaurants the bill can easily exceed 50 euros per person, excluding wine, while in a village trattoria you can usually eat for 15–17 euros per person. It is customary to offer 5–10 per cent of the final bill as a tip.

Restaurants in the larger towns usually close for a spell during the winter and for one full day each week. However, many never close at all.

The Osteria del Teatro in Foligno (p163), decorated in rustic fashion

THE PRODUCE OF UMBRIA

THE COOKERY of Umbria consists of dishes deriving from an ancient tradition, occasionally re-interpreted by chefs. The region yields excellent produce of all kinds, from crops cultivated using the latest methods to those grown according to ancient tradition.

Umbrian wine and olive oil are today among the best-known and most respected anywhere, and this is also the region where some of the

world's best truffles, both black and white types, and best cured meats can be found. The tiny village of Castelluccio in the Monti Sibillini even gives its name to a renowned and tasty variety of lentil.

Good freshwater fish come from Lake Trasimeno and other lakes around Umbria, while excellent meats are brought in from the neighbouring region of Le Marche.

TOP RESTAURANTS

IN RESPONSE TO THE growing number of discerning tourists, several prestigious restaurants have opened in Umbria. Such places alone can make a trip to the region worthwhile.

The most famous of these is the restaurant of chef Gianfranco Vissani, in Baschi on the shores of Lago di Corbara (see p161), but there are other restaurants worthy of note, including the Postale of Marco Bistarelli in Città di Castello (see p157). Tables at these and other top-class restaurants are in high demand, so booking ahead as far as possible is a necessity.

TRATTORIAS

MORE MODEST, but certainly still interesting for lovers of good food, the typical

Specialities of the Lake Trasimeno area, including local wine and oil

Relaxing outside a restaurant in the heart of Assisi

Umbrian trattoria was once found in every town and village. Sadly, however, the proliferation of fast food outlets and pizzerias catering to tourists has elbowed out many traditional restaurants.

The best way to find an old-fashioned trattoria is to ask around among the locals. The older generation in particular prefer this kind of restaurant to a touristy place.

AGRITURISMO

THE FOOD SERVED on farms catering for tourists is often derived from the fresh ingredients produced on the owner's land. Menus are often varied and well-flavoured. Furthermore, the properties often have lots of space, as well as play areas, perfect for small children who grow restless at the table.

COOKERY COURSES

NUMEROUS COOKERY schools, where professionals and amateurs can learn the secrets of Umbria's traditional cuisine, have opened up in recent years. Some *agriturismo* farms also run cookery courses.

BARS AND CAFÉS

EVERY DAY spent in an Umbrian city should begin with a coffee. A bar or café in one of Umbria's famous medieval piazzas will tend to charge higher prices, but the chance to sit and appreciate an unrivalled setting is usually worth the extra cost. Italians like to read the newspaper at

the bar and chat to the other customers. The better cafés also offer a selection of cakes and pastries, as well as home-made ice creams.

A baker's stall at the Mercato delle Gaite festival, Bevagna

LOCAL FESTIVALS

A GOOD OPPORTUNITY to try local specialities and local wines is provided by the traditional fairs and festivals which are held in towns and villages all over Umbria. Such events are always crowded

with visitors, not just Italians. People flock to Norcia (in February) and Città di Castello (in November) to taste the precious truffle, for example, while wine is the attraction at Todi and Torgiano, olives at Spello and "caciucco" (a soup made with lake fish) at Lake Trasimeno.

One event of great interest is the Mercato delle Gaite in Bevagna *(see p104)*. For a full week, the town reverts to the dress and ways of the 14th and 15th centuries, and the local restaurants offer tasty menus that feature ancient dishes and unusual flavours.

In general, prices for food at festival stalls are moderate compared with those charged in a regular restaurant or trattoria; and the atmosphere is sure to be lively as well as of historical interest.

DISABLED PEOPLE

MORE AND MORE places in Umbria, including some of the smarter restaurants, are upgrading their buildings in order to facilitate access for the disabled. Even so, the streets can be steep in Umbria's medieval hill towns, and steps are common.

SMOKING

AS IN MANY other parts of Italy, restaurants do not often have separate areas for smokers and non smokers. This is often because the eating area is simply too small.

The Festa di San Benedetto in Norcia, held in March

What to Eat and Drink

Moraiolo olives

Pasta, soups, meat and fish make up the typical gastronomic fare of central Italy, and of Umbria. Some flavours are very traditional, such as spelt, lentils, sausages and cured meats (especially in Norcia), wild boar and fish from Lake Trasimeno. Breads and cakes follow the peasant tradition: pizza, flat breads and sweet focaccia finished with sugared almonds, raisins and pine nuts.

Black truffle on crostini is a cheaper but still good way to eat this delicacy.

CEREALS AND VEGETABLES

Many farms in hilly areas grow cereals such as barley and spelt (a type of wheat) as well as different legumes: the famous small lentils, chickpeas (garbanzos) and the forgotten chickling (a type of pea) and various kinds of beans.

Spelt, much used in centuries past, is cooked with vegetables and herbs and served as a side dish or in hearty soups.

Castelluccio lentils are known throughout Italy for their fine flavour and their especially quick cooking time.

APPETIZERS (ANTIPASTI)

Traditionally, these consist of slices of cured meat, olives, pickled vegetables and toasted bread wih toppings (*crostini* or *bruschette*).

Salami coated in black pepper

Sausage

The cured meats and pork sausages of Norcia are renowned. "Norcino" has become synonymous with "pork butcher".

FIRST COURSES (PRIMI)

These usually consist of soups and home-made fresh pasta. Local pasta types include *strangozzi* (or *stringozzi*), *ciriole* and *strascinati*.

Chickpea and bean soup, an old peasant dish, is eaten especially on Christmas Eve.

MUSHROOMS AND TRUFFLES

Wild mushrooms are considered a great delicacy in central Italy, and a range of fresh and dried mushrooms is frequently used in cooking. Fresh mushrooms are available in the autumn when restaurants are often packed with locals tasting seasonal mushroom dishes. Prized black truffles (*tartufi neri*), with a rich flavour and firm texture, are expensive and used sparingly. Porcini mushrooms (ceps) may be served grilled as a main course, used on pizza, in stuffed pasta, or served as a vegetable dish, often sautéed gently with garlic.

Chanterelle
(*Cantarello* or *Gallinaccio*)

Field blewit
(*Agarico nudo*)

Parasol
(*Mazza da tamburo*)

Boletus edulis
(*Porcini*)

Oyster
(*Ostrica*)

Black truffle
(*Tartufo nero*)

MEATS (CARNI)

Lamb, beef, pork and game are common items on Umbrian menus. Among the heartier meats is wild boar. This animal, omnipresent in Mediterranean scrub, is semi-wild, which makes its meat taste richer and more rustic. Pigeons also feature, both farmed and wild, as well as wood pigeon.

Wild boar "alla cacciatora" is a stew with tomato, wine, herbs and aromatics such as juniper, and often olives or mushrooms.

Wood pigeon "alla ghiotta" are spit-roasted and served with a sauce made simply from the cooking juices and red wine.

FISH (PESCE)

The fish from lakes Trasimeno and Corbara reaches even the tables of northern Italy. Try roasted carp, fried sand-smelt and perch.

Tegamaccio, served on the shores of Lake Trasimeno, is a soup made with freshwater fish. It is rich in flavour, garlicky and quite spicy.

CAKES AND BISCUITS

Yeast-risen cakes, such as almond cakes, biscuits, and breads filled with dried fruit round off Umbrian festival meals.

OLIVE OIL

Umbrian olive oil is known all over the world. Extra-virgin olive oil has an intense scent of olives with spicy, peppery notes.

There are five olive oil-producing areas, including Valnerina, Assisi-Spoleto and Trasimeno.

Torcolo dolce is a typical cake from Perugia, made with candied fruit and raisins. It is prepared for the feast days of San Costanzo and San Giuseppe.

WINE

Most Umbrian white wines are dry or medium-dry, while reds are robust, dry and often fairly potent. There are also wines made from dried grapes. The range includes nine DOCs (Assisi, Colli Alto Tiberini, Colli Amerini, Colli Martani, Colli Perugini, Colli del Trasimeno, Montefalco, Orvieto and Torgiano) and two DOCGs (that is, of even higher quality): Montefalco Sagrantino and Torgiano rosso riserva.

Sagrantino, mentioned by Pliny the Elder, is produced entirely from the grape of the same name. It comes in dry (secco) and sweet (passito) versions.

Rubesco, produced in Torgiano, is a full-bodied red which goes well with the meat and game dishes of the region.

Succulent Umbrian grapes

White Orvieto has a strong and ancient tradition. Nowadays, it is generally made dry – and with a slightly bitter taste – but there is also a sweet version.

Grechetto is made from a grape that grows abundantly in Umbria. Varying in taste from area to area, this wine is a good aperitif, and also goes well with lake fish.

Choosing a Restaurant

THE RESTAURANTS below have been selected across a wide range of price categories, for the quality of the food, good value and enjoyable atmosphere. They are divided into two sections, Northern and Southern Umbria, and are then listed alphabetically by town. Rural restaurants are generally listed under the name of the nearest main town.

	CREDIT CARDS	PARKING	OUTSIDE TABLES	TRADITIONAL COOKING	FISH DISHES

NORTHERN UMBRIA

ASSISI: *Brilli Bistrot* €€
Via Los Angeles 83. (075 804 3433.
This romantic restaurant offers a mixture of typical seasonal dishes and delicious, innovative combinations. Try the fillet of turkey with honey, served with pears, rocket (arugula) and pecorino cheese. ● *Tue; Aug.* & ▤

AE DC MC V	●		●	

ASSISI: *La Fortezza* €€
Vicolo della Fortezza 2/b. (075 812 418 or 075 812 993.
A busy and reputable restaurant in a medieval palazzo. The menu consists of dishes that combine traditional Umbrian flavours with those of the Trentino region. Black truffles, vegetables and cheeses accompany pasta dishes and meat-based main courses. Good wine list.
● *Thu; Feb, Jul (10 days).* ▤ ▯

AE DC MC V	●		●	

ASSISI: *Stalla* €€
Via Eremo delle Carceri 8, Fontemaggio. (075 812 317.
Simple Umbrian cuisine is served up in this former stables, all done out in wood and stone. Typical little *torte* (grilled flat bread) come with meat or vegetables, *strangozzi* and *bigoli* (pasta) with game. ● *Mon.*

AE DC MC V	●	■	●	

ASSISI: *Trattoria Pallotta* €€
Vicolo della Volta Pinta 3. (075 812 649.
A family-run trattoria with a hospitable atmosphere. Among the traditional dishes try the *strangozzi alla Pallotta* with mushrooms and black olives, and the grilled meats. ● *Tue; Feb or Mar.* ▤ ▯

AE DC MC V			●	

ASSISI : *Dei Cavalieri* €€€
Petrignano, Via Matteotti 47. (075 803 0011.
An elegant, welcoming restaurant in a 14th-century hamlet 5 km (3 miles) northwest of Assisi. Fish dishes, or recipes based on cheese, meat and vegetables. Good salami and other local produce. ● *Mon; Jan.* &

AE DC MC V	●	■	●	■

ASSISI: *Buca di San Francesco* €€€
Via Brizi 1. (075 812 204.
Set in the spacious cellar of a 14th-century building, this well-known restaurant serves good traditional food and some original specials. Excellent salami and main courses based on various meats. ● *Mon; Jul.* &

AE DC MC V		■	●	

ASSISI: *Medioevo* €€€
Via Arco dei Priori 4b. (075 813 068.
This elegant restaurant in the old part of Assisi has an attractive beamed dining room that dates back to the Middle Ages. Excellent Umbrian prosciutto and main dishes based on meat. ● *Wed; Jan, Jul.* ▤

AE DC MC V	●		●	■

ASSISI: *San Francesco* €€€
Via San Francesco 52. (075 812 329.
The traditional menu varies according to the season: carpaccio of porcini mushrooms, stuffed duck and beef fillet with truffles. ● *Wed; 1–14 Jul.* ▯ ▤

AE DC MC V	●	■	●	

ASSISI: *Le Silve* €€€
Armenzano. (075 801 9000.
A welcoming restaurant attached to Le Silve hotel *(see p144)*, 10 km (6 miles) east of Assisi, with a garden and terrace. Elegantly creative cooking with a good choice of starters and main courses. ● *Mon.* ▯

AE DC MC V	●	■		

ASSISI: *Umbra* €€€
Via degli Archi 6. (075 812 240.
A modern restaurant serving traditional food and wine. Good *cappelletti* (pasta) with black truffle, *crostini* (toasted bread with different toppings) and *rocciata di Assisi* (fruit and nut biscuits). ● *Sun; Jan–Mar.*

AE DC MC V		■	●	

		Credit Cards	Parking	Outside Tables	Traditional Cooking	Fish Dishes

Price categories are for a 3-course meal with wine, bread and cover charge.
€ under 25 euros
€€ 25–35 euros
€€€ 35–45 euros
€€€€ 45–55 euros
€€€€€ over 55 euros

CREDIT CARDS
American Express, Diners Club, MasterCard, Visa
PARKING
Parking places or garage run by the restaurant.
OUTSIDE DINING
The option of eating outside, on a terrace, in a garden, or at pavement tables.
TRADITIONAL COOKING
Restaurant serving traditional Umbrian cooking.
FISH DISHES
Restaurant serving fish and seafood dishes.

CITTÀ DI CASTELLO: *Altotiberina* €
Piazza Gabriotti. 075 855 3089.
A wine bar in an old palazzo where you can sample salami, cheeses and crostini, complemented by local wines. Also a pizzeria. ● *Tue.*
Credit cards: AE DC MC V

CITTÀ DI CASTELLO: *Amici Miei* €
Via del Monte 2. 075 855 9904.
A rustic but welcoming restaurant specializing in traditional Umbrian cuisine. Limited selection of regional wines. ● *Wed; 20 Dec–10 Feb.*
Outside Tables ●; Traditional Cooking ●

CITTÀ DI CASTELLO: *Bersaglio* €€
Via Vittorio Emanuele Orlando 14. 075 855 5534.
A traditional Umbrian restaurant offering specials with wild mushrooms and truffles, and almond tarts with coffee cream. ● *Wed; 1–14 Jan, 1–14 Jul.*
Credit cards: AE DC MC V; *Parking ●; Outside Tables ■; Traditional Cooking ●*

CITTÀ DI CASTELLO: *Terme di Fontecchio* €€
Fontecchio 4. 075 852 0614
In a pleasant spot just east of the city, and once home to thermal baths, this hotel restaurant offers a tasting menu of typical Umbrian dishes. ● *Tue.*
Credit cards: AE DC MC V; *Parking ●; Outside Tables ■; Traditional Cooking ●*

CITTÀ DI CASTELLO: *Le Logge* €€€
Via Bufalini 1/B. 075 855 0331.
Attached to the Tiferno Hotel, in a 16th-century palazzo, this elegant restaurant has a menu that combines traditional recipes and innovative cooking. Round the meal off with chocolate flan in white chocolate sauce. Open for dinner only. ● *L; Sun; Aug.*
Credit cards: AE DC MC V; *Parking ●; Traditional Cooking ●; Fish Dishes ■*

CITTÀ DI CASTELLO: *Il Postale* €€€€€
Via R. de Cesare 8. 075 852 1356.
The top restaurant in the city, thanks to chef Marco Bistarelli. One of the three menus is fish-based, but mainly recipes are based around pheasant, guinea fowl, foie gras and pigeon. Good desserts. ● *Sat L, Mon.*
Credit cards: AE DC MC V; *Parking ●; Outside Tables ■; Traditional Cooking ●; Fish Dishes ■*

DERUTA: *L'Antico Forziere* €€
Casalina, Strada Statale 45E, Via Della Rocca 2. 074 972 4314.
This elegant inn serves traditional cuisine with a good choice of appetizers, grilled meats and home-made desserts. ● *Mon; last 2 weeks Jan.*
Credit cards: AE DC MC V; *Parking ●; Outside Tables ■; Traditional Cooking ●*

GUBBIO: *Piatto d'Oro* €
Branca, Via Ponte Rosso 205. 075 925 6238.
Family-run trattoria about 10 km (6 miles) southeast of Gubbio, serving traditional home-made food. Try the gnocchi with goose. ● *Fri.*
Credit cards: AE DC MC V; *Parking ●; Traditional Cooking ●*

GUBBIO: *San Martino* €
Via dei Consoli 8, Piazza San Martino. 075 927 3251.
A small trattoria serving good food. Try the aubergine-stuffed ravioli with courgettes (zucchini) and the grilled meats. ● *Tue; Feb.*
Credit cards: AE DC MC V; *Traditional Cooking ●*

GUBBIO: *Alcatraz* €€
Santa Cristina 53. 075 922 9938.
A centre for *agriturismo*, 3 km (2 miles) southwest of Gubbio, where they produce their own pasta, oil and wine. Welcoming atmosphere and simple meals using seasonal produce. ● *Mon–Fri Oct–Mar.*
Credit cards: AE DC MC V; *Parking ●; Outside Tables ■; Traditional Cooking ●*

GUBBIO: *Castello di Cortevecchio* €€
Nogna. 075 924 1017.
Friendly *agriturismo* farm, set in lovely countryside, with small dining room. Try *cappellacci* (pasta) with ricotta and herbs. ● *Mon; Jan–Feb.*
Parking ●; Outside Tables ■; Traditional Cooking ●

GUBBIO: *Dolce Vita* €€
Santa Cristina. 075 922 9932.
This friendly restaurant southwest of the city is well worth seeking out. Good regional cooking. Booking essential. ● *Mon.*
Parking ●; Outside Tables ■; Traditional Cooking ●

Price categories are for a 3-course meal with wine, bread and cover charge.
€ under 25 euros
€€ 25–35 euros
€€€ 35–45 euros
€€€€ 45–55 euros
€€€€€ over 55 euros

CREDIT CARDS
American Express, Diners Club, MasterCard, Visa.
PARKING
Parking places or garage run by the restaurant.
OUTSIDE DINING
The option of eating outside, on a terrace, in a garden, or at pavement tables.
TRADITIONAL COOKING
Restaurant serving traditional Umbrian cooking.
FISH DISHES
Restaurant serving fish and seafood dishes.

	CREDIT CARDS	PARKING	OUTSIDE TABLES	TRADITIONAL COOKING	FISH DISHES
GUBBIO: *Fabiani* €€ Piazza 40 Martiri 26. ☎ 075 927 4639. In an old palazzo surrounded by a garden, this restaurant offers *cappellacci* (pasta) with truffles, *lonzino* (pork) in a walnut sauce and *crespelle* (pancakes) with berries among its specialities. ● *Tue; Jan.* ♿ 🍴	AE DC MC V	●	■	●	
GUBBIO: *Federico da Montefeltro* €€ Vie Della Repubblica 35. ☎ 075 927 3949. There is a family atmosphere at this restaurant, located in a palazzo with a pretty garden outside. A love of tradition and a talent for creativity inspires the menu. Try the shin of pork or the mutton, which are both beautifully prepared. ● *Thu.* 🍴	AE DC MC V		■	●	
GUBBIO: *Fornace di Mastro Giorgio* €€€€ Via Mastro Giorgio. ☎ 075 922 1836. Romantic atmosphere and excellent service. The menu is based primarily on the typical produce of the area, including cheese, olive oil and wine. ● *Tue, Wed L; Jan, Jul.* ♿ 🍴	AE DC MC V			●	
GUBBIO: *Park Hotel ai Cappuccini* €€€€ Via Tifernate. ☎ 075 922 0134. Light and delicate dishes which range from the traditional to the international. Tart of spelt with black truffle is particularly noteworthy, as is the wide selection of desserts. ● *Mon.* ♿ 🍽 🍴	AE DC MC V	●	■	●	
GUBBIO: *Taverna del Lupo* €€€€ Via Giovanni Ansidei 6. ☎ 075 927 4368. Typical local food prepared with great care, using fresh and high-quality ingredients. Game and truffles feature large in season. Meat dishes are embellished with local black truffle and *formaggio di fossa* (mature pecorino cheese). ● *Mon.* ♿	AE DC MC V		■	●	
GUBBIO: *Villa Montegranelli* €€€€ Monteluiano. ☎ 075 920 0185. Attached to a hotel, in an 18th-century villa on the outskirts of Gubbio, this restaurant has an elegantly rural atmosphere. Try the *crostini* with porcini mushrooms, and the exquisite desserts made with nuts and ricotta. ● *Wed.* 🍴	AE DC MC V		■	●	
ISOLA MAGGIORE (LAKE TRASIMENO): *Da Sauro* €€ Via Guglielmi 1. ☎ 075 826 168. This hotel restaurant is on an island in Lake Trasimeno, reached by a pleasant boat ride from Tuoro sul Trasimeno. Excellent dishes based on fish from the lake, including eel and carp, along with other typically Umbrian recipes and home-made desserts. ● *Wed; Nov.* ♿	AE DC MC V		■		■
MAGIONE: *Oasi La Valle* €€ Via Lungolago Alicata, San Feliciano. ☎ 075 847 6292. A hotel restaurant by Lake Trasimeno, just south of Magione. The local dishes on the menu include fillets of perch in sweet and sour sauce and smoked tench. ● *Tue; Nov.* 🍽 🍴	AE DC MC V	●	■		■
MAGIONE: *Riva del Sole da Cesare* €€ Strada Provinciale San Feliciano, Monte del Lago, Via Gandhi. ☎ 075 840 0185. Surrounded by a garden, this restaurant offers traditional cuisine and fish dishes. Delicious sea bass with black truffles. ● *Tue; Jan.*		●		●	■
MAGIONE: *Rosso di Sera* €€ Via Papini 31, San Feliciano. ☎ 075 847 6277. An appealing wine bar and a good place from which to watch the sunset by the shores of Lake Trasimeno. It offers a menu with satisfying fish and other dishes, plus a good selection of wines. ● *Tue.* 🍴		●	■	●	■

MONTE SANTA MARIA TIBERINA: *I Muri*   €€
Gioiello, I Muri. **(** 075 857 1001.
Agriturismo farm in the Umbrian hills west of Città di Castello, offering wonderful views as well as mostly traditional cooking using the freshest ingredients. The spaghetti with olives and basil is a Neapolitan recipe.

NOCERA UMBRA: *La Costa*   €
Costa 3. **(** 0742 810 042.
This pretty farmhouse is in a lovely position, surrounded by lush countryside about 5 km (3 miles) north of Nocera Umbra. A good place to try traditional local food. ● *Mon L.* &

NOCERA UMBRA: *Piazza Grande*   €€
Campo d'Arco, Via Fano. **(** 0742 812 034.
Traditional restaurant serving home cooking: you can try excellent snails with wild fennel or a tasty stuffed pigeon. ● *Wed.* &

PACIANO: *Locanda della Rocca*   €€
Viale Roma 4. **(** 075 830 236.
An elegant restaurant in an old palazzo. A fine selection of cheeses could round off a meal of local dishes. Open for dinner only. ● *Tue, L; Jan–Feb.*

PASSIGNANO SUL TRASIMENO: *Il Fischio del Merlo*   €€€
Calcinaio 17a, SS 75 bis. **(** 075 829 283.
A comfortable and welcoming spot overlooking Lake Trasimeno. The menu includes some of the oldest recipes from the lake area, many featuring fish, of course. ● *Tue.* & ▤

PERUGIA: *Aladino*   €
Via delle Prome 11. **(** 075 572 0938.
A very popular family-run restaurant offering Sardinian dishes: *pane carasau* (thin flat bread) with buffalo milk cheese and *salamino piccante* (spicy sausage), *spaghetti alla bottarga* (fish roe) and wild boar *alla sarda* ("Sardinian style"). Excellent *tortelli* (pasta) of wild mushrooms and truffle. Open for dinner only. ● *L, Mon; Aug.* ▤

PERUGIA: *Osteria Fiorucci*   €
Via Fabretti 27. **(** 075 573 5273.
A small trattoria with a friendly atmosphere and serving traditional Umbrian cookery. Choose from a range of excellent wines and cheeses. Pasta includes *strangozzi* and *spaghettoni*, while main courses are meat-based. ● *Sun; Aug.* ▮

PERUGIA: *La Taverna*   €
Via delle Streghe 8. **(** 075 572 4128.
This welcoming dining room in an old palazzo is very popular. Typical Umbrian food, plus more inventive dishes, including *baccalà* (salt cod) *alla perugina*. The wines, cheeses and desserts are all delicious.
● *Mon.* & ▤

PERUGIA: *Altro Mondo*   €€
Via C. Caporali 11. **(** 075 572 6157.
The fried lamb is the signature dish at this friendly restaurant. Also on the menu are Castelluccio lentils on toast. ● *Sun; Aug, Dec.* ▤

PERUGIA: *Cesarino*   €€
Piazza IV Novembre 5. **(** 075 572 8974.
A trattoria-cum-pizzeria in a medieval palazzo that can get very busy. Hot appetizers, good-quality meat and fine wines. Finish with *meringa semifredda* (meringue and ice cream). ● *Wed; Jan or Feb.* ▮

PERUGIA: *Dal Mi' Cucco*   €€
Corso Garibaldi 12. **(** 075 573 2511.
Typical surroundings and good value in old Perugia. If you don't book, you can expect the owner to suggest you go for a walk around the block rather than stand in line. Genuine Perugian cooking is on offer. ● *Wed.* ▤

PERUGIA: *Giancarlo*   €€
Via Dei Priori 36. **(** 075 572 4314.
Set in an old palazzo, this popular trattoria has offered a menu of traditional recipes for more than 20 years: *tagliatelle* with porcini mushrooms, grilled meats of various kinds, fresh wild mushrooms and a good crème caramel. ● *Fri; Aug–Sep.*

For key to symbols see back flap

	Legend
Price categories are for a 3-course lete meal with wine, bread and cover charge. € under 25 euros €€ 25–35 euros €€€ 35–45 euros €€€€ 45–55 euros €€€€€ over 55 euros	**CREDIT CARDS** American Express, Diners Club, MasterCard, Visa. **PARKING** Parking places or garage run by the restaurant. **OUTSIDE DINING** The option of eating outside, on a terrace, in a garden, or at pavement tables. **TRADITIONAL COOKING** Restaurant serving traditional Umbrian cooking. **FISH DISHES** Restaurant serving fish and seafood dishes.

	Credit Cards	Parking	Outside Tables	Traditional Cooking	Fish Dishes
PERUGIA: *Giò Arte e Vini* €€ Via Ruggiero d'Andreotto 19. 075 573 1100. A wine bar, restaurant and hotel. Offers a wide choice of wine by the bottle and glass. Good choice of food, too, based on local vegetables, cheeses, sausages and salami. ● *Sun D, Mon L.*	AE DC MC V	●		●	
PERUGIA: *La Lanterna* €€ Via U. Rocchi 6. 075 573 6397. Carefully prepared and elegantly presented food is served in this restaurant in the historic centre, just behind the cathedral. Try the incredibly delicate ravioli with orange and rose petals or the more hearty *agnolotti* (pasta) *alla norcina.* ● *Wed.*	AE DC MC V		■	●	
PERUGIA: *Osteria del Gambero* €€ Via Baldeschi 17. 075 573 5461. Despite the name of this rustic restaurant ("The Prawn"), the menu does not offer only fish and seafood, but also the best of Umbrian traditional cooking. Open for dinner only. ● *L, Mon; Jan, 15–30 Jun.*	AE DC MC V		■	●	■
PERUGIA: *Piazzetta* €€ Via Deliziosa 3. 075 573 6012. A cordial family atmosphere reigns at this restaurant, located in an old Perugian palazzo. New and traditional dishes fill the menu, leaving diners only with the difficult task of making a choice. Make sure you save room for one of the delicious desserts. ● *Tue; Jan.*	AE DC MC V		■	●	
PERUGIA: *Rosetta* €€ Piazza Italia 19. 075 572 0841. An excellent hotel-restaurant with a kitchen that produces traditional Umbrian food. The speciality of the house is an excellent rice dish, *risotto alla Fregoli* (with meat, chicken livers and peas), but this must be ordered in advance. ● *Mon.*	AE DC MC V		■	●	
PERUGIA: *La Bocca Mia* €€€ Via U. Rocchi 36. 075 572 3873. This restaurant has a romantic atmosphere and serves good Umbrian cooking, dominated by wild mushrooms, as well as seafood. Try *linguine* with broad (fava) beans and pecorino cheese to start with, followed by grilled young pork with seasonal vegetables. ● *Sun; Aug.*	AE DC MC V	●		●	
PERUGIA: *Decò* €€€ Ponte San Giovanni, Via del Pastificio 8. 075 599 0950. A modern, comfortable restaurant, with a hotel and meeting rooms and a good menu of fish dishes. Particularly good are the sautéed steamed sea bass, the *linguine* with red mullet and *taglierini* with prawns. ● *Sun D; Aug.*	AE DC MC V	●	■	●	■
PERUGIA: *Osteria dell'Olmo* €€€ Olmo, Strada Olmo, Stazione Ellera 8. 075 517 9140. An elegant restaurant in an old palazzo, with a large garden. Innovative and international dishes are served, according to the chef's mood. There is a vast selection of first courses, including rainbow ravioli with scented herbs. Mushrooms and cheese feature prominently in the house specialities. ● *Mon.*	AE DC MC V	●	■		
PERUGIA: *San Lorenzo* €€€€ Piazza Danti 19/A. 075 572 4314 or 075 572 1956. In the historic centre of Perugia, in front of the cathedral and the Fontana Maggiore. The chef prepares imaginative food, re-interpreting traditional regional dishes and classic Umbrian recipes. Excellent galantine of pigeon stuffed with egg and breadcrumbs. Booking advised. ● *Sun in winter.*	AE DC MC V	●	■	●	

PETRIGNANO: *Cavalieri* €€ — AE DC MC V
Via Aeroporto-Petrignano 47. 075 803 0011.
Located in a village about 5 km (3 miles) west of Assisi, this is a place in which to try out creative, elegant dishes and variations on traditional Umbrian cuisine such as cutlets of lamb stuffed and wrapped in pork caul, or *tortelli* stuffed with turbot and served with a sauce of prawns, fresh tomato and basil. ● *Mon, Tue.*

SAN GIUSTINO: *Galleria* €€ — AE DC MC V
Lama, Via Tifernate 34. 075 858 2586.
This restaurant, just off the road between Città di Castello and San Giustino (close to the Tuscan border), offers traditional Umbrian food alongside some Puglian dishes and pizzas. An interesting tasting menu is offered, too, as well as an excellent range of spirits and liqueurs to round off the meal. ● *Mon; Jul–Aug.*

TORGIANO: *Tre Vaselle* €€€€€ — AE DC MC V
Via Garibaldi 48. 075 988 0447.
This hotel-restaurant in an old house right in the town serves traditional cuisine and makes the most of the excellent local produce. The grilled meats are excellent, or you may like to try the purée of beans and the chicory with Torgiano olive oil, or the egg pasta triangles stuffed with truffle, served with truffle fondue. Delicious desserts and wines.

UMBERTIDE: *Cerretino* €€ — MC V
Calzolaro, Via Colonnato 3. 075 930 2166.
Agriturismo farm, about 10 km (6 miles) northwest of Umbertide, with ample space outside and good views of the Umbrian hills. Light dishes based on recipes typical of the region and authentic flavours. Excellent meat-based main courses: try the *rollé di tacchino* (rolled turkey). ● *L, Sun D; Jan–Feb.*

UMBERTIDE: *Abbazia di Montecorona* €€€ — AE DC MC V
Montecorona. 075 941 1810.
Situated in the charming atmosphere of an old abbey, in a thoroughly romantic setting, this restaurant offers typical Umbrian dishes as well as good fish and seafood specials. Risotto with pears and gorgonzola or a soup of spelt and chicory are two excellent restorative dishes for cold winter days. ● *Mon; Jan.*

SOUTHERN UMBRIA

AMELIA: *Carleni* €€ — AE DC MC V
Via P. Carleni 21. 0744 983 925.
Annexed to a delightful hotel in the heart of the medieval town of Amelia, this restaurant offers *fettuccine* with hare, fillet steak with mushrooms and truffles and, to finish, apple tart. Good wine list. ● *Tue; Jan, Feb.*

ARRONE: *Rossi* €€ — AE DC MC V
Voc. Isola Casteldilago 7. 0744 388 394.
This trattoria is in the Valnerina, 14 km (9 miles) west of Terni. It is worth stopping here to try the best prawns in the valley, especially those in *salsa verde* (herby green sauce). ● *Fri.*

BASCHI: *Vissani* €€€€€ — AE DC MC V
Civitella del Lago, SS 448, km 6600. 0744 950 396 or 0744 950 206.
This is one of Italy's best and most expensive restaurants, with a menu that changes with the the seasons and with the inspiration of the chef Gianfranco Vissani. Expect delicacies such as suckling pig, lobster and oysters, prepared in an inventive and exquisite manner. ● *Wed, Thu L, Sun D; Aug–Sep.*

BEVAGNA: *El Rancho* €€ — AE DC MC V
Via Flaminia 55. 0742 360 105.
Mushrooms, mushrooms and yet more mushrooms in this friendly hotel-restaurant. Used to flavour pasta and other first courses, mushrooms also turn up in main courses or as a side dish. Efficient service. ● *Mon.*

BEVAGNA: *Nina* €€ — AE DC MC V
Piazza Garibaldi, 6. 0742 360 161.
A welcoming, family-run trattoria with home cooking and regional cuisine, grilled meat and old recipes. Excellent *cappelletti tartufati* (truffle-stuffed pasta). ● *Tue; Jul.*

Price categories are for a 3-course meal with wine, bread and cover charge.
€ under 25 euros
€€ 25–35 euros
€€€ 35–45 euros
€€€€ 45–55 euros
€€€€€ over 55 euros

CREDIT CARDS
American Express, Diners Club, MasterCard, Visa.
PARKING
Parking places or garage run by the restaurant.
OUTSIDE DINING
The option of eating outside, on a terrace, in a garden, or at pavement tables.
TRADITIONAL COOKING
Restaurant serving traditional Umbrian cooking.
FISH DISHES
Restaurant serving fish and seafood dishes.

	Credit Cards	Parking	Outside Tables	Traditional Cooking	Fish Dishes
BEVAGNA: *Ottavius* €€ Via del Gonfalone 1. **(** 0742 360 555. Welcoming restaurant in a vaulted medieval room, serving excellent Umbrian food that makes the most of seasonal produce. A wide variety of grilled meats, to be washed down with wine chosen from a long wine list. ● *Mon; Jul.* & ♟	AE DC MC V			●	
BEVAGNA: *Poggio dei Pettirossi* €€ Madonna delle Grazie, Pilone 301. **(** 0742 361 740. Although this friendly farm, about 2 km (1 mile) southwest of Bevagna, isn't easy to find, it is worth seeking out to enjoy the view and the food. Enjoy a plate of home-made pasta, a *torta* (flat bread with a topping) or a focaccia and an honest glass of wine. ● *Mon.*	AE DC MC V	●		●	
BEVAGNA: *Orto degli Angeli* €€€ Via Dante Alighieri 1. **(** 0742 360 130. A very pleasant setting in an old building. Variations on local traditional food. Good selection of regional wines. ● *Tue; Jan–Feb.* ▤ ♟	AE DC MC V	●	▣	●	
CAMPELLO SUL CLITUNNO: *Castello di Poreta* €€ Poreta. **(** 0743 275 810. A pretty hotel-restaurant just south of Campello. Ideal for trying regional specialities and variations, such as buckwheat ravioli with aubergine (eggplant) and taleggio cheese. The bread is home-made. ● *Mon.* & ♟		●	▣	●	
CAMPELLO SUL CLITUNNO: *Trattoria Pettino* €€ Pettino 31. **(** 0743 276 021. In a hilly setting, up a winding road northeast of Campello, this restaurant is in a renovated old house. It serves delicious *bruschetta*, truffles and a wide range of specials. ● *Tue.*		●	▣	●	
CANNARA: *Perbacco* €€ Via Umberto I 14. **(** 0742 720 492. A romantic trattoria in a village 7 km (4 miles) north of Bevagna. It offers, along with regional specialities, an excellent choice of wines, cheese, oils, spirits and liqueurs. Duck wrapped in pork is a local delicacy. ● *Mon; mid-Jul–mid-Aug.* & ♟	AE DC MC V	●	▣	●	
CIVITELLA DEL LAGO: *Trippini* €€€€ Via Italia 14. **(** 0744 950 316. A warm, intimate restaurant with a lovely view over the hills and Lago di Corbara. Top-quality food using local vegetables and meat such as lamb, duck and goose. Good selection of cheeses, to be eaten with the home-made jams and preserves. Also a pizzeria. ● *Mon.* ♟	AE DC MC V	●		●	
FERENTILLO: *Piermarini* €€€ Via F. Ancaiano 23. **(** 0744 780 714. The cooking in this restaurant is thoroughly traditional. The black truffle dominates the menu when in season, from November to February. There are also excellent wines and desserts, the latter being especially good over the Christmas period. ● *Sun D, Mon; Sep.* ▤ ♟	AE DC MC V	●	▣	●	
FOLIGNO: *Il Bacco Felice* €€ Via Garibaldi 33. **(** 0742 341 019. This typical trattoria has a friendly and informal atmosphere, and prices are moderate for the tasty, genuinely Umbrian food. Good soups, meat and snails. ● *Sun L, Mon; Aug.* ♟	AE DC MC V	●		●	
FOLIGNO: *Lieta Sosta* €€ Colfiorito, Via Adriatica 230. **(** 0742 681 321. Family-run trattoria in Colfiorito, 20 km (12 miles) northeast of Foligno, offering both hotel guests and non-residents a good range of cold meats and sausages accompanied by tasty *bruschetta*, cheeses and grilled meats.	MC V	●	▣	●	

FOLIGNO: *Angelo dell'Albergo Guesia* €€
Ponte Santa Lucia 46. (0742 311 515 or 0742 660 216.
An elegant and comfortable hotel-restaurant. The menu consists of regional dishes, including good fish dishes. ● Mon. & ☐

FOLIGNO: *Da Remo* €€ MC V
Via Filzi 10. (0742 340 522.
A well-established restaurant in a villa near the railway station, serving home-cooked old recipes. Fresh pasta served with seasonal sauces, lamb, pigeon and pork are the specialities of the house. ● Sun D, Mon; Aug. ☐

FOLIGNO: *Le Mura* €€ AE DC MC V
Via Mentana 25. (0742 354 642.
Home-made food is provided in this welcoming hotel-restaurant. Soups, pasta and imaginative vegetable dishes precede or accompany a delicious range of grilled meats. ● Tue; Jul.

FOLIGNO: *Sparafucile* €€ MC V
Largo Carducci 30. (0742 342 602.
Situated in a fine old palazzo adjacent to the cathedral, this small trattoria offers dishes often based around fish, such as soup of *cicerchie* (chickling, a type of pea) and *baccalà* (salt cod), or *strangozzi* with baby squid. Good selection of wines, cheeses and oils. ● Wed; Nov. ☐

FOLIGNO: *Osteria del Teatro* €€€ AE DC MC V
Via Petrucci 8. (0742 350 745.
This small, elegant restaurant with a vaulted ceiling can accommodate little more than 40 covers. Typical regional recipes, excellent sausages and salami, and *strangozzi* with truffles in the right season. A good selection of wines ● Wed; Aug. ▤ ☐

FOLIGNO: *Villa Roncalli* €€€€ AE DC MC V
Sant'Eraclio, Via Roma 25. (0742 391 091.
Surrounded by a shady garden, this enchanting hotel-restaurant is housed in a lovely 17th-century villa just south of Foligno. Good regional dishes prepared with the freshest seasonal ingredients. Excellent home-made bread and desserts. ● Mon; Jan, Aug. ▤ ☐

GUALDO CATTANEO: *Noci* €€€ AE DC MC V
Grutti, Via Torino. (0742 983 71.
A windy 8-km (5-mile) drive west from Bevagna. A lively family trattoria with a pretty garden and generous portions. Excellent gnocchi served with porcini mushrooms or plums. ● Fri; Aug, Christmas.

LUGNANO IN TEVERINA: *Frateria dell'Abate Loniano* €€ MC V
San Francesco 6. (0744 902 180.
A charming 13th-century monastery, with an enchanting view, a short distance west of Amelia. Tables are set out in the old refectory. The menu offers a variety of local produce, cooked according to traditional recipes. ● Wed; Nov.

MONTEFALCO: *Coccorone* €€ AE DC MC V
Largo Tempestivi. (0742 379 535.
An elegant but unpretentious family-run trattoria in an old palazzo with an open fire in winter. Excellent food, including grilled meats, game in season, delicious home-made pastas and *crespelle* (stuffed pancakes). ● Wed.

MONTEFALCO: *Enoteca Federico II* €€ AE DC MC V
Piazza del Comune 1. (0742 378 902.
A wine bar-cum-trattoria with a young clientele and lively atmosphere, with a good range of Umbrian specialities. Tasty snacks, sausages and salami, cheeses and, of course, wine. ● Wed.

MONTEFALCO: *Villa Pambuffetti* €€€ AE DC MC V
Via della Vittoria 20. (0742 379 417.
Elegant and romantic restaurant in a 19th-century villa hotel-inn, with views over the lovely garden. Regional cuisine offering a good range of tasty, authentic dishes. ● Mon, Tue D, Sun D; Jan–Mar, 1 Nov; 20 Dec. & ☐

NARNI: *Cavallino* €€ AE DC MC V
Via Flaminia Romana 220. (0744 761 020.
Family atmosphere and home cooking in the Umbrian tradition, including interesting pastas such as *manfricoli* and *ciriole*, pigeon and grilled meats, washed down with local wines. ● Tue; Jul, Christmas.

Price categories are for a 3-course meal with wine, bread and cover charge.
€ under 25 euros
€€ 25–35 euros
€€€ 35–45 euros
€€€€ 45–55 euros
€€€€€ over 55 euros

Credit Cards
American Express, Diners Club, MasterCard, Visa.
Parking
Parking places or garage run by the restaurant.
Outside Dining
The option of eating outside, on a terrace, in a garden, or at pavement tables.
Traditional Cooking
Restaurant serving traditional Umbrian cooking.
Fish Dishes
Restaurant serving fish and seafood dishes.

	Credit Cards	Parking	Outside Tables	Traditional Cooking	Fish Dishes
Norcia: *Dal Francese* €€ Via Riguardati 16. *0743 816 290.* This rustic trattoria serves regional specialities, including home-made salami. Dishes with black truffles when in season. ● *Fri (winter); Jun, Nov.*	AE DC MC V	●		●	
Norcia: *Granaro del Monte* €€ Via Alfieri 12. *0743 816 513 or 0743 816 504.* Hotel-restaurant in an old pawnbrokers. Specializes in grilled meats, prepared on the open fire. Also try the *risotto alla castellana tartufato* and the trout with crushed chickpeas (garbanzos). ● *Tue.*	AE DC MC V	●	■	●	
Orvieto: *Ancora* €€ Via di Piazza del Popolo 7. *0763 342 766.* This elegant, 30-year-old restaurant has a traditional menu offering a good choice of game and grilled meats. Anyone wanting to sample the house speciality, *palombaccio* (wood pigeon) *alla leccarda*, should order the dish in advance. Also a wood-fired pizzeria. ● *Thu; Jan.*	AE MC V	●	■	●	
Orvieto: *Le Grotte del Funaro* €€ Via Ripa Serancia 41. *0763 343 276.* This elegant restaurant is carved out of the tufa caves in the medieval quarter. Excellent local cuisine, particularly pasta and grilled meats, as well as pizzas and a good selection of wines, spirits and liqueurs. ● *Mon; Jul.*	AE DC MC V	●		●	
Orvieto: *Maurizio* €€ Via del Duomo 78. *0763 341 114.* A smart, spacious dining room. The menu is based on local food and grilled meats. The *cosciotto d'agnello* (leg of lamb) is recommended. ● *Tue; Feb.*	AE DC MC V	●		●	
Orvieto: *La Badia* €€€€ La Badia 8. *0763 301 959.* Entering this restaurant, part of a 13th-century monastery (and hotel), you have the feeling of stepping back in time. Fittingly, the menu offers some of the most traditional recipes in the area, including game roasted over an open fire. ● *Mon & Tue L, Wed; Jan–Feb.*	AE DC MC V	●	■	●	
Orvieto: *Osteria dell'Angelo* €€€ Corso Cavour 166. *0763 341 805.* A tiny place but one of Orvieto's best restaurants. Diners can choose from fish and seafood or meat-based dishes from three very different menus. The combinations are adventurous but always well-judged and the ingredients are of excellent quality. Bookings advisable. ● *Mon; Jul.*	AE MC V	●	■	●	■
Orvieto: *Giglio d'Oro* €€€€ Piazza Duomo 8. *0763 341 903.* In a perfect position, next to the cathedral, this elegant restaurant offers traditional cooking and a good selection of wines. ● *Wed.*	AE DC MC V	●	■	●	
Orvieto: *Sette Consoli* €€€€ Piazza Sant'Angelo 1a. *0763 343 911.* A fascinating restaurant created from the old sacristy of the church of Sant'Angelo. Numerous tempting gastronomic ideas, often using game or other local meat. Try the *menu degustazione*. The wine cellar is among the best in Italy. ● *Sun D, Wed (Sep–Jun); Feb.*	AE DC MC V	●	■	●	■
Orvieto: *Trattoria Etrusca* €€€ Via Lorenzo Maitani 10. *0763 344 016.* Minestrone, Chianina beef carpaccio and mushrooms or *piccione all'orvietana* (pigeon in red wine) are some of the specialities in this highly reputable restaurant. Warm family atmosphere in the medieval vaulted dining room. ● *Mon; Feb, Aug.*	AE DC MC V			●	

ORVIETO: *Villa Ciconia* €€ | AE DC MC V
Via dei Tigli 69. **[** *0763 305 582.*
In a 16th-century villa, this pleasant restaurant offers a wide range of dishes based on wild mushrooms and truffles, when in season, to be washed down with a good red Orvieto classico. ● *Mon.* & ▯

PRECI: *Castoro* €€ | AE DC MC V
Via Roma. **[** *0743 991 27.*
This rustic restaurant, in the fortified village of Preci in the Valnerina, 16 km (10 miles) north of Norcia, has a good reputation for its dishes with wild mushrooms. Try the spaghetti with ultra-fresh truffle, when in season. Pizza is also available. ● *Thu.*

SAN GEMINI: *Porta* €€ | AE MC V
Via Roma 54–56. **[** *0744 334 060.*
An ancient and welcoming restaurant serving rustic and fish-based dishes. Good ravioli with sea bass and a prawn sauce. ● *Mon.* ▯

SCHEGGINO: *Del Ponte* €€ | AE DC MC V
Via di Borgo. **[** *0743 611 31 or 0743 612 53.*
This pleasant restaurant, with a small hotel alongside, honours the gastronomic specialities of the Valnerina: a particular type of black truffle, trout and freshwater crayfish. ● *Mon; 1–14 Sep.* &

SPELLO: *Il Cacciatore* €€ | AE DC MC V
Via Giulia 42. **[** *0742 651 141.*
A restaurant housed in a friendly inn with lovely views. Home-made *pappardelle* (wide, flat noodles) with goose and grilled meats are the specialities of the house. ● *Mon–Sat L, Sun D; Nov.*

SPELLO: *Il Molino* €€ | AE DC MC V
Piazza Matteotti 6/7. **[** *0742 651 305.*
Housed in rooms within a medieval palazzo, this elegant restaurant offers traditional and innovative cuisine. Try the *tagliatelle "strascicate"* (with puréed vegetables) and the home-made bread. ● *Tue.* & ▯

SPELLO: *Pinturicchio* €€ | AE DC MC V
Largo Mazzini 8. **[** *0742 301 033.*
A typical Umbrian trattoria housed in a medieval palazzo. A rich array of regional specials is on offer, with especially good *tagliatelle* with truffles and an excellent selection of cheeses. ● *Tue; Jul.* &

SPELLO: *La Bastiglia* €€€€ | AE DC MC V
Piazza Vallegloria 7. **[** *0742 651 277.*
A very popular restaurant in a restored palazzo-inn. Excellent and genuinely traditional food is served on the terrace, with a panoramic view. Booking advisable. ● *Wed; Thu L; 2 weeks in Jan, 1 week in Jul.* ▯

SPOLETO: *Corso Flaminio* €€ | AE DC MC V
San Giacomo di Spoleto, Corso Flaminio 113. **[** *347 033 4744.*
A small trattoria in a village 8 km (5 miles) north of the city. Generous portions of home-made food and pizza. ● *Mon; Aug.*

SPOLETO: *Enoteca Provinciale* €€ | AE DC MC V
Via Aurelio Saffi 7. **[** *0743 220 484.*
This wine bar and restaurant offers a menu of simple local dishes, such as spelt soup, *strangozzi "alla spoletina"* or a delicate *frittatina* (light omelette) with black truffle. Good choice of wines by the glass. ● *Tue.* ▯

SPOLETO: *Ferretti* €€ | MC V
Monteluco 20. **[** *0743 498 49.*
A small hotel-restaurant up a winding road east of the city. Excellent grilled meats, but roasts and desserts are the pride of the kitchen. ● *Tue.* ▯

SPOLETO: *Festival* €€ | AE DC
Via Brignone 8. **[** *0743 220 993.*
The hot appetizers, the sausages and cured meats and the *strangozzi tartufati* (pasta with truffle) are crowned by excellent desserts. ● *Fri; Feb.*

SPOLETO: *Madrigale* €€ | DC MC V
Strettura, Strada Flaminia, km 117. **[** *0743 541 44.*
The restaurant, 16 km (10 miles) south of Spoleto, is large, comfortable and reasonably atmospheric, both inside and in the garden. Seasonal dishes (such as game) and local specialities, as well as pizzas. ● *Tue.* ▯

For key to symbols see back flap

Price categories are for a 3-course meal with wine, bread and cover charge.

€ under 25 euros
€€ 25–35 euros
€€€ 35–45 euros
€€€€ 45–55 euros
€€€€€ over 55 euros

CREDIT CARDS
American Express, Diners Club, MasterCard, Visa.
PARKING
Parking places or garage run by the restaurant.
OUTSIDE DINING
The option of eating outside, on a terrace, in a garden, or at pavement tables.
TRADITIONAL COOKING
Restaurant serving traditional Umbrian cooking.
FISH DISHES
Restaurant serving fish and seafood dishes.

Restaurant	Credit Cards	Parking	Outside Tables	Traditional Cooking	Fish Dishes
SPOLETO: *Mercato* €€ Piazza del Mercato 29. 0743 453 25. Creativity and balanced flavours are the hallmarks of this small family restaurant. Eat here if you want to try an excellent truffle fondue, snails, or a good plate of thinly sliced beef with rocket (arugula). ● Tue; Nov. 🍷	AE DC MC V	●	■		
SPOLETO: *I Pini* €€ Via 3 Settembre 1. 0743 481 56. Open for nearly half a century, this restaurant guarantees to provide good-quality meat and seasonal local dishes. ● Mon. ♿	AE DC MC V	●	■	●	
SPOLETO: *Caffè della Signoria* €€€ Piazza della Signoria 5. 0743 463 33. When the weather permits, you should eat lunch or dinner in the pretty garden outside. Dishes to try include the galantine of guinea fowl with truffle, which is delicious. Booking required. ● Wed; Jan. ♿		●	■	●	
SPOLETO: *Sabatini* €€€ Corso Mazzini 52/54. 0743 221 831. The chef, who is also the owner of this classy restaurant, concentrates on regional traditions. *Strangozzi alla spoletina* or mousse of egg and truffle are among his specialities. ● Mon; Jan, Aug. 🍷	AE DC MC V			●	
SPOLETO: *Tric Trac* €€€ Piazza Duomo 10. 0743 445 92. With tables looking out across the Piazza del Duomo, this restaurant is known for its imaginative cooking. Start with wholemeal pasta with wild fennel and courgettes (zucchini) and finish with strawberry ice cream with green peppercorns. ● Wed (winter). 🍷	AE DC MC V	●		●	
SPOLETO: *Il Panciolle* €€€€ Vicoli degli Eroli 1. 0743 455 98. You can have a satisfying meal here eating only bread and cheese, but it would be a shame not to try the *bigoli alla smollicata* (speciality pasta) or the spit-roasted lamb. ● Wed; early Nov–early Dec. 🍷	AE DC MC V		■	●	
SPOLETO: *Il Tartufo* €€€€ Piazza Garibaldi 24. 0743 402 36. The floor in one of the dining rooms dates from the Roman era. Among the regional delicacies on offer are truffles, barley soup and duck in Sagrantino wine sauce. Friendly, cordial atmosphere. ● Sun D, Mon; Jan, Jul. ♿	AE DC MC V	●		●	
STRONCONE: *Taverna di Porta Nova* €€ Via Porta Nova 1. 0744 604 96. This restaurant, just south of Terni, is in the cellars of an old palazzo and is always refreshingly cool in summer. Umbrian food and pizza. ● Wed; 1–14 Aug.	AE DC MC V	●		●	
TERNI: *Da Carlino* €€ Via Piemonte 1. 0744 420 163. Carlino offers rustic, robust food, such as *crostini* with local salami, *tagliatelle* with truffle or duck sauce, roast lamb and *involtini di fagioli* (meat parcels with beans). ● Mon; Aug.	AE DC MC V	●	■	●	■
TERNI: *Gatto Mammone* €€ Vico Catina 15. 0744 400 863. A place with a very pleasant atmosphere, with excellent cooking and a carefully assembled wine list. ● Sat, Sun L; Aug. 🍷	AE DC MC V	●	■	●	
TERNI: *Graziano* €€ Via Alfonsine 17–19. 0744 800 090. Grilled or boiled meats of all kinds and a good choice of pecorino cheese are offered in this trattoria, part of a small hotel. ● Sun; 2 weeks in Dec.		●	■	●	

TERNI: *Gulliver* €€ | AE DC MC V
Via Sant'Alò 10. 0744 441 106.
Creative dishes based on local ingredients. Among the specialities are snails, fried courgette (zucchini) flowers, *tagliolini* with prawns and courgettes, and lasagne with taleggio cheese and radicchio. ● Sun.

TERNI: *Melograno dell'Hotel Garden* €€ | AE DC MC V
Via Bramante 2. 0744 300 375.
The restaurant is part of an elegant, well-maintained, contemporary hotel. Traditional cooking features beautifully fresh fish, as well as tasty and authentic *tagliatelle* with porcini mushrooms and fresh tomato, and an excellent carpaccio of smoked meats. Good service. ● Sun D.

TERNI: *Mora* €€ | AE DC MC V
Via San Martino 44. 0744 421 256.
Small trattoria offering simple, authentic and tasty versions of traditional recipes. The menu is based essentially on the cuisine of Terni and a range of grilled meats. ● Mon; Aug.

TERNI: *Somaru* €€ | AE DC MC V
Via C. Battisti 106. 0744 300 486.
Imaginative dishes based around local ingredients. Among the specialities are hand-made pasta and roast guinea fowl. The *spaghetti alla Checca* is particularly recommended. ● Mon; Aug.

TERNI: *Villa Graziani* €€ | AE DC MC V
Papigno, Villa Valle 11. 0744 676 53 or 0744 671 38
Expect a good welcome at this restaurant, located in a lovely 18th-century palazzo just outside Terni. Anyone eating here for the first time should try the pasta and chickpeas (garbanzos), kid with truffle and, to finish off, a delicious Grand Marnier mousse. Also a pizzeria. ● Sun D; Mon; Aug.

TODI: *Jacopone* €€ | AE DC MC V
Piazzetta Jacopone 3. 0758 942 366.
A rustic place a stone's throw from Piazza del Popolo. The house specialities include the *pasticcio Jacopone* (a pasta bake) and *strangozzi* with truffle. ● Mon.

TODI: *La Mulinella* €€ | MC V
Vasciano, Ponte Naia 29. 0758 944 779.
In the countryside just south of Todi, and offering a good view up to the town, La Mulinella serves simple but authentic meals. The *tagliatelle* with goose sauce, potato gnocchi with wild mushrooms and turkey with grapes are particularly recommended. ● Wed; Nov.

TODI: *Lucaroni* €€ | AE DC MC V
Via A. Cortesi 57. 0758 873 70.
Local fish, meat and game, including hare, duck and lamb with truffles, are on offer. Good puddings include *budino alla crema* (cream pudding) with hot chocolate. ● Tue.

TODI: *Umbria* €€€ | AE DC MC V
Via San Bonaventura, 13. 0758 942 737.
The restaurant is housed in part of a small medieval palazzo, with beams and candelabra. A menu of elegant Umbrian traditional dishes makes use of black truffle from Norcia and includes a delicious dish of duck stuffed with lentils. Excellent *antipasti*. Good wine list. ● Tue.

TREVI: *Maggiolini* €€ | AE DC MC V
Via San Francesco 20. 0742 381 534.
There is a romantic atmosphere in this elegant restaurant, housed in a historic palazzo. Meat-lovers will feel completely at home, but vegetarians are also well catered for, with vegetable-based appetizers, *bruschetta*, pasta stuffed with truffles, or in season, celery. ● Tue.

TREVI: *Osteria La Vecchia Posta* €€
Piazza Mazzini 14. 0742 381 690.
A family trattoria with a menu of dishes centred around black truffles. ● Thu; Feb.

TREVI: *Taverna del Pescatore* €€€ | AE DC MC V
Pigge, SS Flaminia Vecchia, Via Chiesa Tonda 50. 0742 780 920.
This taverna is a temple to river produce, with its famous dishes of freshwater crayfish, to try with a delicate lemon sauce. ● Wed; Jan.

For key to symbols see back flap

SHOPPING IN UMBRIA

THE SMALL SHOPS LINING the narrow streets of the historic centres of Umbria's towns and the craft workshops seen in small Umbrian villages make the region a wonderful place for shopping. It is not simply a question of buying traditional furniture, ceramics or textiles; it is also possible to track down workshops producing new and modern interpretations of ancient crafts, created by real masters of their art. Their fame is such that there are

A basket-maker at work

many schools for artisans in Umbria, which are attended by students from all over the world. The street markets, which may be permanent or weekly, are often excellent places to find good handicrafts, as well as more everyday items. Shops are, in general, open in the morning from 9am to 1pm and in the afternoon from 3 to 8pm. In the major tourist centres, such as Perugia and Assisi, shops are often open on Sunday as well.

Pottery shop in Deruta, a town famous for its ceramics

CERAMICS

THE ANCIENT ART of making pottery is one of the most traditional of Umbrian crafts. It was practised by the Etruscans and then resumed in the Middle Ages.

The ceramics of Deruta are among the most famous in Umbria, for their sheer quality and their bright colours. Today, the introduction of new styles and designs has breathed fresh life into a series of workshops run by artist-potters, whose work can be seen in Perugia, Orvieto, Deruta, Gubbio and Umbertide.

WOOD

THE WOODWORKERS of Umbria are not simply carpenters or restorers. Umbrian artisans working in wood, though famous for their solid and traditional furniture, have also introduced some individual

lines, such as wooden models (Perugia), sculpture (Orvieto) and modern furniture (Assisi). Most carpentry workshops are keen to produce furniture and other items for individual customers. However, these custom-made pieces can be very costly.

TEXTILES AND EMBROIDERY

FOR SOME YEARS now in Umbria the tradition of hand-weaving fabric, using methods and designs dating back as far as the Middle

Worker with a hand loom used in the production of typical Umbrian textiles

Ages, has been making a comeback. Rugs, bedspreads, and household linens, all with an antique feel, are regaining popularity in the shops of many Umbrian towns.

Another well-known tradition is that of "punto Assisi", or Assisi embroidery. Less widespread but equally fine is embroidery on tulle, originating from Panicale, south of Lake Trasimeno.

ANTIQUES

TRADITIONAL UMBRIAN taste, a sense of the past, and increasing numbers of visitors have helped antiques shops and galleries to prosper. Items on sale range from antique books and other printed material to statues, furniture, jewellery, carpets and even icons. There are, in addition, regular antiques markets, such as those held in Assisi, Todi and Perugia.

WINE AND OLIVE OIL

UMBRIAN WINE companies vary considerably in size, from the small vineyard owner to large modern industrial units. Wine is a serious matter in Umbria and the quality of its red and white wines now rivals the world's best.

Vineyards can often be visited, and wines tasted and purchased on site. In some cases the wine tasting, with sampling of cheeses and salami included, commands a fee and must be booked in advance. Apart from the traditional wine cooperatives, the most famous places to go to are the Lungarotti company in Torgiano; Antinori, not far from Orvieto; and Decugnano dei Barbi, near Corbara.

In Umbria, the production of olive oil is an ancient and much-respected tradition. A good proportion of the oil made in Umbria is bottled with the quality mark DOP (Denominazione di Origine Protetta – or protected denomination of origin), which guarantees the origin of the olives used and the method of pressing. The best places to buy oil are at the olive presses *(frantoi)*, which can be visited in November and December; here you can see how the olives are made into olive oil in a matter of hours. The price of a good-quality oil bought on site will be at least twice that of any everyday extra-virgin oil bought in an ordinary shop.

Delicatessen in Norcia, a typical shop selling local produce

GASTRONOMY

ANOTHER POPULAR BUY is the traditional produce of the region. The cured meats – especially those from Norcia, although they can be found almost everywhere – are one of the top delicacies. The variety is impressive: salami, hams and sausages, cured or fresh. Bottled vegetables in oil or brine are widely available, as are locally made jams.

Focaccia with cheese (which is traditional at Easter) is particularly good in southern Umbria, and Umbrian sheep's milk cheeses, both mature and fresh, are also excellent.

Cereals and vegetables are another important and popular Umbrian staple, and are often grown organically. In addition to the lentils of Castelluccio, look for spelt *(farro)* and chickling *(cicerchia)*, a type of pea.

DIRECTORY

CRAFTS

**Aldo Ajo'
Maioliche d'Arte
(ceramics)**
Via della Cattedrale 20, Gubbio.

**L'Antica Deruta
(ceramics)**
SS E45, Deruta.

**Artigianato
Ferro Artistico
(ironwork)**
Via Baldassini 22, Gubbio.

**Astolfo sulla Luna
(papier mâché)**
Via Flaminia 148, Foligno.

**Bottega d'Arte
(tapestry)**
Corso Vannucci 38, Perugia.

**Bottega del legno
di Gualverio
Michelangeli
(woodwork)**
Via Michelangeli 3, Orvieto.

**Ceramiche
artigiane
(ceramics)**
Via Storelli 42, Gualdo Tadino.

**Ceramiche Rometti
(ceramics)**
Via Garibaldi 73, **Umbertide**.

**La Fucina
(metalwork)**
Fontanelle di Bardano, **Orvieto**.

**Laboratorio
Tela Umbra
(textiles)**
Via Sant'Antonio 3, Città di Castello.

**Maestri Librai
Eugubini
(books)**
Via dei Consoli 41, Gubbio.

**Mastri Cartai
Editori (paper)**
Via Alessi 4, Perugia.

**La Spola
(general crafts)**
Via Garibaldi 66, Torgiano.

**Tessuto Artistico
Umbro
(textiles)**
Piazza del Comune 1, Montefalco.

ANTIQUES FAIRS

**Assisi Antiquariato
(Apr–May)**
Centro Umbriafiere Bastia Umbria.

**Rassegna
antiquaria
(end Oct–early Nov)**
Rocca Paolina, Perugia.

**Rassegna
antiquaria d'Italia
(end Mar–mid-Apr)**
Palazzo Vignola, Todi.

W *www.umbria2000.it*
for information.

GASTRONOMY

L'Agricola Goretti
Corso Vannucci 32, Perugia.

Bottega Barbanera
Piazza della Repubblica 34, Foligno.

**Cantina Terre
de' Trinci**
Via Fiamenga 57, Foligno.

**Macelleria Giulietti
(meat products)**
Corso Cavour 13, Città di Castello.

**Pasticceria Muzzi
(cakes and biscuits)**
Via Roma 38, Foligno.

**Fratelli Ansuini
(cured meats)**
Via Anicia 105, Norcia.

**Pasticceria Sandri
(cakes and biscuits)**
Strada del Pino 4, Perugia.

**La Spezieria
Bavicchi (spices)**
Piazza Matteotti 32, Perugia.

Giò Arte e Vini
Via Ruggero d'Andreotto 19, Perugia.

**Urbani Tartufi
(truffles)**
SS Valnerina, 31.3 km, Santa Anatolia di Narco.

What to Buy in Umbria

THE VARIED CRAFTS OF UMBRIA, derived from tradition but still open to new ideas, can be found either in shops or actually at the artists' own workshops. Old-fashioned ceramics sit side by side with works by great contemporary artists such as Cagli and Leonardi. Antique linen, lovingly produced by hand on a loom, is piled up next to more up-to-date and fashionable knitwear produced by Umbrian factories. It would also be impossible to ignore the delicious food of the region. Salami, of course, but also preserves, lentils, black truffles and chocolate, enabling visitors to take home something of the flavour of Umbria.

Potter at work in his studio

CERAMICS

Ceramics production – of which Deruta is the capital – is inspired by techniques and designs from a centuries-old tradition. An interesting new and flourishing trend is for new artists to make modern pieces, which have been inspired by their own imagination and by the study of new production methods.

Whistle from Ficulle

Vases and jars in painted majolica

BASKETS

The reeds that grow around Lake Trasimeno are gathered for use today, as they were in centuries past. A sturdy but flexible plant material, the reed is used to make all kinds of objects. Baskets, mats and traps for fishing on the lake are on sale in the towns of Passignano, Castiglione del Lago and Tuoro.

Basket and lid   **Basket for fruit**

TEXTILES AND EMBROIDERY

In several studios in Perugia, and in a few other towns, it is possible to buy household linen, fabrics and carpets, woven on a loom according to ancient methods. Umbrian embroidery and lace (made in Assisi, Panicale and Orvieto) are still widely available.

Detail from antique fabric

Cashmere wool is used to make high-quality garments. The most famous company name is that of Brunello Cucinelli.

Ars panicalensis is the name given to the technique of embroidering on tulle, originating in Panicale and now done throughout Umbria. The pieces have the delicacy of lace.

KNITWEAR

Umbria is a region with a series of small but dedicated knitwear companies producing garments using different types of wool. Clothes made from cashmere wool are particularly desirable.

BOOKBINDING

The old traditions of bookselling, bookbinding and book restoration are by no means dead in Umbria. Bookplates, diaries, notebooks, and albums are made with paper that reproduces the designs and colours of the Renaissance, a tradition that began with the followers of St Francis.

Book plate

WOOD

A man called Michelangeli launched the trend for good-quality woodwork in Orvieto. There is now a small but flourishing trade in wooden statues and animals, as well as garden sculptures. Items made from olive wood are now a tourist attraction in Assisi.

Hand-made wooden aeroplane

PORK SAUSAGES AND SALAMI

The meat and salami of Norcia are superb. You can choose from hams (made from pig or wild boar), fresh sausages, cured pork sausage, *capocollo* (made with neck of pig), and wild boar salami among many other delicacies. Good salami from small producers is found all over the region.

Shop selling a selection of fine hams, sausages and salamis

The prized black truffle

White truffle

TRUFFLES

The world's most prized type of black truffle *(tartufo nero)* grows in the Valnerina, especially around Norcia, and is gathered from November to March. The white truffle, gathered from October to December, is rare but less prized.

CHOCOLATE AND SWEETS

The manufacture of chocolate in Perugia dates back to the early 1900s, though the famous Perugina chocolates are no longer made exclusively in Umbria. Traditional sweets can be found all over the region.

PERUGINA

Baci Perugina, individually wrapped hazelnut chocolates, are the bestselling line of a business established in 1907. Their introduction led to a fresh appreciation of Italian confectionery. "Baci" means kisses and each sweet wrapper contains a little quotation about love, in four languages. Historic Perugina adverts are on display in Perugia's Museo Storico.

SURVIVAL
GUIDE

PRACTICAL INFORMATION

Along with an exceptional variety of landscapes, museums and places of historical and artistic interest, Umbria can offer a good range of services. The distances between the main centres are not great, making this, therefore, an ideal place for visitors eager to explore. The museums and galleries are, in general,

Regione dell' Umbria logo

modern, well run, welcoming and accessible to all (an increasing number have access for people with disabilities). The regional authority, Regione dell'Umbria, can offer a wide range of maps and lists of events through the various tourist offices. Banks and medical services are widely available throughout the region.

Mountain biking in the hills around Gubbio

WHEN TO VISIT

Umbria is one of the richest regions in Italy in terms of its attractions (natural and man-made) and its calendar of traditional, cultural and religious events. As a result, Umbria attracts large numbers of visitors between May and September. If you have the option, it is certainly best to arrange to visit either in May and June or September and October, thereby avoiding the crowded peak summer months. In summer, Umbria can also be exceedingly hot. In winter, when snow falls in the mountains, temperatures are low and the winds cold.

TOURIST INFORMATION

The two provinces that form Umbria – Perugia and Terni – each have their own Azienda di Promozione Turistica (APT), responsible for the promotion of tourism in that particular province. There is a tourist office in every town of a decent size. In smaller centres, offices

called Pro Loco are able to supply historical or cultural information, in addition to information about restaurants and lodgings. Specialist tour guides providing individual attention are available in some towns, too. In addition,

Tourist office (APT) sign

there are numerous organizations which deal with all kinds of sporting events and activities (*see pp20–1*). For those planning a cycling holiday, and for lovers of mountain biking, the APT provides a booklet called *Umbria in bicicletta* ("Umbria by bicycle").

Informa Giovani, set up by the Comune di Perugia (the Perugia town council), is aimed at young people, and can provide suggestions as well as addresses relating to culture, sport, music, wildlife, holidays, work opportunities, and youth associations.

SIGHTSEEING

Museums in Umbria are run either by the local town council or by the Italian government. In general, state

museums are open from 9am to 7pm, and often close on Monday, and on Sunday afternoon. Winter hours tend to be shorter. Museums run by the local authority have more varied timetables, and may even close over lunch. The use of a flash or a tripod is forbidden in most museums.

Church opening hours are unpredictable, but many close between noon and 3 or 4pm. When visiting churches, you should dress suitably. Tourists are discouraged from touring churches during services, and may be excluded from special religious festivals.

COMMUNICATIONS

Post offices can be found in all towns and there is often more than one branch. Main post offices are usually open from 8:30am to 7:30pm Monday to Saturday. Smaller offices, however, are often open in the morning only, from 8:30am to 1:30pm; on Saturday and the last day of the month, these post offices close at noon.

If all you want is stamps (*francobolli*) for postcards and normal letters, you can buy these at any tobacconist's (*tabacchi*) with the black and white T sign.

The number of public telephones has fallen in tandem with the rise of the mobile phone. Those that remain use telephone cards, available from tobacconists and some newspaper kiosks.

Telephone company logo

◁ **The picturesque Piazza del Popolo in Todi**

DIALLING CODES

- To phone another number in Italy you must include the full area code.
- For international calls, country codes are: UK & Ireland 00 39; USA & Canada 0 11 39; Australia 00 11 39.
- For reverse charge calls, dial 170.
- For directory enquiries dial 12 (for Italy), or 176 (international).
- For the British Operator, dial 17200 44.
- US Operators: 172 10 11 (AT&T); 172 10 22 (MG Worldphone); 172 18 77 (Sprint).
- Australian Operators: 172 10 61 (Telstra); 172 11 61 (Opus).

TAX EXEMPTION

VALUE ADDED TAX (IVA in Italy) ranges from 12–35 per cent. Non-EU citizens can claim an IVA rebate, provided the total expenditure is over €155. It is easiest to get a refund if you shop where you see the "Euro Free Tax" sign. Show your passport, complete a form, and the IVA will be deducted from your bill. Or show your purchases and their receipts at customs upon departure; they will stamp the receipts. Send these to the vendor and a refund should then be sent to you.

STUDENT INFORMATION

AN INTERNATIONAL Student Identity Card (ISIC) can be used to get a reduction on admission charges to many museums and other tourist attractions. The ISIC card also gives access to a 24-hour phone helpline. For discount travel and information, visit any branch of the Centro Turistico Studentesco (CTS).

ELECTRICAL ADAPTORS

THE VOLTAGE IN ITALY is 220 volts, with two-pin round-pronged plugs. It is worth buying adaptor plugs before you leave as they are difficult to find in Italy. Most hotels with three or more stars have hairdriers and shaving points in all bedrooms, but check the voltage first, to be safe.

ITALIAN TIME

ITALY IS ONE HOUR ahead of Greenwich Mean Time (GMT). The time difference is: London: –1 hour; New York: –6 hours; Perth: +7 hours; Auckland: +11 hours. These figures may vary briefly in summer with local time changes. Italy uses the 24-hour clock (eg 10pm=22:00).

CONVERSION CHART

Imperial to Metric
1 inch = 2.54 centimetres
1 foot = 30 centimetres
1 mile = 1.6 kilometres
1 ounce = 28 grams
1 pound = 454 grams
1 pint = 0.57 litre
1 gallon = 4.6 litres

Metric to Imperial
1 centimetre = 0.4 inch
1 metre = 3 feet 3 inches
1 kilometre = 0.6 mile
1 gram = 0.04 ounce
1 kilogram = 2.2 pounds
1 litre = 1.8 pints

DIRECTORY

ITALIAN STATE TOURIST OFFICES ABROAD

Canada
1 Bloor Street East, Suite 907, South Tower, Toronto M4W 3R8.
☎ 416-925-4882.

United Kingdom
1 Princes St, London W1B 8AY.
☎ 020 7408 1254.

United States
630 Fifth Avenue, Suite 1565, New York, NY 10111.
☎ 212-245-4822.

STATE TOURIST OFFICES IN UMBRIA

Regional Tourist Office (APT)
Via Mazzini 21, Perugia.
☎ 075 575 951.

Assisi
☎ 075 812 450.
FAX 075 813 727.
@ info@iat.assisi.pg.it

Orvieto
☎ 0763 341 772.
FAX 0763 344 433.
@ info@iat.orvieto.tr.it

Perugia
☎ 075 573 6458.
FAX 075 573 9386.
@ info@iat.perugia.it

Spoleto
☎ 0743 238 921.
FAX 0743 238 941.
@ info@iat.spoleto.pg.it

Trasimeno
☎ 075 965 2738.
@ info@iat.castiglione del lago.pg.it

OTHER TOURIST INFORMATION

Associazione guide turistiche (tour guides)
Via Porta Pernici 21, Assisi.
☎ 075 815 228.

Centro Turistico Studentesco (CTS)
Viale Sempione 6, Città di Castello.
☎ 075 855 3353.
W www.cts.it

Informa Giovani
Via Idalia 1, Perugia.
☎ 075 572 06 46.
W www.comune. perugia.it/informagiovani

EMBASSIES AND CONSULATES

Canada
Via Zara 30, Rome.
☎ 06 445 981.

United Kingdom
Via XX Settembre 80a, Rome.
☎ 06 4220 0001.
Lungarno Corsini 2, Florence.
☎ 055 284 133.

United States
Via Vittorio Veneto 121a, Rome.
☎ 06 46 741.

WEBSITES

Regione Umbria
W www.umbria2000.it
W www.regione.umbria.it/ tourism

EMERGENCIES

General emergencies
☎ 113.

Carabinieri (police)
☎ 112.

Fire service
☎ 115.

Car breakdown
☎ 116.

Ambulance
☎ 118.

Hospital
Via Bonacci Brunamonti, Perugia.
☎ 800 118 020 or 075 57 81.

Health and Safety

U MBRIA IS A safe region. However, if you are in diffculties, each town has a police headquarters, open 24 hours a day. Medical care in Umbria can be excellent, but be sure to take out medical insurance.

Police vehicle, equipped for off-road use

Vehicle used by the Vigili del Fuoco for smaller fires

HOSPITALS AND PHARMACIES

P HARMACIES are open from 9am–1pm and 4–8pm, Monday to Friday, and mornings only on Saturdays.

Every Umbrian city has its own hospital. In emergencies, go to the *Pronto Soccorso* (Casualty) or telephone for help. EU citizens are entitled to free treatment if they have filled in an E111 form before leaving home, but making a claim is a bureaucratic process. Always ensure that your travel insurance includes medical cover.

POLICE

I N ITALY the forces of law and order are organized into two divisions: the *Carabinieri* and the police *(Polizia)*, to which can be added, at urban level, the municipal police, including traffic police *(Vigili Urbani)*. Traffic police can also deal with minor matters and can provide information

Pharmacy sign

and deal with emergency situations. They wear a dark uniform in winter and a light one in summer, with the city coat of arms usually on the pocket. *Carabinieri* are responsible for public order. They wear black trousers with a red stripe down the side, and a white band across the body. Patrols are often seen on the streets.

A team of *carabinieri* in traffic police uniform

The duties of the *Polizia* are more wide-ranging and are, in general, concerned with criminal investigations. The uniform is blue, with a white belt and hat. To report a theft or other serious problem, go to the nearest police station or dial 113.

FIREFIGHTERS

I N SUCH A GREEN and wooded region as Umbria, problems with fires are perhaps inevitable, even if the fairly damp climate and the scarcity of winds do not favour the spread of fire. Even so, particularly if you are planning an outdoor holiday, be sure to observe all the standard countryside code practices, especially with regard to not lighting a fire outside the designated areas and making sure cigarettes are completely extinguished.

Municipal policeman

The region has many fire stations, and fire engines respond rapidly to alarm calls. Firefighters also attend to other kinds of emergencies.

PERSONAL SAFETY

U SE COMMON SENSE to keep safe. Do not carry large sums in cash and, if you have valuables, leave them in the safe at your hotel if possible. Pickpockets frequent main railway stations and crowded tourist sights. If travelling by car, lock the vehicle and don't leave any items in view.

It is essential to arrange full insurance cover before you travel, and you may wish to keep a separate photocopy of personal documents so that you can request duplicates in the event of theft.

In Umbria, whether in town or countryside, there are no areas which need to be avoided. It is safe to walk around town streets in the evenings, and even late at night. And there is no reason why unaccompanied women should feel any unease.

Banking and Local Currency

FOREIGNERS ARRIVING in Umbria may change currency in a number of ways, but it is still wise to arrive with euros in your pocket. Credit cards are widely accepted for purchases and can be used to withdraw money.

Sign at a cash machine, useful for withdrawing cash with a debit card

BANKS AND CURRENCY EXCHANGE

IN THE LARGER towns there are bureaux de change as well as currency-converting machines. It is also possible to change money in hotels and in travel agencies, but you'll get a better exchange rate in the banks. Commission charges can be hefty, so it's worth shopping around.

Italian banks are normally open from 8:30am to 1:30pm, and then from 3pm to 4pm,

from Monday to Friday, but these hours may vary from place to place; banks often close early the day before a public holiday. Your hotel reception or the tourist office should be able to help with information. Opening hours of bureaux de change and other places are much more variable. Some form of identification will be needed for all kinds of money transactions.

All towns have cashpoint (ATM) machines *(bancomat)*, which allow you to take money out with a debit card or a credit card and a PIN number. VISA, American Express, MasterCard and Diners Club are the most commonly seen credit cards and there should be no problems getting them accepted.

THE EURO

SINCE 1 JANUARY 2002 the euro (€) has been the sole official currency in 12 of the 15 member states of the European Union. The 12 are Austria, Belgium, Finland, France, Germany, Greece, the Irish Republic, Italy, Luxembourg, the Netherlands, Portugal and Spain.

Euro notes are identical on one side (that is, the value side) throughout these 12 countries., and feature architectural drawings of fictitious monuments. The coins' other side is unique to each country. Both notes and coins are valid within each of the 12 countries, no matter where they originated.

Logo of the Banca dell'Umbria

You may find that some locals, not having formed a clear idea of exactly how much a euro is worth, still talk about prices in lira. It is best not to carry euro notes of large denominations since not all businesses have large amounts of change.

Banknotes and Coins
Banknotes come in seven denominations. The 5-euro note is grey, the 10-euro is pink, the 20 is blue, the 50 orange, the 100 green, the 200 yellow and the 500 purple. There are eight different coins. The 1- and 2-euro coins are silver and gold; those worth 50, 20 and 10 cents are gold, while the 5-, 2- and 1-cent coins are bronze.

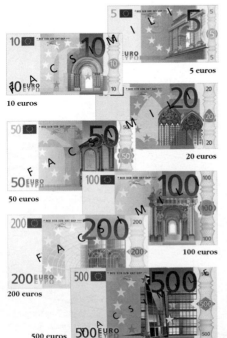

5 euros

10 euros

20 euros

50 euros

100 euros

200 euros

500 euros

2 euros

1 euro

50 cents

20 cents

10 cents

5 cents

2 cents

1 cents

TRAVEL INFORMATION

Logo of state railway
Ferrovie dello Sato

U MBRIA LIES at the geographical heart of Italy. Despite the hills and the mountains of the Apennines, road and rail infrastructures are well maintained and well organized; this, combined with the relatively small size of the region, makes it easy and straightforward to travel from one place to another by car. Road and tourist signs are helpful and up-to-date. Driving and parking can be difficult in towns, but buses and taxis are plentiful, and most towns are small enough to be explored easily on foot. The railway network has few branch lines but there are frequent and reliable connections by coach where there are no trains. Umbria itself is easily reached by air or coach. Ferries link the villages on the shores of Lake Trasimeno as well as the lake islands.

Hiring a car, a practical and convenient way of getting around Umbria

ARRIVING BY AIR

T HE UMBRIAN Regional Airport of Sant'Egidio is 12 km (7 miles) from both Perugia and Assisi. Scheduled Alitalia flights arrive here from Milan Malpensa and Rome, the main Italian international airports, as well as some charter flights. Buses running between the airport and the centre of Perugia are timed to coincide with the arrival of scheduled flights. Taxis are also available at the airport, as is car hire: the major companies (Avis, Europcar and Hertz), offer pre-booked fly-drive arrangements.

One option is to fly to Rome or another nearby airport, such as Ancona or Pisa, and take the train or drive from there. Rome to Perugia by car, for example, takes two hours.

TRAVELLING BY CAR

T HE AUTOSTRADA del Sole (A1) from Milan, via Florence, skirts Umbria along the Tuscan border before continuing on to Rome. At the Val di Chiana exit a road runs east to Perugia. Other useful exit points are Chiusi Chianciano, Orvieto and Orte, from where a fast road runs to Terni and links up with the Via Flaminia. The latter is the most important state road in Umbria, running from north to south. The condition of the roads is good; only within the Apennines does driving becomes more challenging.

A car is by far the best way to explore Umbria, enabling you to reach the most remote villages and making it easier to enjoy the scenery.

Car hire is expensive and should be booked ahead. You must be over 21 and have held a licence for at least a year. Visitors from outside the EU may need to show an international licence.

A toll is payable for use of the motorways (*autostrade*). Tolls are high, but you can usually pay by credit card.

Note that petrol stations may close at lunch time and rarely stay open late.

TRAVELLING BY TRAIN

T HE MOST IMPORTANT railway line as far as Umbria is concerned is the Milan–Rome line, which stops at Orte, Orvieto and the rail junction at Terontola. Two super-fast EuroStar (ES) trains a day link Rome and Milan with Perugia, but do not stop at any of the other Umbrian stations on this line: for Terontola and Orte you need to travel by Inter-City (IC) train or a slower local service. Terni, Foligno and Spoleto are on the Orte–Ancona line. From Terontola a branch line runs to Perugia and Foligno, stopping at a few places on Lake Trasimeno and passing close to Assisi. A local line from Terni to Perugia serves Todi and goes on to Città di Castello and beyond to Sansepolcro, in Tuscany.

The main problem with travelling around Umbria by train is that railway stations can be some distance from the hill town after which they are named. Rolling stock is improving, but while InterCity trains are usually modern and air-conditioned, branch line carriages may still be ancient.

It is advisable to buy tickets before departure, because if

A train run by the state company Ferrovie dello Stato

you pay on the train there will be a surcharge. Be sure to validate both outward and return tickets in the machines provided on the platform, before boarding the train, or you will be fined. Always check before doing so that the train you plan to board stops at the station you want: InterCity and EuroStar trains stop only at major stations, and may also require the payment of a first- or second-class supplement (which can be paid for on the train but is more expensive).

Fares are still among the cheapest in Europe, but check in advance with Rail Europe *(see box)* for details of money-saving passes.

TRAVELLING BY COACH

INTERCITY coach travel can be faster than travelling by train. Perugia is the main hub for coach services. It has direct links to several Italian cities, with stops in various Umbrian towns en route. A daily service from Roma Tiburtina, Rome's main coach station, stops in Todi, Assisi and Deruta en route to Perugia. There are daily coaches between Rome and Gubbio and Città di Castello, as well Norcia. Perugia is accessible by coach from Florence.

Coaches from Perugia to Assisi run six or seven times a day, while Todi has around five services a day and Gubbio ten. Coach services are often reduced at weekends, particularly on Sundays, and also vary between summer and winter.

Ferry logo

TOWN BUSES

IN PERUGIA the Azienda Perugina di Mobilità operates services within the city and out to the suburbs, among them buses linking the train terminal with the coach station. Tickets are valid for different lengths of time and prices vary accordingly. Bus tickets can be purchased from newspaper kiosks and *tabacchi*. Season tickets are also available, including tourist tickets that are valid for 24 or 48 hours.

In Assisi, regular buses link the railway station, 5 km (3 miles) away at Santa María degli Angeli, to the centre. In Todi, too, the railway station is linked to the town by bus. At Terni, buses run by the Azienda Trasporti Pubblici (ATC) serve the town and also travel as far as the Cascata delle Marmore.

TAXIS

HIRE A CAB ONLY from an official taxi stand or else reserve it by phone. If you telephone, the meter will run from the time of your call. Extra is charged for each piece of luggage put in the boot, for rides at night, on Sundays and public holidays, and for airport trips (fix a price before you set off).

FERRIES

ON LAKE TRASIMENO ferries link Castiglione del Lago, the islands of Isola Polvese, Isola Maggiore and Isola Minore, as well as Tuoro sul Trasimeno and Passignano sul Trasimeno.

DIRECTORY

AIRPORTS

Perugia
Aeroporto Regionale Umbro di Sant'Egidio.
📞 075 592 141.
🖥 www.airport.umbria.it

GENERAL TRANSPORT INFORMATION

📞 800 512 141 (free).
🖥 www.umbriatransporti.it

RAIL INFORMATION

📞 892021.
🖥 www.trenitalia.it

Rail Europe
📞 08705 848 548 (UK).
🖥 www.raileurope.co.uk

📞 1-877-257-2887 (US).
🖥 www.raileurope.com

COACH INFORMATION

Società Umbro Laziale Gestione Autolinee
📞 075 500 9641.

BUS INFORMATION

Azienda Perugina di Mobilità (APM)
📞 075 506 781.

ATC Terni
📞 0744 492 711.

CAR HIRE

Hertz
📞 075 500 2439.
🖥 www.hertz.com

Avis
📞 075 500 0395.
🖥 www.avis.com

Europcar
📞 075 573 1704.
🖥 www.europcar.it

TAXIS

Assisi	📞 075 804 0275.
Foligno	📞 0743 220 489.
Orvieto	📞 0763 342 613.
Perugia	📞 075 500 4888.
Spoleto	📞 0742 344280.
Terni	📞 0744 425 294.
Todi	📞 075 894 2525.

One of the ferries linking the islands and towns on Lake Trasimeno

General Index

Acknowledgments

DORLING KINDERSLEY would like to thank all those whose contribution and assistance have made the preparation of this book possible.

SPECIAL THANKS

Archivio Electa-Milano, Assessorato del Turismo Regione Umbria, APT di Perugia, APT di Assisi, APT di Foligno, APT di Spoleto, Consorzio del Parco del Lago Trasimeno, Consorzio del Parco del Monte Cucco, Ente Parco dei Monti Sibillini, Guido Stecchi for consultation and help with pages 154–5, and all the companies who have assisted with their products.

PHOTOGRAPHY

Ghigo Roli (Modena).

TRANSLATOR

Fiona Wild

EDITOR

Emily Hatchwell

PHOTOGRAPHY PERMISSIONS

The publisher would like to thank all the churches, museums, hotels, restaurants, art galleries, parks and all those who supplied material and contributed to the publication of this guide, too numerous to be named individually. While every effort has been made to contact the copyright holders, we apologize for any omissions and will be happy to include them in subsequent editions of this publication.

PICTURE CREDITS

t = top; tl = top left; tlc = top left centre; tc = top centre; tr = top right; cla = centre left above; ca = centre above; cra = centre right above; cl = centre left; c = centre; cr = centre right; clb = centre left below; cb = centre below; crb = centre right below; bl = bottom left; b = below; bc = bottom centre; bcl = bottom centre left; br = bottom right; (d) = detail

FABRIZIO ARDITO (Rome): 2–3, 14tl, 30tr, 33bl, 61tl, 61cr, 69tc, 71tr, 86br, 89c, 92tr, 92bl, 131cr, 134cl, 135tc, 137cr.

ADRIANO BACCHELLA (Milan): 14c.

CORBIS: Elio Ciol 15b.

DAVID CAPASSO (Modena): 42bl, 103cl, 104tl, 105cr.

GIOVANNI FRANCESIO (Mantua): 54tl, 54cr, 56 all photos, 57 all photos, 63t, 63b, 64 all photos, 65 all photos, 66tr, 66bl, 67tl, 67cr, 67b, 82c, 82br, 83cl, 83cr, 94 all photos.

ROBERT HARDING PICTURE LIBRARY: T. Gervis 14b.

TIM JEPSON: 13b.

MARCO MANDIBOLA (Milan): 51b, 61bc, 78c, 100bl, 102tl, 105bl, 130b.

GUIDO MANNUCCI (Florence): 33cr, 91cl.

MARKA (Milan): D. Donadoni96, 153b, 172–3; R. Gropozzo 153t; Sechi 140–1

PETER NOBLE: 176b

ANNA SERRANO (Rome): 14cb, 16tr, 16crb, 17bl, 32tc, 32cr.

GUIDO STECCHI (Milan): 154cla, 154cra, 154bl.

Additional Photography:
John Heseltine

Jacket:
Front – CORBIS: Elio Ciol cr; Staffan Widstrand cl; MARKA (Milan): D.Donadoni c; L. Fioroni main image.
Back – DK PICTURE LIBRARY: John Heseltine t/b; Spine – MARKA (Milan); L. Fioroni.

DORLING KINDERSLEY SPECIAL EDITIONS

Dorling Kindersley books can be purchased in bulk quantities at discounted prices for use in promotions or as premiums. We are also able to offer special editions and personalized jackets, corporate imprints, and excerpts from all of our books, tailored specifically to meet your own needs.

To find out more, please contact: (in the United Kingdom) – Sarah.Burgess@dk.com or SPECIAL SALES, DORLING KINDERSLEY LIMITED, 80 STRAND, LONDON WC2R 0RL;

(in the United States) – SPECIAL MARKETS DEPARTMENT, DK PUBLISHING, INC., 375 HUDSON STREET, NEW YORK, NEW YORK 10014.

Phrase Book

IN AN EMERGENCY

Help!	**Aiuto!**	*eye-yoo-toh*
Stop!	**Fermate!**	*fair-mah-teh*
Call a doctor.	**Chiama un medico**	*kee-ah-mah oon meh-dee-koh*
Call an ambulance.	**Chiama un' ambulanza**	*kee-ah-mah oon am-boo-lan-tsa*
Call the police.	**Chiama la polizia**	*kee-ah-mah lah pol-ee-tsee-ah*
Call the fire brigade.	**Chiama i pompieri**	*kee-ah-mah ee pom-pee-air-ee*
Where is the telephone?	**Dov'è il telefono?**	*dov-eh eel teh-leh-foh-noh?*
The nearest hospital?	**L'ospedale più vicino?**	*loss-peh-dah-leh pee-oovee-chee-noh?*

COMMUNICATION ESSENTIALS

Yes/No	**Si/No**	*see/noh*
Please	**Per favore**	*pair fah-vor-eh*
Thank you	**Grazie**	*grah-tsee-eh*
Excuse me	**Mi scusi**	*mee skoo-zee*
Hello	**Buon giorno**	*bwon jor noh*
Good bye	**Arrivederci**	*ah-ree-veh-dair-chee*
Good evening	**Buona sera**	*bwon-ah sair-ah*
morning	**la mattina**	*lah mah-tee-nah*
afternoon	**il pomeriggio**	*eel poh-meh-ree-joh*
evening	**la sera**	*lah sair-ah*
yesterday	**ieri**	*ee-air-ee*
today	**oggi**	*oh-jee*
tomorrow	**domani**	*doh-mah-nee*
here	**qui**	*kwee*
there	**la**	*lah*
What?	**Quale?**	*kwah-leh?*
When?	**Quando?**	*kwan-doh?*
Why?	**Perchè?**	*pair-keh?*
Where?	**Dove?**	*doh-veh*

USEFUL PHRASES

How are you?	**Come sta?**	*koh-meh stah?*
Very well, thank you.	**Molto bene, grazie.**	*moll-toh beh-neh grah-tsee-eh*
Pleased to meet you.	**Piacere di conoscerla.**	*pee-ah-chair-eh dee coh-noh-shair-lah*
See you soon.	**A più tardi.**	*ah pee-oo tar-dee*
That's fine.	**Va bene.**	*va beh-neh*
Where is/are ...?	**Dov'è/Dove sono ...?**	*dov-eh/doveh soh-noh?*
How long does it take to get to ...?	**Quanto tempo ci vuole per andare a ...?**	*kwan-toh tem-poh chee voo-oh-leh pair an-dar-eh ah...?*
How do I get to ...?	**Come faccio per arrivare a ...?**	*koh-meh fah-choh pair arri-var-eh ah..?*
Do you speak English?	**Parla inglese?**	*par-lah een-gleh-zeh?*
I don't understand.	**Non capisco.**	*non ka-pee-skoh*
Could you speak more slowly, please?	**Può parlare più lentamente, per favore?**	*pwoh par-lah-reh pee-oo len-ta-men-teh pair fah-vor-eh?*
I'm sorry.	**Mi dispiace.**	*mee dee-spee-ah-cheh*

USEFUL WORDS

big	**grande**	*gran-deh*
small	**piccolo**	*pee-koh-loh*
hot	**caldo**	*kal-doh*
cold	**freddo**	*fred-doh*
good	**buono**	*bwoh-noh*
bad	**cattivo**	*kat-tee-voh*
enough	**basta**	*bas-tah*
well	**bene**	*beh-neh*
open	**aperto**	*ah-pair-toh*
closed	**chiuso**	*kee-oo-zoh*
left	**a sinistra**	*ah see-nee-strah*
right	**a destra**	*ah dess-trah*
straight on	**sempre dritto**	*sem-preh dree-toh*
near	**vicino**	*vee-chee-noh*
far	**lontano**	*lon-tah-noh*
up	**su**	*soo*
down	**giù**	*joo*
early	**presto**	*press-toh*
late	**tardi**	*tar-dee*
entrance	**entrata**	*en-trah-tah*
exit	**uscita**	*oo-shee-ta*
toilet	**il gabinetto**	*eel gah-bee-net-toh*
free, unoccupied	**libero**	*lee-bair-oh*
free, no charge	**gratuito**	*grah-too-ee-toh*

MAKING A TELEPHONE CALL

I'd like to place a long-distance call.	**Vorrei fare una interurbana.**	*vor-ray far-eh oona in-tair-oor-bah-nah*
I'd like to make a reverse-charge call.	**Vorrei fare una telefonata a carico del destinatario.**	*vor-ray far-eh oona teh-leh-fon-ah-tah ah kar-ee-koh dell dess-tee-nah-tar-ree-oh*
I'll try again later.	**Ritelefono più tardi.**	*ree-teh-leh-foh-noh pee-oo tar-dee*
Can I leave a message?	**Posso lasciare un messaggio?**	*poss-oh lash-ah-reh oon mess-sah-joh?*
Hold on.	**Un attimo, per favore**	*oon ah-tee-moh, pair fah-vor-eh*
Could you speak up a little please?	**Può parlare più forte, per favore?**	*pwoh par-lah-reh pee-oo for-teh, pair fah-vor-eh?*
local call	**la telefonata locale**	*lah teh-leh-fon-ah-ta loh-kah-leh*

SHOPPING

How much does this cost?	**Quant'è, per favore?**	*kwan-teh pair fah-vor-eh?*
I would like ...	**Vorrei ...**	*vor-ray*
Do you have ...?	**Avete ...?**	*ah-veh-teh.. ?*
I'm just looking.	**Sto soltanto guardando.**	*stoh sol-tan-toh gwar-dan-doh*
Do you take credit cards?	**Accettate carte di credito?**	*ah-chet-tah-teh kar-teh dee creh-dee-toh?*
What time do you open/close?	**A che ora apre/ chiude?**	*ah keh or-ah ah-preh/kee-oo-deh?*
this one	**questo**	*kweb-stoh*
that one	**quello**	*kwell-oh*
expensive	**caro**	*kar-oh*
cheap	**a buon prezzo**	*ah bwon pret-soh*
size, clothes	**la taglia**	*lah tah-lee-ah*
size, shoes	**il numero**	*eel noo-mair-oh*
white	**bianco**	*bee-ang-koh*
black	**nero**	*neh-roh*
red	**rosso**	*ross-oh*
yellow	**giallo**	*jal-loh*
green	**verde**	*vair-deh*
blue	**blu**	*bloo*
brown	**marrone**	*mar-roh-neh*

TYPES OF SHOP

antique dealer	**l'antiquario**	*lan-tee-kwah-ree-oh*
bakery	**la panetteria**	*lah pah-net-tair-ree-ah*
bank	**la banca**	*lah bang-kah*
bookshop	**la libreria**	*lah lee-breh-ree-ah*
butcher's	**la macelleria**	*lah mah-chell-eh-ree-ah*
cake shop	**la pasticceria**	*lah pas-tee-chair-ee-ah*
chemist's	**la farmacia**	*lah far-mah-chee-ah*
delicatessen	**la salumeria**	*lah sah-loo-meh-ree-ah*
department store	**il grande magazzino**	*eel gran-deh mag-gad-zee-noh*
fishmonger's	**la pescheria**	*lah pess-keh-ree-ah*
florist	**il fioraio**	*eel fee-or-eye-oh*
greengrocer	**il fruttivendolo**	*eel froo-tee-ven-doh-loh*
grocery	**alimentari**	*ah-lee-men-tah-ree*
hairdresser	**il parrucchiere**	*eel par-roo-kee-air-eh*
ice-cream parlour	**la gelateria**	*lah jel-lah-tair-ree-ah*
market	**il mercato**	*eel mair-kah-toh*
news-stand	**l'edicola**	*leh-dee-koh-lah*
post office	**l'ufficio postale**	*loo-fee-choh pos-tah-leh*
shoe shop	**il negozio di scarpe**	*eel neh-goh-tsioh dee skar-peh*
supermarket	**il supermercato**	*su-pair-mair-kah-toh*
tobacconist	**il tabaccaio**	*eel tab-bak-eye-oh*
travel agency	**l'agenzia di viaggi**	*lah-jen-tsee-ah dee vee-ad-jee*

SIGHTSEEING

art gallery	**la pinacoteca**	*lah peena-koh-teb-kah*
bus stop	**la fermata dell'autobus**	*lah fair-mah-tah dell ow-toh-booss*
church	**la chiesa**	*lah kee-eh-zah*
	la basilica	*lah bah-seel-i-kah*
closed for the public holiday	**chiuso per la festa**	*kee-oo-zoh pair lah fess-tah*
garden	**il giardino**	*eel jar-dee-no*
library	**la biblioteca**	*lah beeb-lee-oh-teb-kah*
museum	**il museo**	*eel moo-zeb-oh*
railway station	**la stazione**	*lah stah-tsee-oh-neh*
tourist information	**l'ufficio turistico**	*loo-fee-choh too-ree-stee-koh*

STAYING IN A HOTEL

Do you have any vacant rooms?	**Avete camere libere?**	*ah-veh-teh kah-mair-eh lee-bair-eh?*
double room	**una camera doppia**	*oona kah-mair-ah dob-pee-ah*
with double bed	**con letto matrimoniale**	*kon let-toh mah-tree-moh-nee-ab-leh*
twin room	**una camera con due letti**	*oona kah-mair-ah kon doo-eh let-tee*
single room	**una camera singola**	*oona kah-mair-ah sing-goh-lah*
room with a bath, shower	**una camera con bagno, con doccia**	*oona kah-mair-ah kon ban-yoh, kon dot-chah*
porter	**il facchino**	*eel fah-kee-noh*
key	**la chiave**	*lah kee-ah-veh*
I have a reservation.	**Ho fatto una prenotazione.**	*oh fat-toh oona preh-nob-tah-tsee-ob-neh*

EATING OUT

Have you got a table for ...?	**Avete una tavola per ... ?**	*ah-veh-teh oona tah-voh-lah pair ...?*
I'd like to reserve a table.	**Vorrei riservare una tavola.**	*vor-ray ree-sair-vah-reh oona tah-voh-lah*
breakfast	**colazione**	*koh-lah-tsee-ob-neh*
lunch	**pranzo**	*pran-tsoh*
dinner	**cena**	*cheh-nah*
Enjoy your meal.	**Buon appetito.**	*bwon ah-peh-tee-toh*
The bill, please.	**Il conto, per favore.**	*eel kon-toh pair fah-vor-eh*
I am a vegetarian.	**Sono vegetariano/a.**	*soh-noh veh-jeh-tar-ee-ab-noh/nah*
waitress	**cameriera**	*kah-mair-ee-air-ah*
waiter	**cameriere**	*kah-mair-ee-air-eh*
fixed price menu	**il menù a prezzo fisso**	*eel meh-noo ah pret-soh fee-soh*
dish of the day	**piatto del giorno**	*pee-ab-toh dell jor-no*
starter	**antipasto**	*an-tee-pass-toh*
first course	**il primo**	*eel pree-moh*
main course	**il secondo**	*eel seh-kon-doh*
vegetables	**il contorno**	*eel kon-tor-noh*
dessert	**il dolce**	*eel doll-cheh*
cover charge	**il coperto**	*eel koh-pair-toh*
wine list	**la lista dei vini**	*lah lee-stah day vee-nee*
rare	**al sangue**	*al sang-gweh*
medium	**al puntino**	*al poon-tee-noh*
well done	**ben cotto**	*ben kot-toh*
glass	**il bicchiere**	*eel bee-kee-air-eh*
bottle	**la bottiglia**	*lah bot-teel-yah*
knife	**il coltello**	*eel kol-tell-oh*
fork	**la forchetta**	*lah for-ket-tah*
spoon	**il cucchiaio**	*eel koo-kee-eye-oh*

MENU DECODER

l'abbacchio	*lah-back-kee-oh*	lamb
l'aceto	*lah-cheh-toh*	vinegar
l'acqua	*lah-kwah*	water
l'acqua minerale gasata/naturale	*lah-kwah mee-nair-ab-leh gah-zah-tah/nah-too-rah-leh*	mineral water fizzy/still
l'aglio	*labl-yoh*	garlic
al forno	*al for-noh*	baked
alla griglia	*ah-lah greel-yah*	grilled
l'anatra	*lah-nah-trah*	duck
l'aragosta	*lah-rah-goss-tah*	lobster
l'arancia	*lah-ran-chah*	orange
arrosto	*ar-ross-toh*	roast
la birra	*lah beer-rah*	beer
la bistecca	*lah bee-stek-kah*	steak
il brodo	*eel broh-doh*	broth
il burro	*eel boor-oh*	butter
il caffè	*eel kah-feh*	coffee
il carciofo	*eel kar-choff-oh*	artichoke
la carne	*la kar-neh*	meat
carne di maiale	*kar-neh dee mah-yab-leh*	pork
la cipolla	*lah chee-poll-ah*	onion
i fagioli	*ee fah-job-lee*	beans
il formaggio	*eel for-mad-joh*	cheese
le fragole	*leh frah-goh-leh*	strawberries
frutta fresca	*froo-tah fress-kah*	fresh fruit
frutti di mare	*froo-tee dee mah-reh*	seafood
i funghi	*ee foon-gee*	mushrooms
i gamberi	*ee gam-bair-ee*	prawns
il gelato	*eel jel-lab-toh*	ice cream
l'insalata	*leen-sah-lab-tah*	salad
il latte	*eel labt-teh*	milk
i legumi	*ee leh-goo-mee*	vegetables

lesso	*less-oh*	boiled
il manzo	*eel man-tsoh*	beef
la mela	*lah meh-lah*	apple
la melanzana	*lah meh-lan-tsah-nah*	aubergine
la minestra	*lah mee-ness-trah*	soup
l'olio	*loll-yoh*	oil
l'oliva	*loh-lee-vah*	olive
il pane	*eel pab-neh*	bread
il panino	*eel pah-nee-noh*	roll
le patate	*leh pah-tab-teh*	potatoes
patatine fritte	*pah-tah-teen-eh free-teh*	chips
il pepe	*eel peb-peh*	pepper
la pesca	*lah pess-kah*	peach
il pesce	*eel pesh-eh*	fish
il pollo	*eel poll-oh*	chicken
il pomodoro	*eel poh-moh-dor-oh*	tomato
il prosciutto cotto/crudo	*eel pro-shoo-toh kot-toh/kroo-doh*	ham cooked/cured
il riso	*eel ree-zoh*	rice
il sale	*eel sah-leh*	salt
la salsiccia	*lah sal-see-chah*	sausage
secco	*sek-koh*	dry
succo d'arancia/di limone	*soo-koh dah-ran-chah/dee lee-moh-neh*	orange/lemon juice
il tè	*eel teh*	tea
la tisana	*lah tee-zab-nah*	herb tea
il tonno	*ton-noh*	tuna
la torta	*lah tor-tah*	cake
l'uovo	*loo-oh-voh*	egg
l'uva	*loo-vah*	grapes
vino bianco	*vee-noh bee-ang-koh*	white wine
vino rosso	*vee-noh ross-oh*	red wine
il vitello	*eel vee-tell-oh*	veal
le vongole	*leh von-goh-leh*	baby clams
lo zucchero	*loh zoo-kair-oh*	sugar
gli zucchini	*lyee dzo-kee-nee*	courgettes
la zuppa	*lah tsoo-pah*	soup

NUMBERS

1	**uno**	*oo-noh*
2	**due**	*doo-eh*
3	**tre**	*treh*
4	**quattro**	*kwat-roh*
5	**cinque**	*ching-kweh*
6	**sei**	*say-ee*
7	**sette**	*set-teh*
8	**otto**	*ot-toh*
9	**nove**	*nob-veh*
10	**dieci**	*dee-eh-chee*
11	**undici**	*oon-dee-chee*
12	**dodici**	*dob-dee-chee*
13	**tredici**	*tray-dee-chee*
14	**quattordici**	*kwat-tor-dee-chee*
15	**quindici**	*kwin-dee-chee*
16	**sedici**	*say-dee-chee*
17	**diciassette**	*dee-chah-set-teh*
18	**diciotto**	*dee-chot-toh*
19	**diciannove**	*dee-chah-nob-veh*
20	**venti**	*ven-tee*
30	**trenta**	*tren-tah*
40	**quaranta**	*kwah-ran-tah*
50	**cinquanta**	*ching-kwan-tah*
60	**sessanta**	*sess-an-tah*
70	**settanta**	*set-tan-tah*
80	**ottanta**	*ot-tan-tah*
90	**novanta**	*nob-van-tah*
100	**cento**	*chen-toh*
1,000	**mille**	*mee-leh*
2,000	**duemila**	*doo-eh mee-lah*
5,000	**cinquemila**	*ching-kweh mee-lah*
1,000,000	**un milione**	*oon meel-yob-neh*

TIME

one minute	**un minuto**	*oon mee-noo-toh*
one hour	**un'ora**	*oon or-ah*
half an hour	**mezz'ora**	*medz-or-ah*
a day	**un giorno**	*oon jor-noh*
a week	**una settimana**	*oona set-tee-mah-nah*
Monday	**lunedì**	*loo-neh-dee*
Tuesday	**martedì**	*mar-teh-dee*
Wednesday	**mercoledì**	*mair-koh-leh-dee*
Thursday	**giovedì**	*joh-veh-dee*
Friday	**venerdì**	*ven-air-dee*
Saturday	**sabato**	*sab-bah-toh*
Sunday	**domenica**	*dob-meh-nee-kah*

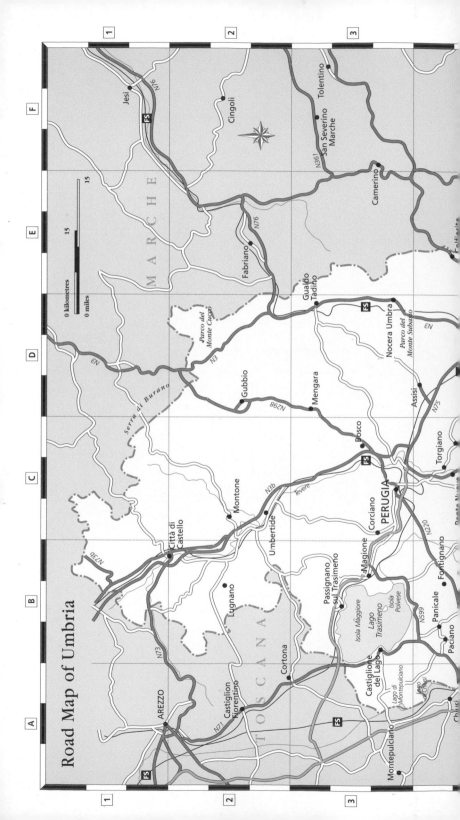

Road Map of Umbria